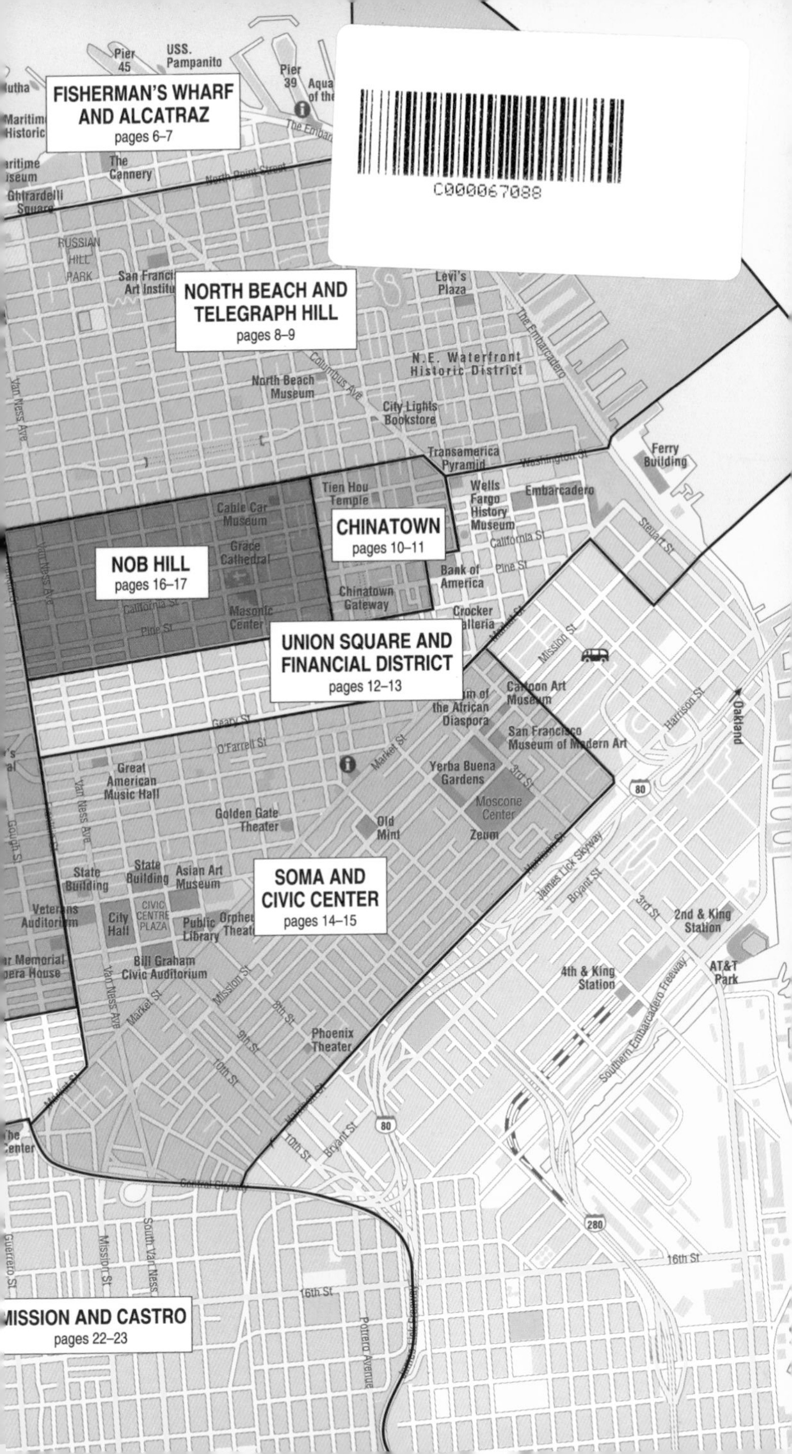

FISHERMAN'S WHARF AND ALCATRAZ
pages 6–7
NORTH BEACH AND TELEGRAPH HILL
pages 8–9
CHINATOWN
pages 10–11
NOB HILL
pages 16–17
UNION SQUARE AND FINANCIAL DISTRICT
pages 12–13
SOMA AND CIVIC CENTER
pages 14–15
MISSION AND CASTRO
pages 22–23
Pier 45
USS. Pampanito
Pier 39
The Cannery
North Point Street
Ghirardelli Square
RUSSIAN HILL PARK
Levi's Plaza
The Embarcadero
N.E. Waterfront Historic District
North Beach Museum
Columbus Ave
City Lights Bookstore
Van Ness Ave
Transamerica Pyramid
Washington St
Ferry Building
Tien Hou Temple
Wells Fargo History Museum
Embarcadero
Cable Car Museum
Grace Cathedral
California St
Stewart St
Bank of America
Pine St
Chinatown Gateway
Masonic Center
Crocker Galleria
Mission St
Cartoon Art Museum
the African Diaspora
San Francisco Museum of Modern Art
Harrison St
Oakland
Geary St
O'Farrell St
Market St
Great American Music Hall
Yerba Buena Gardens
3rd St
80
Moscone Center
Golden Gate Theater
Old Mint
Zeum
Gough St
James Lick Skyway
Bryant St
State Building
Asian Art Museum
CIVIC CENTRE PLAZA
City Hall
Public Library
Veterans Auditorium
2nd & King Station
AT&T Park
Bill Graham Civic Auditorium
4th & King Station
Southern Embarcadero Freeway
8th St
9th St
10th St
Phoenix Theater
280
16th St
Central Skyway
Guerrero St
Mission St
South Van Ness
Potrero Avenue

SAN FRANCISCO
smartguide

Part of the Langenscheidt Publishing Group

Contents

Areas

Below: all aboard at the Cable Car turnaround.

A–Z

Left: the Golden Gate Bridge, wreathed in the famous fog.

Below: a sunbathing sea lion at Fisherman's Wharf.

Atlas

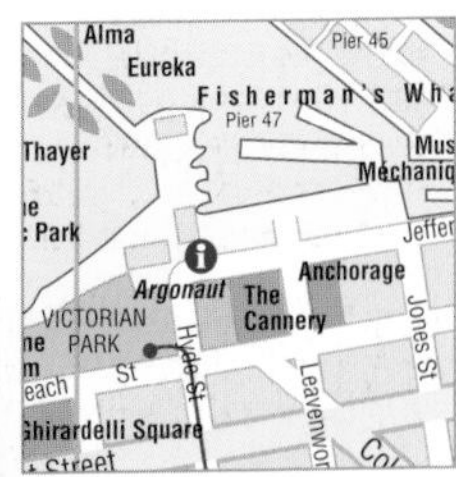

San Francisco

Locals are proud of their City by the Bay, and who can blame them? Built on fog-capped, sloping hills and surrounded by sparkling waters, San Francisco is often called the most beautiful American city. It is also idiosyncratic: many are drawn west by the allure of the city's open-minded character, fertile ground for idealists and entrepeneurial gold-prospectors alike.

San Francisco Facts and Figures

Population of city: **808,844 (7 million in Bay area)**
Area: **47.3 miles**
Major ethnic groups: **White (44.1 percent); Asian (32.9 percent); Hispanic (13.7 percent)**
Annual visitors: **15.7 million**
Number of restaurants: **4,375**
Tallest building: **Transamerica Pyramid (853ft)**
Cable car riders per year: **7.9 million**
Miles of shoreline: **29.5 miles**
Islands within city limits: **12**
Number of hills: **43**
Steepest street: **Filbert (between Leavenworth and Hyde) with 31.5 percent gradient**
Official ballad: ***I Left My Heart in San Francisco***

The City by the Bay

San Francisco has been enticing dreamers for the last century and a half. Gold in the 19th century and technology in the 20th made this city an economic boomtown, while conversely, its non-conformist ethos has put it at the center of important countercultural movements. This combination is tantalising; today, space in this compact city is at a premium and the cost of property is the second highest in the US, close behind New York City.

The threat of earthquakes and the reality of frequent fog do nothing to deter the many who fall in love with San Francisco; the city offers enough diversity of culture to ensure most will find something to suit them. Foodies, politicos, film buffs, aspiring poets, jazz-fiends, and 1960s nostalgists can find plenty to get their teeth into. All this nestles in the San Francisco peninsula, alongside the natural splendors of the Pacific Ocean, and there's no denying that the city's looks are beguiling; many even argue that the fog is romantic.

The San Franciscans

Perhaps more importantly, however, the local people are welcoming, taking an immense pride in their home, and promoting a stronger sense of a community than is found in most other cities of a similar stature.The term 'multicultural' certainly applies here: San Francisco is home to truly diverse demographics, representing all ethnicities, sexual persuasions, and proclivities. The Chinatown area is famous, but San Francisco also has a vibrant Hispanic-origin population, and large communities of people of Italian, Japanese and Russian descent. Indeed, only 35 percent of San Franciscans were born in California, while 39 percent were born outside of the US.

Many are attracted to the city by its liberal spirit. Mutal tolerance towards all is part of the city's ethos, not to mention public policy. This is perhaps all the more impressive as San Francisco is a small city, only seven square miles of overlapping and interrelating yet highly distinctive neighborhoods. For instance, the Mission, traditionally the

Below: park festivals are still a part of the summertime in San Francisco.

nexus of the city's Chicano culture, is increasingly popular with lesbian couples, suits, and bar-prowling hipsters, while the adjoining Castro is the epicenter of the city's significant gay community.

Today, there are rich pickings for nightlife, culture, and particularly food, as San Francisco boasts a world-class restaurant scene. While the average earnings enable enough eating out to sustain the city's eating establishments, and the general standard of living is high, at the other end of the spectrum, there is a big homelessness problem. It's estimated that San Francisco has the highest number of homeless people per capita in the country. Recent initiatives are making a difference, but visitors will undoubtedly notice the many down and outs.

Tales of the City

Throughout its dramatic history, San Francisco has often taken center stage culturally and politically: the Gold Rush, the Beatniks, the summer of love, the gay rights movement, the dot-com boom, then bust. Yet no matter what dramas befall this beautiful city, its charms just seem to grow. Some come to absorb the city's legacy, others to shop and eat, or to investigate Alcatraz; most want to ride up steep hills in an iconic cable car and admire the views. Whichever side of San Francisco intrigues, most find it's hard not to leave your heart here.

Highlights

▲ **Alcatraz** 'The Rock' is the world's most legendary penitentiary, once used to incarcerate the likes of Al Capone.

▶ **Mission Dolores** San Francisco was founded on the site of this adobe chapel.

▲ **Ferry Building Market** A foodie's paradise at this mouth-watering gourmet emporium, housed in an historic building.

▶ **M.H. de Young Memorial Museum** Striking architecture and culture amid the green of Golden Gate Park.

▲ **Chinatown** A fascinating city within a city, and the place to come for dim sum.

▶ **Golden Gate Bridge** The enduring, defining symbol of San Francisco.

Fisherman's Wharf

Fisherman's Wharf is filled with knick-knack stores, carnival-esque attractions, and scores of tourists, making it easy to forget that it represents the maritime past that is so integral to San Francisco's character. In the maritime present, it is still the place to pick up a ferry to Alcatraz or Angel Island, as well as across the Bay. Back on dry land, if crowds and trinkets hold no appeal, visit the waterfront in the evening when the stores have closed and everyone has gone home. Then, accompanied only by barking sea lions and the city's lights on the bay, it is much easier to enjoy the saltiness of this once bustling harbor.

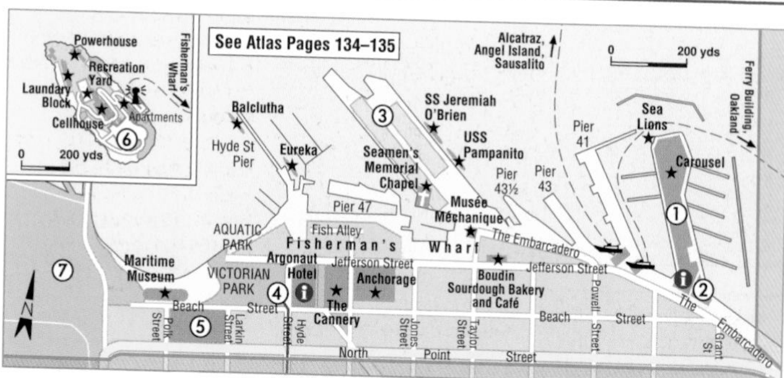

Jefferson Street and Pier 39

Jefferson Street is the main drag of Fisherman's Wharf, and home to multiple street vendors hawking boiled shellfish and clam chowder in an edible sourdough bowl, alongside several more expensive seafood restaurants. Vintage streetcars on the F-Line provide a direct route downtown.

The height of the cacophony is **Pier 39** ①, built from old wharves and anchoring the 45-acre Fisherman's Wharf. This is where you will find the double-decker carousel, depicting famous local landmarks, and some of the city's most famed inhabitants: 600 barking and sunbathing sea lions who camp out on pontoons in the water below.

To get even closer to the bay's sealife, you can descend into the nearby **Aquarium of the Bay** ② and view local sharks, other fish and crustaceans from an underwater, glass tunnel.

SEE ALSO CHILDREN, P.40

Below: flying the flag for this tourist hot-spot.

Pier 45

Today, **Pier 45** ③ and Fish Alley form the working heart of Fisherman's Wharf. From here, fishermen depart in the predawn hours and return mid-morning. Their catch is packed and sold in the tin-roofed sheds on Fish Alley. Often these fishermen guide or captain the many bay tours that launch from here in the afternoon. Pier 45 is also home to the submarine USS *Pampanito* and the **Liberty Ship SS *Jeremiah O'Brien***, which participated in the Normandy Invasion of D-Day.

Also on Pier 45, at the end of Taylor Street, the **Musée Méchanique** is an exercise in nostalgia, an arcade packed with vintage games, antique slot machines and dubious fortune-tellers. Nearby stands

Left: sea lions soak up sun and attention at Pier 39.

Tucked away amid a network of piers and boats, the tiny Fishermen's and Seamen's Memorial Chapel is dedicated to those lost at sea in North California. Once a year there is ceremony blessing San Francisco's fishing fleet.

the flagship **Boudin Sourdough Bakery and Café**. In addition to buying the bread here for a picnic or eating in the café, you can also watch it being made in the two-story, glassed-in bakery.
SEE ALSO CHILDREN, P.40; FOOD AND DRINK, P.55

Ships, Ferries, and Cable Cars

Hyde Street Pier is the original Ferry terminal for Sausalito and Berkeley, and has an impressive array of 19th-century sailing vessels, including one of the original trans-bay ferries, the *Eureka*, and the steel hulled *Balclutha*, a Scottish square-rigged sailing ship. The pier is part of the **National Maritime Park**, the smallest national park in the country. Its Visitor Center is located across the street in the **Argonaut Hotel**, itself housed inside a historic building.

Victorian Park is frequently filled with lines for the **Powell-Hyde Cable Car**, whose terminus ④ is here; be warned, the crowds mean that the wait to board a cable car from here can be a long one. On the other side of the hotel, the **Cannery**, once the largest fruit and vegetable cannery in the world, is now a popular shopping center. **Ghirardelli Square** ⑤ sits just west and is another shopping complex. It is named for the original Ghirardelli Chocolate Factory, which opened just 13 days before the legendary gold was struck at Sutter's Mill.

Below: the impressive USS *Pampanito*.

Fisherman's Wharf is the place to catch a ferry across the bay to destinations including Sausalito, Oakland, and Angel Island, not to mention **Alcatraz** ⑥; ferries depart for 'The Rock' from Pier 41. This infamous, former maximum-security prison remains one of the biggest tourist draws in the city.
SEE ALSO ALCATRAZ, P.32; FOOD AND DRINK, P.55; HOTELS, P.68; SHOPPING, P.112; TRANSPORTATION, P.122–3

Aquatic Park and Fort Mason

Perched above **Aquatic Park**, one block west of the Hyde Street Pier, is the **San Francisco National Maritime Museum**, reopening after renovation in 2009. Built in the 1930's with the rest of Aquatic Park, it resembles a beached ocean liner in the art deco style of its day. The romantic Aquatic Park prominade leads to the Municipal Pier and on to **Fort Mason** ⑦, one of the city's earliest military installations, dating back to the 1850s. Fort Mason offers stunning views of the Golden Gate Bridge, while its rugged shore below is the last original bay coastline in the city.
SEE ALSO MUSEUMS AND GALLERIES, P.88

North Beach and Telegraph Hill

Named 'Little City' by its earliest settlers, North Beach is a colorful, compact, Italian neighborhood bursting with bars, restaurants, and sidewalk cafés. Tucked into the valley between Russian Hill and Telegraph Hill, North Beach is best known for its excesses in literature, food, libations, and sex. This is where you will find the ghosts of the city's famed Beat past, as well as the best espressos in the city, as the neighborhood's Italian roots are still much in evidence.

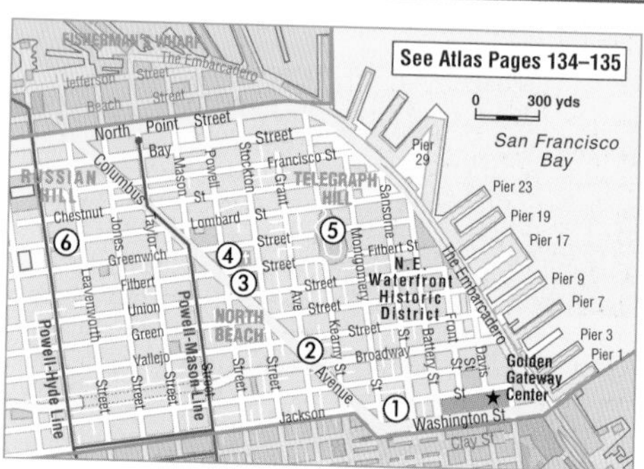

Above: the legendary bookstore, City Lights.

The Barbary Coast

Despite its name, North Beach borders no water, but when the neighborhood earned its name and reputation, the bay lay roughly at today's Bay Street.

Approaching North Beach from the Financial District, sandwiched between Jackson and Pacific streets and to the east of Montgomery Street, **Jackson Square** ① is worth a visit. Built in the 1850s, its brick architecture was able to withstand the 1906 earthquake and the following fire. It is one of the best representations of mid-19th-century San Francisco. Despite its quaint tree-lined blocks filled with chic galleries and design studios, Jackson Square was once the most notorious red light district in the city, known as the Barbary Coast.

The intersection of Columbus, Broadway, and Grant Avenue gamely carries on this tradition. It is jam-packed with strip-clubs, adult video parlors, and racy late-night clubs, including the Hungry I, which helped launch the careers of Woody Allen and Bill Cosby. Carol Doda made history at the Condor Club, performing the first topless (1964) then bottomless (1969) act in the country, while descending from the ceiling on top of a piano. For years, Ms. Doda's three-story visage, complete with neon red nipples, anchored the corner of Broadway and Columbus Avenue. Nearby, the gritty **Saloon**, opened in 1861, is the oldest bar in the city, and home to some of the city's best jazz and blues acts.

SEE ALSO MUSIC AND DANCE, P.91

Beats and Books

In the post-World War II period, rents were low, the jazz and coffeehouse scene was lively, and the neighborhood's character was lascivious; North Beach became the natural west-coast hub of beat poets, writers, and artists. This heritage is still visible today: **City Lights Bookstore** ②, Lawrence Ferlinghetti's National Literary Landmark, is both a bookstore and a publishing house, which first gained notoriety in 1956 when it published Alan Ginsburg's poem, *Howl* and subsequently won the obscenity case brought

Left: cars snake down crooked Lombard Street.

During 1906 earthquake and fire, North Beach was completely destroyed. It was quickly rebuilt with little of the architectural flourishes for which San Francisco is famous. These simple and understated Victorian and Edwardian buildings came to be fondly known as '1906 specials'.

Irish stevedores were some of the earliest inhabitants of Telegraph Hill, using the rickety network of stairs to get to and from work at the docks every day. They were replaced by Italian immigrants, and later, bohemians who liked the views and seclusion of the rustic hill.

against it, in a landmark ruling. Next door sits **Vesuvio Café**, a beatnik haunt that saw everyone from Bob Dylan to Dylan Thomas.

Up Columbus Avenue, in the heart of North Beach, sits **Washington Square** ③. While dogs and sunbathers dominate in the afternoon, early mornings belong entirely to Chinese tai-chi practitioners. Across the street, the 80-year old Romanesque Church of **Sts Peter and Paul** ④, picturesque with its gleaming white twin spires, gives daily Mass in Italian, Chinese, and English. Columbus and the narrow Grant Avenue are the two dominant commercial streets, the former filled with delis, restaurants, and cafés that spill out onto the sidewalks, while Grant retains many family-run Italian businesses and remains the centre of North Beach's social world.

SEE ALSO BARS AND CAFÉS, P.35; CHURCHES, P.44; LITERATURE, P.79; PARKS AND GARDENS, P.98

Below: local character at North Beach's Café Trieste.

Telegraph Hill and Russian Hill

Telegraph Hill got its name in 1849 when it became the site of the first telegraph on the west coast. Today, lush with winding staircases, gardens, and birdsong (including the famous flock of wild red-headed conures), it is one of the most exclusive districts in San Francisco.

Erected in 1933 and resembling the nozzle of a fire hose, **Coit Tower** ⑤ is a monument to the firefighters of the 1906 earthquake. It commands panoramic views, and its interior is illustrated with murals, in the style of Diego Rivera *(see picture, p.66)*.

To the west is the leafy and genteel Russian Hill. Named for the Russians buried here in the early days of San Francisco, it is bisected by the Powell-Hyde Cable Car and lined with elegant bistros and boutiques. It is also home to heart-stopping hills, including Filbert Street, deemed the steepest in the city, and the famous 'crookedest street in the world', **Lombard Street** ⑥, constructed with eight hairpin turns.

SEE ALSO WALKS AND VIEWS, P.124, 127

Chinatown

San Francisco's Chinatown is one of those rare tourist attractions that is also a dynamic community. With 75,000 residents tightly packed into 24 square blocks, Chinatown is as close as you can get to a city within a city, complete with its own banks, schools, law offices, video stores, and sweatshops, sadly reminiscent of those at the turn of the 20th century. Not that you see this on main thoroughfare Grant Avenue, which feels in many ways like a Disney version of 'Chinatown', but do not be fooled: behind the tourist-oriented commercialism exists a thriving, insular, and in many ways, impenetrable community.

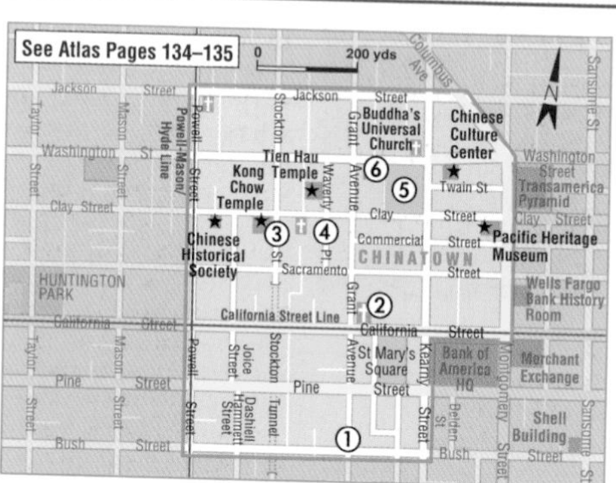

Above: checkers is a serious activity in Portsmouth Square.

'Little Canton'

Despite Chinatown's 'otherness', it has been a significant part of San Francisco's history since the earliest days of the Gold Rush. Due to political upheaval and widespread famine in Southern China in the 1850s, it is estimated that as many as 30,000 Chinese came to California to find their fortunes in the gold fields of the Sierras or to find work on the Transcontinental Railroad. As many as half decided to stay in San Francisco. These immigrants quickly set up a commercial district near the then center of town, Portsmouth Square.

By the mid-19th century, 'Little Canton', as it was then known, was filled with hotels and boarding houses as well as at least six restaurants (of both Chinese and non-Chinese food), as well as 33 retail stores and 15 pharmacies. The latter's herbal remedies served a vital purpose in a quickly growing city with few doctors.

Christened 'Chinatown' in 1853 by the local press, it was also notorious as a den of vice. Brothels, opium dens, and gambling rings were legendary, and often exaggerated to justify the anti-Chinese racism rampant in 19th-century California. This discrimination and hostility reached a boiling point in the aftermath of the 1906 earthquake and fire, which leveled the ramshackle Chinatown. Seeing the opportunity to seize the valuable downtown real estate, as well as to eradicate what they saw as a blight on the city, San Francisco's leaders tried to relocate Chinatown to the windswept Hunter's Point in the distant south-east corner of the city. However, the residents of Chinatown would have no such thing, and due to their steadfastness and the intervention of the Dowager Empress on behalf of her distant subjects, Chinatown was rebuilt in its original spot, in the heart of the city.

SEE ALSO HISTORY AND ARCHITECTURE, P.65

Grant Avenue

The 'official' entrance of Chinatown is through the ornately decorated jade-tiled **gate** ① at the intersection of Bush

Left: bustling Grant Street.

> Every year in early spring, Chinatown sees the biggest Chinese New Year celebration outside of Asia, drawing thousands into the cramped neighborhood. During the festivities, firecracker wrappers litter every alleyway, as venders fill the streets, and the spectacular parade, complete with the 201-ft Golden Dragon, seals the celebration.

Street and Grant Avenue near Union Square. A gift from Taiwan in 1970, it is modeled after a traditional village gate, and marks the beginning of Chinatown's glitzy emporiums, Cantonese restaurants, and stores hawking silks, jade, carved teak, and other Chinese bric-a-brac. The busy main drag, **Grant Avenue**, is packed with souvenir shops, but there are some respites along the way; **Old St Mary's Church** ②, at the intersection of Grant Avenue and California Street, was established in 1853, making it the oldest Catholic church in the city.
SEE ALSO CHURCHES, P.44; SHOPPING, P.112

Around Chinatown

It is worth stepping off Grant Avenue to experience the richer flavors of Chinatown. **Stockton Street** ③ is its working center, filled with Chinese owned and operated businesses, countless dollar stores, and open-air markets. Many temples of different faiths sit atop buildings (to place them closer to heaven) throughout Chinatown, frequently acting as both an active house of worship and a community center. They are open to visitors, but be respectful and prepared to leave an offering. **Waverly Place** ④, just off Clay Street between Stockton Street and Grant Avenue, is known as the 'Street of Painted Balconies' and offers a brief reprieve from Chinatown's frenetic hum. Here, stores sell 'real' Chinese goodies – lychee wine, pickled ginger and herbal remedies. The **Tien Hau Temple** (125 Waverly) is believed to be the oldest Chinese temple in the country.

Portsmouth Square ⑤ is steeped in history and often considered the birthplace of San Francisco. In 1846, it was where Captain John Montgomery first raised the American flag. A year later, it was the site of San Francisco's first school. And a year after that, it was the place where Sam Brannan, owner of San Francisco's first newspaper, the *California Star*, announced that gold had been discovered in the Sierra foothills. Today, it is where children play, and old men go to spend their day arguing politics, while playing checkers and mahjong at the small tables dotting the square.

The pagoda-like Chinese Telephone Exchange building on Washington Street, where the *California Star* was once printed, is now home to the **Bank of Canton** ⑥.
SEE ALSO CHURCHES, P.44; FOOD AND DRINK, P.54

Below: going to the bank, Chinatown style.

Union Square and Financial District

Banks, designer labels, chic bars, exclusive restaurants, top-end hotels, the theater, and art galleries all define this commercial mecca. In the heart of the west coast's financial hub in downtown San Francisco, the hum of cable cars is an atmospheric background noise to socialites shopping for their next gala and theatergoers attending the latest play. Weekdays downtown are dominated by a smart-looking set shuffling between the office, trips for lattes, the gym, and high-powered martini lunches.

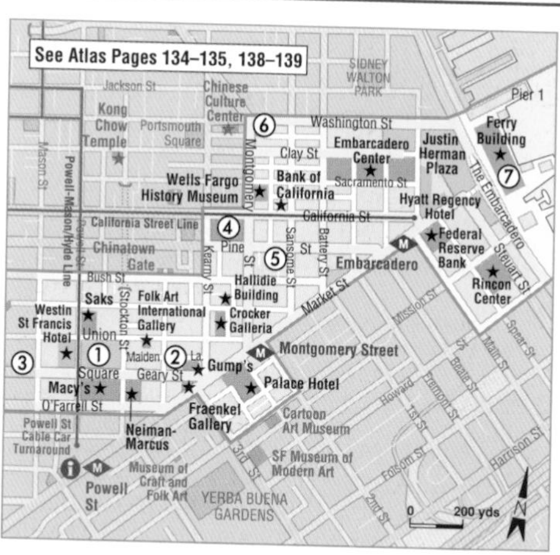

Above: multitasking on the move downtown.

Union Square ①

Gump's, Macy's, Neiman-Marcus, Saks Fifth Avenue, the many international luxury retailers from Cartier to Hermes, and hometown institutions such as Shrieve's give this shopping district enough swank to hold up to any other cosmopolitan city.

Redesigned in 2002, Union Square has a sleek modern look of gray and pink granite, and provides a place of repose for the weary shopper. In spite of its appearance, the square is as old as San Francisco itself. First deeded for public use in 1850, it got its name a decade later when it was used to rally support for the Union cause during the Civil War. At the square's center is a 90-ft Corinthian column, topped by a bronze Victory commemorating the successful Manila Bay campaign during the Spanish-American War.

The square is ringed by high-end hotels; particular standouts include the **Sir Francis Drake Hotel**, home of the lavish Harry Denton Starlight Room, and the **Westin St Francis Hotel**, which was built in 1904.

Nearby is Maiden Lane, a pedestrian-only alleyway studded with boutiques, sidewalk cafés, and the Frank Lloyd Wright designed **Xanadu Gallery** ②. Maiden Lane's tongue-in-cheek name originated from its notorious red-light past, known for having the cheapest prostitutes on the Barbary Coast.

Wedged between Union Square, Market Street, Civic Center, and the Tenderloin, is the city's Theater District. At its heart lies the historic **Geary Theater** built in 1910. It is home to San Francisco's **American Conservatory Theater** ③, whose season runs roughly from September through June. They perform an assortment of theater classics as well as original productions. The three other large theaters, the **Orpheum**, the **Golden Gate**, and the

Left: the distinctive Transamerica Pyramid.

Snaking through the Financial District is the hidden French Quarter of San Francisco. Alleyways such as Belden Place and Claude Alley are full of French bistros, and the area is particularly lively each year on Bastille Day (July 14).

Curran, attract larger national shows, often New York companies running performances before they debut on Broadway.

SEE ALSO HOTELS, P.72; MUSEUMS AND GALLERIES, P.87; SHOPPING, P.112; THEATER AND CABARET, P.118

Financial District

Considered to be the financial capital of the west coast, the soaring Financial District owes its great heights to the gold struck in the Sierra Nevada. The banks of 'Wall Street West' turned the miners' gold into money by minting currency. Bank of America and Wells Fargo both began and are headquartered here. The **Bank of America Building** ④ is the second tallest building in the city; the polished black granite sculpture by Masayuki Nagare just outside it is locally known as the 'Bankers Heart'. The **Wells Fargo Museum** celebrates the bank's rich history and role in the Gold Rush.

Other historic and architectural gems include: the old world **Palace Hotel**, which initially made news in 1875 for supposedly being fire proof (definitively disproved in 1906), but has since become known for its opulent Garden Court, the site of the celebration following the opening session of the United Nations; the 1930 **Pacific Stock Exchange** ⑤, illustrated by muralist Diego Rivera; and the **Transamerica Pyramid** ⑥, the tallest building in the city, which redefined San Francisco's skyline when it was built in 1972.

SEE ALSO HISTORY AND ARCHITECTURE, P.67; HOTELS, P.74; MUSEUMS AND GALLERIES, P.88

Below: it is always time to eat at the Ferry Building.

Embarcadero

Only recently has the waterfront become incorporated into the Financial District. For years the Embarcadero Freeway turned the waterfront into a mess of concrete and abandoned wharves; it collapsed during the Loma-Prieta Earthquake in 1989, opening up this vital area to redevelopment and rebirth. Since then, the Embarcadero has been lined with palm trees, given tracks for the historic F-line streetcars, and seen the renovation of the **Ferry Building** ⑦. Opened in 1898 and with a 230-ft tower modeled after Seville's Cathedral, it is the transit center for ferries bringing people to and from work every day, and more recently, the epicenter of San Francisco's sustainable food movement. Redevelopment has made this landmark into a mouthwatering gourmet emporium with a range of dining options, as well as food merchants and a farmers' market.

SEE ALSO FOOD AND DRINK, P.54

SoMa and Civic Center

Firmly rooted in the life of the city are the grandiose Civic Center and the energetic SoMa (South of Market) districts. Awash with civic life, they are underpinned by city government, cultural institutions, public spaces, the visual and expressive arts, cutting edge restaurants, and a thriving late-night club scene. Bordering the two neighborhoods is the edgier Tenderloin district, while nearby Hayes Valley is a smart locale packed with upscale eateries and trendy design stores.

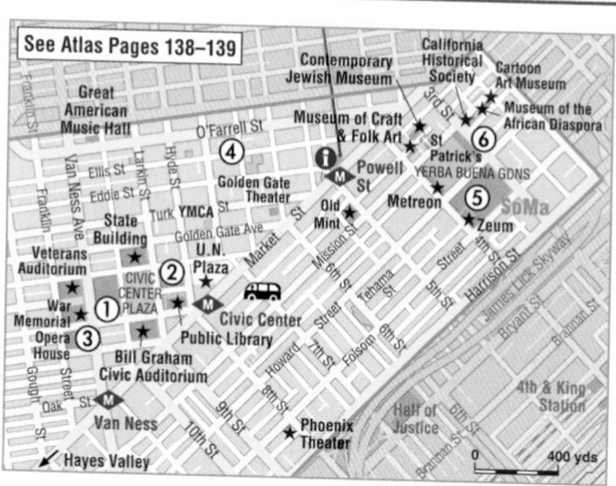

Above: performance is part of the scenery at Yerba Buena park.

Civic Center

San Francisco's Civic Center is dominated by Arthor Brown Jr's beaux arts **City Hall** ①. Built in 1914, it was influenced by the City Beautiful movement of the 1890s and is perhaps the grandest seat of city government in the United States, eclipsing even New York's, and representing the city's optimism at the end of the century. City Hall was the scene of the murders of Harvey Milk and Mayor George Moscone in 1978, and in February 2004 found itself at the centre of nation-wide controversy when Mayor Gavin Newsom granted marriage licenses to same-sex couples; around 4,000 flocked to City Hall to exchange their vows before the Supreme Court of California shut down proceedings.

Brown was also responsible for many other Civic Center buildings, including the Veterans Auditorium, home to the **Herbst Theater**, the **War Memorial Opera House** (the birthplace of the United Nations), and the old Main Public Library Building, now the location of the **Asian Art Museum** ②, which has one of the world's largest collections of Near and Far East art.

The Civic Center also includes the new Main Public Library, the State Building, the ultramodern **Louise M. Davies Symphony Hall** ③, and the Bill Graham Civic Auditorium, named for the famous promoter who was responsible for San Francisco's explosive music scene in the 1960's.

SEE ALSO MUSEUMS AND GALLERIES, P.82; MUSIC AND DANCE, P.90

The Tenderloin

Connecting the Civic Center to Market Street is the United Nations Plaza, host to a **farmers' market** every Wednesday and Sunday. This is also the tip of the grimy Tenderloin, a neighborhood that extends along Market Street to Union Square. Known for drugs, prostitution, criminal activity, and the down and out, it is also home to some great old San Francisco architecture, inexpensive but fantastic ethnic food, and historic sites, including the **Glide Memorial Methodist Church** ④, dedicated to serving the homeless

Left: the road to City Hall.

The Mitchell Brothers' O'Farrell Theater is a Tenderloin institution and a San Francisco legend. A pioneer in the adult entertainment industry, Hunter S. Thompson proclaimed it 'the Carnegie Hall of public sex in America'. In 1991 it became infamous when one brother was shot and killed by the other.

while welcoming visitors to its energetic and soulful Sunday sermons, and the historic **Great American Music Hall**, whose voluptuous rococo interior harks back to its bordello past and adds flavor to this world class music venue. The neighborhood is as gritty as it looks, so keep alert during the day and at night it is advisable to hail a cab.
SEE ALSO CHURCHES, P.44; FOOD AND DRINK, P.57; MUSIC AND DANCE, P.92

Hayes Valley

On the other side of the Civic Center, the newly revitalized Hayes Valley is a charming neighborhood to enjoy a coffee, cocktail, or a bit of shopping before, or after, a night at the opera. It is also home to many of the city's top restaurants.

SoMa

Low-slung factories and empty warehouses fill the wide blocks stretching from Market Street to the old working waterfront. Its gradual decay began when San Francisco transferred its shipping industry to the ports of Alameda and Oakland. In the 1950s the area emerged as the center for the gay community's leather subculture. However, the dot-com boom of the 1990s turned the South of Market district into SoMa, a chic area filled with museums, live-work lofts, nightclubs, exciting restaurants, and a ton of artistic and entrepreneurial energy. Since the bust at the turn of the millennium, SoMa has settled down a bit, but it has forever changed into a vital part of San Francisco's cultural life.

Below: the striking San Francisco Museum of Modern Art.

The intersection of Mission and 3rd streets is the nexus of SoMa's museum district, anchored by the **Moscone Convention Center** and **Yerba Buena Center for the Arts** ⑤, a 22-acre complex complete with rolling gardens, an art museum, the children's museum **Zeum**, performance spaces, an ice skating rink, and a beautifully restored 1905 carousel.

Nearby **St Patrick's Church**, established in 1851, stands for a bit of history. Still serving the community, it now performs a Sunday Mass in Tagalog for the local Filipino residents. Across 3rd Street, is the **San Francisco Museum of Modern Art** ⑥. Other museums include the **Museum of the African Diaspora**, the **California Historical Society**, the **Cartoon Art Museum**, and the temporarily located **California Academy of Sciences**.
SEE ALSO CHILDREN, P.41; MUSEUMS AND GALLERIES, P.85–6, 88–9; PARKS AND GARDENS, P.98

Nob Hill

Perched on the highest of San Francisco's many hills, the robber barons of Nob Hill have been looking down at the rest of San Francisco since the late 19th century. Nicknamed the 'hill of palaces' by Robert Louis Stevenson, it has always had a reputation for being home to privilege and refined luxury. While this attitude endures, all but one of the 'palaces' are gone, replaced by the Gothic Grace Cathedral, the beautiful Huntington Park, and elite hotels with spectacular views. Today, Nob Hill is a charming neighborhood filled with elegant apartment buildings, where the lesser mansions once stood.

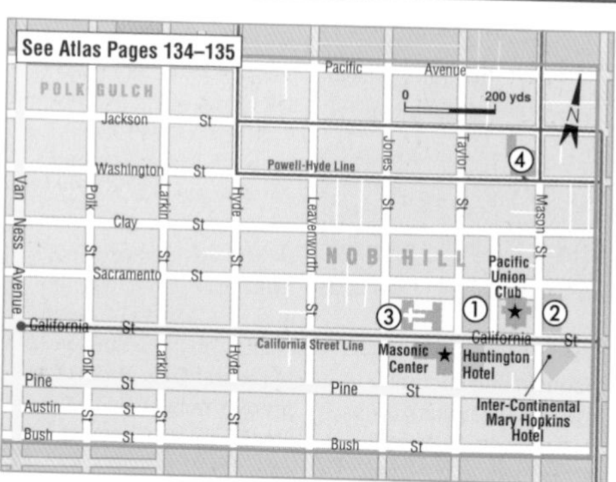

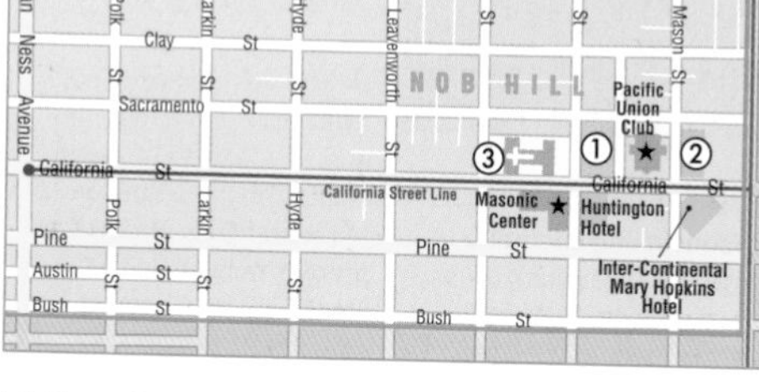

Above: the temples to luxury on Nob Hill.

Fit For a Baron

In 1873, Andrew Smith Hallidie invented the cable car, and turned the once barren 'California Street Hill' into prime real estate. No sooner had the tracks been laid when San Francisco's wealthiest began vying for the best lot, and outdoing each other building opulent and extravagant mansions. The most prominent residents occupied the apex of the hill. These were James Flood, who was one of the kings of the Comstock Silver Load, and the Big Four rail barons, Charles Crocker, Mark Hopkins, Leland Stanford, and Collis Huntington. It did not take long for the name to change to 'Nob Hill', 'nob' being a variation on 'nabob', the Indian word for Moghul prince. But many San Franciscans gave it their own nickname, 'Snob Hill'.

Thus there was little love lost, when the fire following the 1906 earthquake consumed the neighborhood. The sole surviving estate, the interior ravaged by the fire, belonged to James Flood. Holding court next to the genteel greenery of **Huntington Park** ①, it is now home to the **Pacific Union Club**, which keeps up the fine elitism of its forbearers and does not admit women into the club.
SEE ALSO PARKS AND GARDENS, P.98

Hotels and Cathedrals

From the ashes of the great Hopkins, Stanford, and Huntington mansions have sprung world famous luxury hotels. Across from the old Flood mansion now stands the **Huntington Hotel** and the **Inter-Continental Mark Hopkins Hotel**. Between them is the imposing **Fairmont Hotel** ②, which had been scheduled to open just before the earthquake of 1906. Surviving the quake but not the fire, it was quickly rebuilt, opening a year to the day after the devastating event. The stratospheric rates keep these hotels exclusive, but all are welcome to view their elegant lobbies, or to enjoy a cocktail.

The estate of Charles Crocker was the only one of the Big Four not to become a hotel. Instead, the Crocker family donated the property to the Episcopal Diocese, who built **Grace Cathedral** ③. Its

Left: parking is for experts only on a hill this steep.

car system. It also contains a museum detailing the cars' history and viewing the inner workings of this historic and uniquely mechanical system.

Centrally located, Nob Hill is a wonderful, if athletic, place to walk and enjoy its great views. Strolling the lesser streets and alleyways, it is easy to spy the neighborhood of Dashiell Hammett, who set many of his stories here, in particular, *The Maltese Falcon*. In Nob Hill, Hammett saw all the components that help define the old San Francisco: wealth, power, criminals, and style.
SEE ALSO CHURCHES, P.45; HOTELS, P.74; LITERATURE, P.78; MUSEUMS AND GALLERIES, P.87; MUSIC AND DANCE, P.92–3

The walls of the 'Room of Dons' inside the Inter-Continental Mark Hopkins Hotel, are covered in nine 7-ft tall murals depicting early California, including a golden Queen Califa for whom the state is named.

Gothic spires can be seen from high spots around the city, but the Cathedral's details deserve a closer look. From the windows, which depict prominent 20th Century figures, to the bronze and gold cathedral doors cast from Lorenzo Ghiberti's *Doors of Paradise*, to Keith Haring's altarpiece in the AIDS Interfaith Memorial Chapel, it suggests a modernism and egalitarianism that is refreshing on Nob Hill.

Across the street is the **Masonic Center**. Commissioned by the California Freemasons after the end of World War II, it is now an event center hosting cultural performances with an underground parking garage available hourly to the public.

Located near the intersection of Chinatown and Nob Hill at the corner of Washington and Mason streets, is the handsome home of the cable cars. Built in 1910, the **Cable Car Museum** ④ is the nerve center of the present cable

Polk Gulch

As Nob Hill slides down to the west, the classic apartment buildings become a little rougher around the edges. Before Castro became the city's gay center, Polk Gulch was it. Today it is where the Tenderloin nips at the well heeled Nob Hill and Russian Hill neighborhoods. Full of energy, Polk Gulch is filled with ethnic restaurants, used bookstores, and several hard-rocking nightspots.

Right: the Masonic Center's distinctive stained-glass imagery.

Central Neighborhoods

Riding the city's crests and valleys from the bay to Market Street, Fillmore Street is an excellent place to penetrate San Francisco's central neighborhoods. Largely residential, these districts all contain their own thriving commercial centers with parks, cafés, restaurants, niche stores and boutiques. Whether affluent, ethnic or edgy, these districts boast some of the best examples of San Franciscan architecture and contain some of its most distinct cultural pockets. Each is unique in character, informed by their location in San Francisco's wild topography, and all deserve a trip off the beaten path.

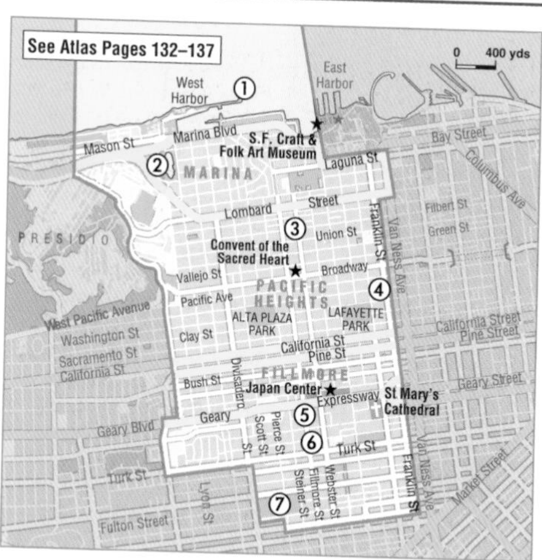

Above: celebrating jazz in the Fillmore District.

Marina and Cow Hollow

The Marina neighborhood is popular with young professionals who make good money in the Financial District and pack out the bars at the weekend. Locals celebrate the Marina's proximity to the bay with the Golden Gate Promenade, where they push baby strollers, walk dogs, or power walk amid harbors stuffed with sailboats, Frisbee throwers on the Marina Green, and native birds and plant species at the recently restored Crissy Field. Farther along the waterfront, the unique **Wave Organ** ① produces unearthly 'music' as waves crash against its 25 pipes that jut into the ocean.

Back on dry land, locals get their lattes on Chestnut Street, where stores, cafés, and an old theater grace this low rise pastel district. At the far end, by the Presidio, the **Palace of Fine Arts** ②, first built for the Pacific International Exposition in 1915, now houses the Exploratorium.

Union Street is another commercial hub, also called Cow Hollow for the cow pastures that used to occupy the softly sloping landscape. Here the 1920s Mediterranean architecture gives way to older Victorians, some of which have been converted into boutiques, bars, and restaurants. **The Vedanta Temple** ③ on Webster Street is a distinctive tribute to religious tolerance; the amalgam of architectural styles is designed to convey that all religions stem from common roots.

SEE ALSO MUSEUMS AND GALLERIES, P.89

Pacific Heights

Sitting high above the Marina is the crown of Pacific Heights, the neighborhood of today's power brokers and social elite, and lined with beautiful, jaw-dropping mansions. While many remain in private hands, others have been converted to schools or

Left: the oft-pictured 'painted ladies' of Alamo Square.

Built on reclaimed land and rubble from the 1906 earthquake, the Marina was one of the worst hit areas when the Loma-Prieta earthquake struck in 1989, though only the markedly newer structures give any clue to this today.

consulates. One of the few open to the public is the Queen Anne-style **Haas-Lilienthal House** (1886) ④, full of Victorian-era antiques.

In addition to **Alta Plaza** and **Lafayette Park**, Fillmore Street is the place to enjoy the luxury of Pacific Heights. For those lighter of pocket, it has a number of secondhand stores where the rich discard last year's fashions.

SEE ALSO PARKS AND GARDENS, P.99

The Fillmore District

It is a steep drop down to the Fillmore District, where the line between the haves and the have-nots cannot be any clearer. Rich in cultural history, the Fillmore has seen better days. Once a thriving African American community, attracting the very best jazz stars of the 1930s and 1940s, it was destroyed by the controversial Urban Redevelopment Program of the 1950s, which filled the area with low-income housing developments. Nonetheless, it is a great neighborhood for seeing live music, particularly at the **Fillmore Auditorium** ⑤, where Bill Graham helped launch the careers of San Francisco's biggest 1960's musical acts.

SEE ALSO MUSIC AND DANCE, P.92

Japantown

Just across the street from The Fillmore is the compact Japantown. It is home to 12,000 Japanese San Franciscans and dominated by the Japan Center, an enormous complex of stores, theaters, sushi bars, restaurants, and the wonderful Japanese-style **Kabuki Springs and Spa**. Its distinguishing feature is its 100-ft high, five tiered, **Peace Pagoda**, given to San Francisco by Japan following World War II. Despite being settled by Japanese immigrants as far back as the 1860s, Japantown was razed during World War II as the US government expelled Japanese Americans to inland internment camps.

SEE ALSO PAMPERING, P.97

The Western Addition

An extension of the Fillmore, the Western Addition also has a long and proud African-American past, and is where you'll find the **St John Coltrane African Orthodox Church** ⑥, newly relocated at 1286 Fillmore Street.

Alamo Square ⑦ is the pinnacle of the Western Addition. This sloping city park fits perfectly into an imagined 19th century past, surrounded by fully restored Victorians. The famous **'painted ladies'** on the eastern side pit a dramatic contrast against the sparkling view of the Financial District and City Hall.

SEE ALSO CHURCHES, P.45; HISTORY AND ARCHITECTURE, P.65; PARKS AND GARDENS, P.99

Below: the Peace Pagoda.

Haight-Ashbury and Golden Gate Park

In 1966, at the intersection of Haight and Ashbury streets, a young, pre-beard Jerry Garcia and the rest of the Grateful Dead posed for one of the era's iconic photos, proclaiming the district to be the epicenter of the quickly emerging counterculture. The brightly painted Victorian houses became hippie crash pads; their presence can still be felt today in this nostalgic neighborhood. Nearby, Golden Gate Park stretches to the sea over 1,000 acres, containing wonderful gardens, museums, and other attractions.

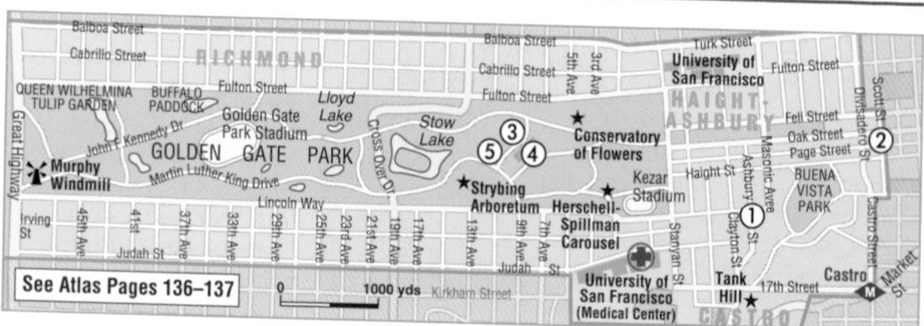

The Haight

Low rents initially attracted the next wave of bohemians following the Beats. By the mid-1960s the neighborhood had filled with headshops, boutiques, bookstores, musicians and artists, but it was 1967 when it gained iconic status, as tens of thousands flocked here for first the 'Human Be-In,' and then the famous 'Summer of Love'. The event catapulted the careers of such San Francisco bands as Jefferson Airplane, Big Brother, and the Holding Company, not to mention the Grateful Dead. The sense of this history is palpable as you walk around Haight Street, particularly from the intersection with **Ashbury Street** ①.

However, while The Haight, as it is known by locals, is considerably steeped in nostalgia, there are plenty of modern day fashonistas, Goths, and young 'hippie' homeless types claiming the neighborhood as their own. Crowded with thrift stores, iconoclastic fashion boutiques, cheap eateries, friendly local bars, the vast **Amoeba** record store, housed in an old bowling alley, and the second-run **Red Vic Movie House**, Haight Street remains a colorful and dynamic place to hang out.

Down several residential blocks, past the city's oldest park, **Buena Vista**, and Divisadero Street, the Lower Haight is considerably grimier and less nostalgic, but some feel it is a more exciting version of the Haight and today it is certainly more progressive. Edgy music and fashion stores sit alongside hip bars and eateries here. At the corner of Page and Scott is **Jack's Record Cellar** ②, the oldest record store in the city.

For a change of tempo and a sunnier neighborhood, visit Cole Valley. Winding up the hill from Upper Haight toward University of California San Francisco Medical School, Cole Valley is filled with charming gingerbread houses, young families, and fabulous places to grab coffee or brunch. A climb up Tank Hill offers spectacular views of the city.

Above: hippies still congregate in the Haight.

SEE ALSO FASHION, P.52–3; HISTORY AND ARCHITECTURE, P.67;

Left: the Conservatory of Flowers, in Golden Gate Park.

MOVIES, P.81; MUSIC AND DANCE, P.93; PARKS AND GARDENS, P.99; WALKS AND VIEWS, P.128

Golden Gate Park

One of the civic wonders of San Francisco, **Golden Gate Park**, is eight blocks wide and 52 blocks long. It represents the aspirations at the end of the 19th century of civic leaders who sought to build a city (and a park) rivaling New York. The dedicated and talented William Hammond Hall converted the once windswept sand dunes into a verdant wonderland, hailed for its botanical variety and naturally unfolding topography. Today it is home to a vast collection of cultural attractions and countless places to picnic, play Frisbee, or catch some sun.

The eastern end of the park has the highest concentration of cultural sites. Built at the turn of the 20th century and landscaped with trees and fountains, the Music Concourse is an outdoor summer music venue seating 20,000 people. Surrounding it are the new **M.H. de Young Memorial Museum** ③, with a striking exterior, home to an impressive collection of art from around the world, ranging from antiquity to the modern era; the **California Academy of Sciences** ④, featuring the **Steinhart Aquarium** and **Morrison Planetarium**, reopening after renovation in late 2008; and the **Japanese Tea Garden** ⑤, a favorite for its subtlety and beauty. Also nearby is the 70-acre **Strybing Arboretum** and the **Conservatory of Flowers**, housed in the oldest building in the park, an elegant copy of the Palm House in London's Kew Gardens.

Crossing 19th Avenue, the park is dotted with a series of lakes and contains horse stables, archery facilities, flyfishing ponds, playgrounds, tennis and bocce ball courses, a polo field, and two windmills, once used to pump water for the entire park.

SEE ALSO CHILDREN, P.42; MUSEUMS AND GALLERIES, P.83, 88; PARKS AND GARDENS, P.99–100

Filled with grand Victorians and large backyards, Haight-Ashbury began as the suburbs, linked by the Haight Street Cable Railroad to the Financial District. In the housing shortage during World War II, many of these single homes were divided into apartments, which were vacated once the war was over, as families left for the suburbs in the 1950s mass 'white flight.'

Below: Bob Dylan gets a nod in a local mural.

Mission and Castro

Pride and Viva La Raza! define these two adjoining neighborhoods, which in many ways provide San Francisco's political and artistic heartbeat. The well-groomed Castro, considered by many to be the gay capital of the world, showcases beautifully restored Victorian and Edwardian homes, while draping its thriving nightlife, love of shopping, and political activism in rainbow flags. Farther east, the Mission dresses itself with colors of the Americas. This working-class Latino neighborhood lures artists, suits, musicians, and hipsters to create one of the most dynamic and diverse districts in the city.

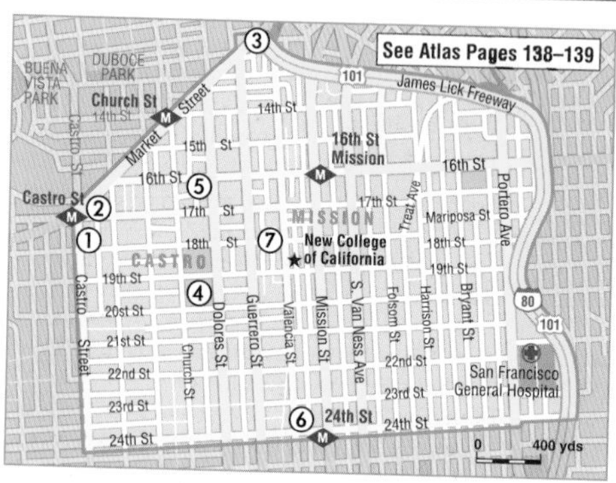

Above: the symbol of Pride flies over a street in the Castro.

The Castro

It was only 30 years ago that the Castro shifted from a working-class, Irish-Catholic neighborhood to being the gay hub of the city, but it is hard now to imagine it any differently. Its tightly packed commercial strip largely caters to the gay community, but there is something for everyone, in particular the **Castro Theater** ①, which exhibits the glamour and class of the neighborhood. Designated a US National Historic Landmark in 1977, this ornate Spanish baroque theater, complete with art deco flourishes, is a revival movie house, and often the host to one of San Francisco's many film festivals. On special nights it features a live organist who plays on an ascending platform before the start of the film. **Twin Peaks** ②, a friendly neighborhood joint, sits proudly at the corner of Castro and Market, and was the first openly gay bar in the US.

The Castro's dedication to community and civil rights is represented at the Charles M. Holmes Campus at **The Center** ③. Located at 1800 Market near the intersection with Hayes Valley, The Center is the nexus for community events, classes and support groups, and information about the local LGBT (Lesbian, Gay, Bisexual, Transgender) community. During the annual Pride celebration in June, this civic commitment becomes a party lasting all weekend. Attracting half a million people, Pride is the highest of high holidays of the gay community, including a huge parade festooned with queens, floats, and high-stepping frivolity.

SEE ALSO GAY AND LESBIAN, P.58–63; MOVIES, P.81

The Mission

Castro residents come to sunbathe and walk their dogs at sunny **Mission Dolores Park** ④, where the district begins, its namesake only two blocks away on the palm-lined Dolores Street. Modestly situated next to the impressive Basilica is the Misión San Francisco de Asís, commonly known as the **Mission Dolores** ⑤. The city's oldest building, it was

Left: Latino color and culture at a Mission taqueria.

Co-founded by author Dave Eggers, 826 Valencia is a non-profit organisation dedicated to helping and encouraging young people to write. It also doubles as a pirate store.

completed just days before the signing of the Declaration of Independence in 1776.

From Dolores Street, The Mission spreads east. Valencia Street is the hipster and bohemian center of the Mission, and is aptly filled with great bookstores, hip bars, internet cafés, and the site of the **New College of California**, an ultra-liberal university. Mission Street's numerous art deco marquees speak of a more prosperous time, but the street is still rich in culture and artistic energy. Full of discount stores, Mexican groceries, and more late night spots, it is an exilarating neighborhood, though a bit less salubrious after dark. While it is a diverse area, the Latino culture for which this area is especially famous can be seen particularly on 24th Street, from Mission to Folsom. Lined with trees and *taquerias*, it has the feeling of being lodged deep in the heart of Latin America.

Murals throughout The Mission express its political consciousness as well as a deep connection to *'La Raza'* (the race, or the people). The **Galeria de la Raza** ⑥ on 24th Street is largely considered the most important Chicano art center in the country.

Meanwhile, the **Women's Building** ⑦ is festooned with brilliant murals and is an important community center. The Women's Movement also took root in this part of the city. Because a two woman household draws in significantly less income than a man/woman, and particularly a man/man household, the Mission's low rents began attracting a strong lesbian community that many credit with shifting the character of this once-rough neighborhood.

Since then, the Mission has become a hub for those trying to make it in the art world and is seen as the new bohemian center. Its numerous bars, cafés, and bookstores are representative of this trend, as well its emerging chic culinary scene.

SEE ALSO CHURCHES, P.45; GAY AND LESBIAN, P.58–63; MUSEUMS AND GALLERIES, P.87; PARKS AND GARDENS, P.101; WALKS AND VIEWS, P.128

Below: the Misión San Francisco de Asís (or Mission Dolores) gives the city its name.

Around San Francisco

Less visited than their central cousins, San Francisco's outlying districts hark back to the city's military and working class foundations. These fringe areas provide green areas and astonishing views of the city, while giving an insight into the lives of many working San Franciscans. They also reach back to San Francisco's natural history. Western places such as Land's End and Ocean Beach preserve the water's wild edge, while the city's southeastern peaks blossom with wildflowers in Spring. Meanwhile, stretching out from the Presidio and South Beach respectively are the photogenic, iconic Golden Gate Bridge and busy, impressive Bay Bridge.

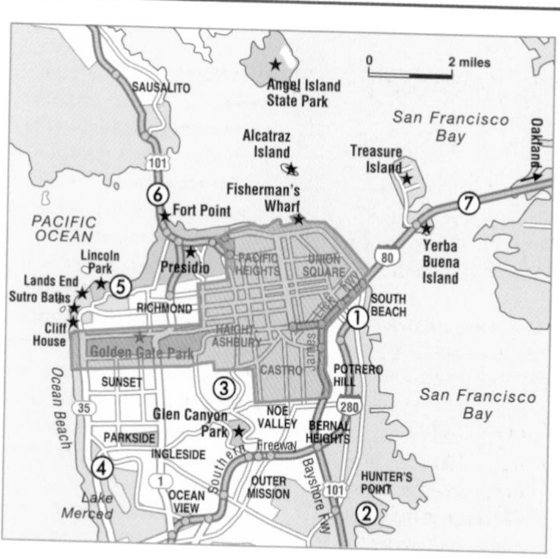

Above: shopping in trendy Noe Valley.

South Beach

The Embarcadero promenade, offering spectacular views of the bay and its namesake bridge, leads to the neighborhood of South Beach, full of redeveloped warehouses. The water line leads from Fisherman's Wharf to the new **AT&T Ballpark** ①, home to the San Francisco Giants.

The **49ers'** home is **Monster Park**, formerly Candlestick Park ②. It is located in Hunter's Point, also the site of the once bustling Naval Shipyard, after whose departure the neighborhood has never quite recovered.

SEE ALSO SPORT, P.117

Potrero Hill to Twin Peaks

Overlooking Hunter's Point, Potrero Hill is a one-time working class neighborhood and a great spot for dinner while enjoying the south end views of the city. Nearby residential neighborhoods include Bernal Heights, packed with families and narrow streets, and Noe Valley, whose 24th Street has a charming assortment of gourmet stores, cafés, and bistros. **Twin Peaks** ③, has an overlook to take in the panoramic view, and residents who are wealthy enough enjoy it year round.

SEE ALSO WALKS AND VIEWS, P.125

Ocean Beach

The 4 miles of Ocean Beach are a wonderful place to play in the sand or take in a sunset. Be aware, the water is very cold and the undertow strong enough to catch even the most experienced swimmers off guard. The **San Francisco Zoo** ④ anchors the south end, with a constant stream of new and exciting exhibits, while the Sutro Baths and the Cliff House overlook the north. The **Cliff House** has gone through a number of remodeling and incarnations due to fires, but is now the location of **Sutro's**, an upscale restaurant with killer views. Public walkways allow appreciation of these without the need for a fat wallet.

SEE ALSO CHILDREN, P.41; RESTAURANTS, P.110

Left: catching some waves at the Presidio's beach.

At sea level, Treasure Island is a great place to ride a bike, take in the phenomenal views of the city, and come eye to eye with the giant cargo ships coming into the Port of Oregon.

Sunset and Richmond

Known as the Avenues, the Sunset and Richmond districts run along either side of Golden Gate Park. Both are vast residential neighborhoods full of Russian, Irish, and Chinese families, with commercial districts filled with bookstores, groceries, and Asian restaurants. Bisecting the Richmond is **Lincoln Park**, home to the **Palace of the Legion of Honor** ⑤. Housed in a beaux art building, the Legion showcases 4,000 years of ancient and European art. From here, it is a short walk to Lands End, the city's most wild section of coastline, complete with arresting views of the Golden Gate.

SEE ALSO MUSEUMS AND GALLERIES, P.83; PARKS AND GARDENS, P.101; WALKS AND VIEWS, P.126

The Presidio

Almost 1,500 acres in size, the Presidio occupies the northwest corner of the city. For more than 200 years, The Presidio was an active military installation, and was turned over to Golden Gate National Parks in 1995. Today it is a rich collection of historic buildings, residential neighborhoods, a few restaurants, and hiking trails which crisscross this vast swath of land.

Out in the bay, to the north of the city, sits **Angel Island**. Once the Quarantine and Immigration stations for the west coast, it processed thousands of Asians attempting to immigrate here, often holding them for several months at a time. The buildings of the station still exist and can be visited on a docent-led tour. Today it is a state park with 13 miles of trails.

SEE ALSO PARKS AND GARDENS, P.101; WALKS AND VIEWS, P.126

Iconic Bridges

The **Golden Gate Bridge** ⑥ is perhaps the most photographed bridge in the world and is popular with bikers, walkers, and drivers alike. Crews work continually from one end to the other and back, sandblasting rust and repainting. Hidden below the bridge is the impenetrable **Fort Point**, a Civil War era fortification built to protect San Francisco Bay from any potential Confederate attack.

The **Bay Bridge** ⑦ is the longest steel high-level bridge in the world and one of its busiest. On its journey downtown from Oakland, it passes through Yerba Buena Island and the adjacent man-made Treasure Island. The latter was created in the late 1930s for the Golden Gate International Exposition and taken over by the Navy shortly thereafter. Recently, it was turned back over to the city and is now San Francisco's newest residential neighborhood.

SEE ALSO HISTORY AND ARCHITECTURE, P.66

Below: a monument to the Giants in South Beach.

Oakland, Berkeley, and the Bay Area

From the Black Panthers to Chez Panisse, the East Bay is in many ways the revolutionary center that San Francisco gets so much credit for. From its lively political culture, vast parklands and outdoor spaces, museums and intellectual centers, and widely diverse demographics, the East Bay is a thriving metropolitan center independent of its scene-stealing neighbor to the west. Oakland and Berkeley are an easy trip across the Bay Bridge, and the BART system makes them particularly accessible.

Above: Jack London's haunt, First and Last Chance Saloon.

Oakland

Much has changed in **Oakland** ① since the indignity of Gertrude Stein's quip, 'There is no there there'. During World War II the industry and ports of Oakland boomed, as did its population, creating the diversity responsible for Oakland's uniquely textured culture. Today, it is one of the most diverse cities in the state with 36 percent of its population African American, 24 percent Caucasian, 22 percent Hispanic, and 15 percent Asian.

Oakland is not a city defined by its skyline, but by its parks and diverse cultural attractions. Near downtown sits **Lake Merritt**, a 155-acre natural salt-water lake, popular with wildlife and picnickers. Close by are the **Oakland Museum of California**, the **African American Museum and Library**, and the restored art deco **Paramount Theater**.

On the waterfront is **Jack London Square**, perhaps Oakland's biggest tourist draw. Named for the city's most famous son, it is a complex of stores, seafood restaurants, and such attractions as the author's rustic cabin, recreated from the logs of the Yukon original, as well as **First and Last Chance Saloon**, one of London's frequent haunts. Farther south on the Nimitz Freeway is the **McAfee Coliseum and Oracle Arena**, home to the Oakland A's, the Golden State Warriors, and the Oakland Raiders.

SEE ALSO LITERATURE, P.78; MUSEUMS AND GALLERIES, P.88; SPORT, P.117

Berkeley

Since the Free Speech Movement in 1964, **Berkeley** ② has been a hot bed of political activism. The university campus, the 'crown of the UC system', is a sprawling temple

Left: a new semester begins at Berkeley University.

> The Marin Headlands are accessible by public transit from San Francisco. Golden Gate Transit makes the trip, as does the number 76 bus.

> Perhaps Oakland's most famous export in the early 1970s was the Black Panthers, who formed in response to police brutality in Oakland's African American neighborhoods. They quickly spread to other big cities and became key figures in the counterculture of that turbulent era.

to education full of earnest students and Nobel Prize-winning professors. The focal point of campus is the 307-ft **Sather Tower**, known as the Campanile, which can be seen from across the bay. The on-site **Berkeley Art Museum** is the largest university art collection of its kind.

Intersecting the campus at Sproul Plaza is **Telegraph Avenue**, long known to be one of the landmarks of the counterculture, as is nearby **People's Park**, the site of a legendary student-police confrontation. Berkeley is a beautiful city filled with elegant Craftsman style homes; a stroll through its leafy streets is a highly recommended treat.
SEE ALSO MUSEUMS AND GALLERIES, P.86

Marin County

A drive over the Golden Gate Bridge or a ferry ride from the Ferry Building or Fisherman's Wharf takes you into Marin County, which is packed with beautiful coastline, rugged hills and attractive towns. **Sausalito** ③ is one of the most worthwhile to visit; it is known as the 'French Riviera' of the west coast, due to its equable climate, art galleries, and restaurants making the most of the great views.

The Bay Area is a rare example of a major metropolitan area that has succeeded in preserving vast amounts of surrounding open space. The magnificent **Marin Headlands** across the Golden Gate from San Francisco attest to this. It is one of several parks in Marin County, which include the **Muir Woods** and the **Point Reyes National Seashore** ④. In the west, open space gives way to dairy farms, ranch land and a windswept coast, while the east is home to upper middle class communities, many of whom make the daily commuter trip into the city.

Below: taking the scenic way to Point Reyes.

Around the Bay Area

In Palo Alto, south from San Francisco, is **Stanford University** ⑤, Berkeley's major rival in sports, academics, and prestige. Major points of interest include the **Hoover Tower** and the **Rodin Sculpture Garden**, which displays 20 bronze castings.

Nearby **Silicon Valley** was once called the Valley of Heart's Delight but is now famed for and synonymous with innovation in technology.

Wine Country

In need of wine for their sacramental duties, the Spanish padres of the California missions can be credited with bringing viticulture to the Napa and Sonoma valleys. However, it was a Hungarian nobleman, Count Agoston Haraszthy, who saw the area's full potential. In 1857, he opened the region's first winery, Sonoma's Buena Vista Winery, which is still in operation. Since then, many winemakers have followed in his footsteps, producing vino recognized around the world for its excellence. A trip to the wine country is a worthwhile excursion from San Francisco, for the region's beauty, cuisine, and sunshine, as well as for its wine.

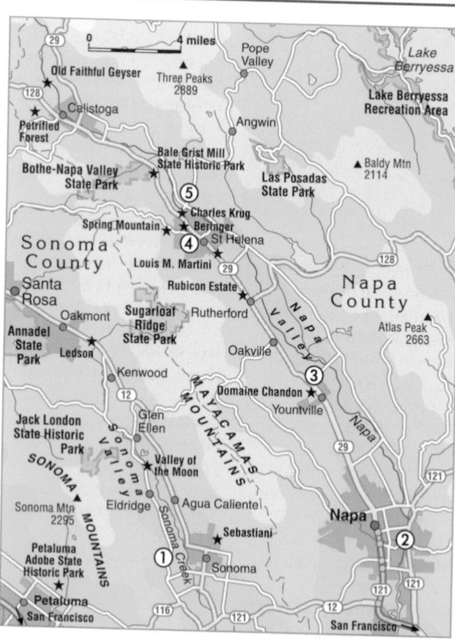

Above: vines at the Ledson Winery in Sonoma County.

Sonoma

Home to the last mission, established in 1832, **San Francisco de Solano Mission** ① in Sonoma is integrally tied to the state of California's earliest beginnings. This will come as no surprise when strolling through the 8-acre main square at the center of the small town. Surrounding the square is a collection of historic sites, including where the first California Republic flag was raised, a collection of Mexican army barracks, and several 19th-century houses, which have been tastefully converted into stores and restaurants. Sonoma was nicknamed **Valley of the Moon** by founding father Mariano Vallejo, and author Jack London used this moniker as a title to one of his books about the area. **Jack London State Historic Park** is the location of the writer's grave and last home, now a museum.

Napa

Just over the Mayacamas Mountains, Napa Valley stretches along the floodplain of the Napa River and State Highway 29. At the base of the valley, Napa has several expensive restaurants, a visitor's center, and a depot to catch the Napa Valley Wine Train, which allows visitors to fully enjoy the best wineries and tasting rooms in relaxed luxury. **Copia** ②, sitting near downtown, is a museum and education center devoted to food, wine, and art. The wine gardens here are both a gar-

Left: at the Sebastiani Winery in Sonoma County.

The Rubicon Estate in Rutherford is owned by the film-maker, Francis Ford Coppola, and worth a stop for the movie memorabilia he has on display here, including his Oscars.

Sonoma is a Patwin word meaning Land of Chief Nose. It may have referred to an influential leader with an unusually large proboscis, or it might have been a premonition of the valley's future as the bouquet of Bacchus.

deners' and an oenophile's delight, designed to represent all the flavours and aromas used to describe different varietals of wine.

Farther north, **Yountville** is where the wine country begins in earnest. Here visitors will find the **Napa Valley Museum** ③, in addition to epicurean institutions such as Thomas Keller's internationally renowned restaurant, **The French Laundry**, and the nearby Domaine Chandon Winery, French makers of sparkling wine.
SEE ALSO RESTAURANTS, P.111

St Helena

The next stop on Highway 29, also called The Great Wine Way, is **St Helena**. The carefully preserved 19th-century downtown is full of chic stores, restaurants, and galleries, including the **Silverado Museum** ④ which celebrates Robert Louis Stevenson, a one-time resident of the area.

The surrounding area is filled with country inns, beautiful parks, and nearly 40 wineries. Historic wineries include: **Louis M. Martini Winery**, run by one of the valley's oldest wine-making families, and **Beringer Vineyards**, started by two brothers in 1876 and whose Rhine House, the location of one of the tasting rooms, was built in 1883. **Charles Krug Winery** is also housed in a historic building (1874) and is the oldest winery in the Napa Valley, opening its doors in 1861.

Of additional historical and culinary note is the **Greystone Mansion** ⑤, a stone winery built in 1883 by mining magnate William Bourne. It is now the west coast headquarters for the New York based Culinary Institute of America.

Calistoga

Rich in mineral springs and hot, therapeutic mud, **Calistoga** offers a decadent reprieve from the valley's Bacchanalian excesses. Throughout the one street downtown day spas mix with bookstores, cafés and hotels. At **Old Faithful Geyser**, 2 miles north of town, visitors can feel (for a fee) the power of Calistoga's subterranean water.

Right: the Ledson vineyard.

寶生
保健藥行
寶生
金山市場

A–Z

In the following section, San Francisco's attractions and services are organized by theme, under alphabetical headings. Items that link to another theme are cross-referenced. All sights that are plotted on the atlas section at the end of the book are given a page number and grid reference.

Alcatraz

Tales of The Rock and its legendary inmates have fascinated Americans since the golden years of the American gangster. Now operated by the National Park Service, anyone can come and go to Alcatraz and explore its famous cellblocks, notorious Segregation Unit, and the 19th-century military garrison standing beneath it all. What is less known about the island is that it was also the site of one of the most significant and prolonged Native American protests in American history, and is now home to a rare and unique variety of plant, animal, and bird life.

'The Rock'

Somber by day and eerily illuminated at night, Alcatraz is a haunting presence in the San Francisco Bay. For prisoners of The Rock, the sounds of the city, from the clang of the cable cars to the light chatter of evening cocktail parties, would float across the water into their cells as haunting reminders of the world outside. Alcatraz was once home to some of the most hardened criminals of the 20th century. But today, the cells of Chicago mob boss Al Capone, the bootlegger Machine Gun Kelly, and Robert Shroud, who was immortalized (ficticiously) by Burt Lancaster in the film *The Birdman of Alcatraz*, are available for all to see.

Originally built as a military garrison in the mid-18th century, Alcatraz was prized for its strategic significance. It began its life as a prison in 1895, when it imprisoned Modoc and Hopi tribe leaders. Responding to the crime wave sweeping the country in the 1920s and 1930s, the federal government decided Alcatraz was fortified enough to house the most violent offenders, and took over the prison in 1934. Alcatraz Federal Penitentiary quickly gained a reputation for its harsh system of earned privileges for the most basic rights, its deadening solitary confinement, and the cold, damp weather. Its severity lead to 39 attempted escapes, and of the 39, two made it to shore only to be picked up immediately, while five others disappeared and are presumed drowned. In 1963, Attorney General Robert Kennedy shut down the crumbling and expensive prison, and it was turned over to the Park Service.

Below: Alcatraz's most famous inhabitant: Al Capone.

Indian Occupation

Six years later, with a trace of irony, a large group of Native Americans under the banner 'Indians of All Tribes' lay claim to the island and occupied it until 1971. Mounted as a protest against the many treaties with Native Americans broken by the US government, the group demanded title to Alcatraz and funds to build an Indian center and university. While the occupation ended with no demands met, it jump-started the Pan-Indian Movement and prompted the US

Recently, the Alcatraz Historic Gardens Project has been busy rebuilding the gardens and natural landscape surrounding the prison. Tended by inmates and prison personnel as a popular pastime, these gardens provided color, as well as hope and reprieve from the harsh world behind the penitentiary's locked doors.

Left: 'The Rock', from the air.

Alcatraz
Pier 33; tel: information: 561-4926, tickets: 981-7625; tours: www.alcatrazcruises.com/website/tour-comparison.aspx, tickets: www.alcatrazcruises.com/website/buy-tickets.aspx; daily; admission charge; metro: F to The Embarcadero and Bay Street; bus: 10, 15, 82X; map p.135 C4

government to adopt a policy of Indian self-determination. Lasting markers of the occupation include graffiti, and the shell of the warden's house that was destroyed by a fire in 1970. The group was helpless to extinguish the blaze as only a few weeks before, the government had cut off their only water source.

Getting to Alcatraz

The most visited attraction in San Francisco, Alcatraz is open daily and easily accessible. Leaving from Pier 33, **Hornblower Cruises** (www.hornblower.com) recently took over the ferry service to the island. All tickets can be purchased online, by phone, or at the ticket office at Pier 33 *(see box, left, for more details)*. Ferries leave roughly every half hour from 9am to 1.55pm and take about 10 to 15 minutes each way. Visitors may take any return ferry until 4.30pm. It is advised to allow at least 2½ hours for the entire trip to get the full experience.

Tickets are pricey ($24.50 for adults, $15.25 for kids 5–11, kids under 5 are free), but cover the transit cost and the 45-minute Cellhouse Audio Tour 'Doing Time', which is available at Pier 33 and at the dock at Alcatraz. Night Tours are also available ($18.75–31.50) Thursday through Monday and depart at 4.30pm. Rated as 'The Best Tour of the Bay Area', it includes a narrated boat tour around the island, guided island tours, and a variety of special activities. During the summer, on weekends, and holidays it is recommended to purchase tickets in advance as they sell out quickly.

Visiting the Park

Once on Alcatraz, there are park rangers to provide assistance and information regarding the variety of tours, which include kid-friendly programs and guided walks through the island's gardens and natural landscape. There is also a museum, two bookstores, and a visitor center located both on the dock and at the main level.

Weather and terrain is another consideration. Located in the middle of the bay, both the island and the ride out there can be plagued with cold and foggy weather, regardless of the time of year. Be sure to wear layers, and comfortable walking shoes to negotiate the uneven walkways and steep, uphill climb from the dock to the main level. For more information visit www.parksconservancy.org/visit/alcatraz/index.asp and www.nps.gov/alcatraz.

Below: cells at the former ultimate maximum-security prison.

Bars and Cafés

San Franciscans spend more per capita on alcohol than any other urbanites in the United States. From Union Square hotel bars, to Irish pubs, punk rock dives, the emerging wine bars, and favorite neighborhood watering holes, San Francisco is a city that loves its cocktails. It also loves its café culture; the importance of Italian-style espresso-based coffees, mouthwatering light meals, and ready Wi-Fi access should not be underestimated. The line between cafés and restaurants, or bars and clubs, is often blurry, so for more suggestions see 'Food and Drink,' 'Nightlife,' and 'Restaurants.'

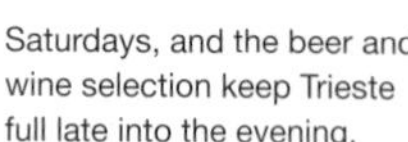

Fisherman's Wharf

Fiddler's Green
1333 Columbus Avenue; tel: 441-9758; Mon–Sat 9.30am–9.30pm; metro: F to Fisherman's Wharf; bus: 10, 30, 47; cable car: Powell-Hyde, Powell-Mason; map p.134 B4
Over shepherd's pie and pints of Guinness, Irish natives mix freely with tourists in this unassuming little bar. The reasonably priced breakfasts are cause enough to come by and escape the area's mayhem.

North Beach and Telegraph Hill

Café Brioche
201 Columbus Avenue; tel: 822-2287; bus: 9, 30, 41, 45; map p.135 C2
Enjoy an expertly made espresso drink with one of Brioche's pastries or sandwiches, made fresh in their South San Francisco bakery. The floor to ceiling windows let in plenty of light, but its warmth comes directly from the friendly service. Cash only.

Caffe Trieste
601 Vallejo Street; tel: 392-6739; www.caffetrieste.com; Fri–Sat 6.30am–midnight, Sun–Thur til 11pm; bus: 9, 30, 45, 41; map p.135 C3
Its rust colored interior is reminiscent of 1950s North Beach, as are the locals who take up residence at most of the café's small round tables. Live opera fills the space on Saturdays, and the beer and wine selection keep Trieste full late into the evening.

Mama's
1701 Stockton Street; tel: 362 6421; Tue–Sun 8am–3pm; bus: 12, 39, 41, 45; map p.134 C3
Legendary favorite for brunch; the line is crazy on the weekend. Big egg dishes and pancakes are some of the offerings at this atmospheric local staple.

Mario's Bohemian Cigar Store
566 Columbus Avenue; tel: 362-0536; daily 10am–11pm; bus: 9, 30, 45, 41; map p.134 C3
Inside this small slice of a café, Mario's serves up delicious small pizzas and baked focaccia sandwiches, as well as espressos, beer, and wine.

Spec's 12 Adler Museum Café
12 William Saroyan Place, off Columbus Avenue; tel: 421-4112; Mon–Fri 4.30pm–2am, Sat–Sun 5pm–2am; bus: 9, 30, 41, 45; map p.135 C2
Since the 1940s, seamen have been leaving behind salty trinkets from their adventures, giving Spec's the right to call itself a

Below: Vesuvio's highly distinctive signage.

Full of legends, **Café Trieste** is believed to be the first place to serve espresso on the west coast. It was opened in 1956 by an Italian émigré who wanted to bring the tastes and smells of Italy to his adopted home. It is also thought to be where Frances Ford Coppola penned *The Godfather.*

museum. Popular with bohemians, Beats, and hippies since it opened, Spec's is a friendly place full of character. Cash only.

Stella

446 Columbus Avenue; tel: 986-2914; www.stellapastry.com; summer: Mon–Wed 7.30am–7pm, Thur 7.30am–10pm, Fri–Sat til midnight, Sun 8.30am–7pm; winter: Mon–Thur 7.30am–7pm, Fri–Sat til midnight, Sun 8.30am–7pm; bus: 9, 30, 39, 41, 45; map p.134 C3

Light, buttery, and delicate, few hold a candle to Stella's pastries. With an ample espresso machine and cozy tables, this tiny store makes savoring these Italian delicacies a real treat.

Tosca

242 Columbus Avenue; tel: 986-9651; Tue–Sun 5pm–2am; bus: 9, 30, 41, 45; map p.134 C3

Classy and harking back to the jazz era, Tosca's red vinyl booths and long elegant bar attracts celebrities, self-styled bohemians, and yuppies alike. Jacketed bartenders knowledgably make drinks, including the house coffee and brandy. Hunter S. Thompson once broke his arm here pirouetting off the bar.

Vesuvio

255 Columbus Avenue; tel: 362-3370; www.vesuvio.com; daily 6am–2am; bus: 30, 45, 41, 9X; map p.134 C3

By far the best time to go to Vesuvio is late in the day, when locals gather to enjoy an afternoon drink or espresso. The narrow, two-story bar is rich in literary history, complete with pictures of James Joyce and the voice of Jack Kerouac booming over the loudspeakers.

Left: alfresco café culture in North Beach.

Chinatown

Li Po Cocktail Lounge

916 Grant Avenue; tel: 982-0072; daily 2pm–2am; bus: 1, 12, 30, 45; map p.134 C2

Passing through the big red doors, patrons will not be surprised to learn that this funky dive bar use to be an opium den. Named for the famous Chinese poet, Li Po is a favorite haunt of both locals and tourists. Cash only.

Union Square and Financial District

Café de la Presse

352 Grant Avenue; tel: 398-2680; www.aqua-sf.com/cdlp; Mon–Thur 7.30am–9.30pm, Fri 7.30am–10pm, Sat–Sun 8am–10pm; bus: 2, 9, 30, 45; map p.135 C1

Join the European literati at the tables spilling out onto the sidewalk at this charming French café. It serves up excellent bistro fare, shots of espresso and glasses of beer and wine. Inside its airy interior, there are international magazines and newspapers for sale. Free Wi-Fi.

Sears Fine Food

439 Powell Street; tel: 986-0700; daily 6.30am–10pm; BART and metro: F, J, K, L, M, N, T to Powell; bus: 30, 38, 45; cable

Below: wine time at Café de la Presse.

Left: spoilt for choice at the Redwood Room.

car: Powell-Hyde, Powell-Mason; map p.134 C1
The Swedish pancakes are the legend here, but this diner boasts a recently extended and tasty menu for brunch (until 3pm each day) and beyond.

Redwood Room at the Clift Hotel
495 Geary Street; tel: 982-6168; www.clifthotel.com/clift_hotel_redwood_room.asp; Sun–Thur 5pm–2am, Fri–Sat 4pm–2am; BART: to Powell; metro: F, J, K, L, M, N, T to Powell; bus: 2, 3, 9, 76; map p.134 C1
Legend has it that this historic San Francisco hotel bar was carved from a single redwood tree. Recently redesigned by Philippe Starck, it still retains its elegance, but now with a modern twist. The nearby Asia de Cuba delivers gourmet bites while young, well-heeled beauties sip their cocktails.

SoMa and Civic Center

21st Amendment
563 2nd Street; tel: 369-0900; www.21st-amendment.com; Sun–Tue 11.30am–9.30pm, Wed–Sat til 10pm; metro: N to 2nd & King; bus: 10, 12, 30, 45, 76; map p.139 E4
With a small beer garden and a lofted, industrial interior, there is plenty of space for beer and baseball enthusiasts to enjoy the charms of this famed SoMa brewery. It also serves excellent pub food made from seasonal and local ingredients.

MOMA Caffe Museo
151 3rd Street; tel: 357-4000; www.sfmoma.org; Thur 10am–9pm, Fri–Tue til 6pm; BART: to Montgomery; metro: F, J, K, L, M, N, T to Montgomery; bus: 9, 30, 31, 45, 71; map p.139 D4
Accessible from the street, the museum's café is a destination in its own right. Stylish and airy, with plenty of sidewalk seating, it serves up coffee, beer, wine, and light café food.

Paragon
701 2nd Street; tel: 537-9020; www.paragonrestaurant.com; daily 11.30am–2am; metro: N to 2nd & King; bus: 10, 30, 45, 76; map p.139 E4
Sit at the polished bar, or at the outside tables on warm evenings, and order from the little black book of a bar menu. Inside, patrons are treated to a list of house cocktails, classic standbys, an impressive collection of spirits, and unmissable small plates.

Nob Hill

Top of the Mark
1 Nob Hill; tel: 616-6916; www.topofthemark.com; Mon–Sat 6.30am–2.30am, Sun 10am–midnight; bus: 1; cable car: California; map p.134 C1
To get the authentic Nob Hill experience, come and sip cocktails in this most elegant of bars. Overlooking all of San Francisco, it makes any visitor feel like a true baron.

Tunnel Top
601 Bush Street; tel: 986-8900; www.tunneltop.com; Mon–Sat 5pm–2am; bus: 2, 30, 45, 76; cable car: California; map p.134 C1
Despite its shady exterior, this bar, hidden appropriately on top of the Stockton tunnel, is warm, modern, and full of thriving thirtysomethings listening to sounds of live DJ's and sipping very reasonably priced drinks.

Central Neighborhoods

Arlequin To Go
384 Hayes Street; tel: 626-1211; Mon–Fri 8am–7pm, Sat 9am–7pm, Sun 9am–6pm; metro: F to Market Street and Van Ness Avenue; bus: 9, 21, 47, 49, 66; map p.138 A3
Do not let the name fool you: this small café opens up to a wide, lush garden in the back, and is a great place to enjoy top quality café food with espresso or a glass of beer or wine.

Bus Stop
1901 Union Street; tel: 567-6905; www.busstopbar.com; Mon–Fri

10am–2am, Sat–Sun 9am–2am; bus: 22, 41, 45; map p.134 A2
In the heart of Cow Hollow, this sports bar quickly fills up with twenty- and thirtysomethings drinking well poured drinks and affordable beer while watching sports and each other.

Cav Wine Bar
1666 Market Street; tel: 437-1770; www.cavwinebar.com; Mon–Thur 5.30–11pm, Fri–Sat 5.30pm–midnight; metro: F, J, K, L, M, N, T to Van Ness; bus: 6, 7, 71; map p.138 B3
Sit at the sleek zinc bar alongside sleek professionals and connoisseurs enjoying Cav's exceptional 300-plus wine list. Recently, Cav has added food, turning this tasting bar into a dinner destination.

Crissy Field Center Café
603 Mason Street; tel: 561-7690; www.parksconservancy.org; daily 9am–5pm; bus: 28, 29, 76; map p.134 B3
Enjoy a latte or a grilled sandwich made from local and organic ingredients while overlooking the newly restored Crissy Field. It is popular with mothers with young children, and sunny weekends can be particularly busy.

Edinburgh Castle
950 Geary Street; tel: 885-4074; www.castlenews.com; daily 5pm–2am, fish and chips served til 11pm; bus: 2, 3, 4, 19; map p.134 B1
A cultural gem in the grimey Tenderloin, this Scottish-run bar hosts local bands and poetry readings upstairs, has a pool table and dart board downstairs, is packed on quiz nights, and has a fantastic Scotch inventory to go with the best fish and chips in the city, delivered from around the corner.

Hemlock Tavern
1131 Polk Street; tel: 923-0923; www.hemlocktavern.com; daily 4pm–2am; bus: 1, 2, 19, 47, 49; map p.134 B1
Cavernous and selling hot peanuts for $1 a bag, it is the natural home for the hipster punk rockers who haunt Polk Gulch. Live music in the back room, plus the outdoor heated smoking lounge, complete with tables and barstools, are extra bonuses.

Noc Noc
557 Haight Street; tel: 861-5811; www.nocnocs.com; daily 5pm–2am; bus: 6, 7, 22, 66; map p.137 E2
The highly stylized interior (aboriginal/Flintstones-esque circa 1986) attracts an easy-going, fun loving crowd. With wine, sake, and 18 beers to choose from, it can be standing room only at the weekend.

Below: locals aren't shy about lingering over coffee.

Likened to Ferlinghetti's City Lights during the 1950's, the **Edinburgh Castle** is considered the current hub of underground literature in San Francisco. Hosting regular readings and the city's annual festival, **Litquake**, it attracts aspiring writers, artists and musicians, alongside literary luminaries such as Irvine Welsh.

San Francisco Art Institute Café
800 Chestnut Street; tel: 749-4567; fall–spring: Mon–Thur 9am–5pm, Fri til 4pm, summer: 9am–2pm; bus: 30; cable car: Powell-Hyde, Powell-Mason; map p.134 B3
Perched on top of the school, this casual café has spectacular views of the Golden Gate, Alcatraz, Angel Island, and the East Bay, and is the place to be on a hot day.

Haight-Ashbury and Golden Gate Park

Cole Valley Café
701 Cole Street; tel 668-5282; www.colevalleycafe.com; Mon–Fri 6am–8.30pm, Sat–Sun 7am–8pm; metro: N to Cole & Carl; bus: 6, 33, 37, 43, 71; map p.137 C2
For neighborhood denizens and tourists alike, this sunny place serves up coffee and light café fare with colorful, hippie flair.

Hobson's Choice
1601 Haight Street: tel: 621-5859; www.hobsonschoice.com; Mon–Fri 2pm–2am, Sat–Sun noon–2am; metro: N to Haight Street; bus: 6, 33, 37, 43, 66; map p.137 D2
Populated by good-looking young people lounging on couches, amid dripping chandeliers and red walls, drinking glasses of rum-infused punch, Hobson's Choice has the decadent vibe of Victorian excess.

Magnolia

1398 Haight Street; tel: 864-PINT; www.magnoliapub.com; Mon–Fri 11am–11pm, Sat–Sun 10am–11pm; bus: 6, 33, 37, 43, 66; map p.137 D2

If the Grateful Dead opened a brewpub, this would be it. Despite the great food, warm and relaxed atmosphere, it is Magnolia's magnificent drafts, which routinely change and are served in glasses designed to best draw out their qualities, that steal the show.

Park Chalet

1000 Great Highway, off John F. Kennedy Drive; tel: 386-8439; www.beachchalet.com; Sun–Thur 9am–10pm, Fri–Sat til 11pm; bus: 5, 18, 31, 38

Located at the western end of Golden Gate Park, the Park Chalet spills out into the park's greenery with outdoor seating, live music, house brewed beer, wine, cocktails, and pub food. It is not unusual to see young families and park visitors lounging on the Chalet's lawn or dancing to the music.

Pork Store Café

1451 Haight Street; tel: 864-6981; daily B and L; bus: 6, 7, 33, 37, 71; map p.137 D2

First opened in 1916 as a butcher shop, the Pork Store is now a classic diner, with a good lunch but an epic breakfast. Window seats provide amusing people-watching in the Haight; avoid on the crowded weekends.

> Many San Franciscan cafés either have wireless internet access or online computers. For complete listings, visit www.bestofsanfrancisco.net/cappuccinocafes.htm. The public libraries (www.sfpl.lib.ca.us) also have access to the Internet, as do the ubiquitous Starbucks, which are particularly concentrated in the Financial District.

Rosamunde Sausage Grill

545 Haight Street; tel: 437-6851; daily 11.30am–10pm; bus: 5, 21, 31, 33, 43; map p.137 E2

Not much happens here besides sausage, but that is enough. With unique and mouth-watering flavors, such as wild boar, duck, chicken, smoked lamb – and, of course, spicy vegan – this is a great spot to grab a quick bite to eat.

Twilight Café and Deli

2600 McAllister Street; tel: 386-6115; Mon–Fri 9am–8pm; bus: 6, 22, 24, 66, 71; map p.137 E3

Syrian food at its best is served in this little café. There is plenty of tahini, chickpeas, garlic, and olive oil to satisfy any Middle Eastern food craving.

Zazie

941 Cole Street; tel: 564-5332; www.zaziesf.com; Mon–Fri 8am–2.30pm, Sat–Sun 9am–3pm, Sun–Thur 5.30–9.30pm, Fri–Sat 5.30–10pm; metro: N to Carl & Cole; bus: 6, 37, 43; map p.137 D1

Charming, well-priced, local bistro-cum-café with plenty of outdoor seating. Standouts among a French-influenced menu are the deservedly popular breakfasts and brunches.

Mission and Castro

Amber

718 14th Street; tel: 626-7827; daily 6pm–2am; metro: F, J, K, L, M, T to Church; bus: 24, 22, 37; map p.138 A2

One of the few smoking bars in the city, Amber's pale interior is small, cozy, and feels like someone's living room. It is marred only by poor ventilation.

Café Flore

2298 Market Street; tel: 621-8579; www.cafeflore.com; Sun–Thur 7am–11pm, Fri–Sat til midnight, kitchen closes at 10pm; metro: F, K, L, M, T to Castro; bus: 24, 22, 37; map p.137 E1

Café Flore has everything you could need or want in a café: a full bar, a well used espresso machine, a light bistro menu, lush garden

Below: the home-grown drinking options are numerous: produce from the nearby wine country, locally brewed beer, and the martini, which some claim was first mixed in San Francisco.

seating and an airy interior. It has an atmosphere that encourages its patrons to stay and chat, or quietly read.

Casanova Lounge
527 Valencia Street; tel: 863-9328; www.casanovasf.com; daily 4pm–2am; bus: 14, 22, 26, 33, 53; map p.138 B1
A rotating lineup of punk rock DJ's keep tattooed hipsters happy as they lounge beneath velvet nude paintings in this low-lit Mission hotspot. Cash only.

Dolores Park Café
501 Dolores Street; tel: 621-2936; www.doloresparkcafe.org; Sat–Thur 7am–8pm, Fri 7am–10pm; metro: F, J, K, L, M, T to Church; bus: 14, 22, 26, 37, 49; map p.138 A1
With wide windows opening on to the sunny Dolores Park, this café, patronized by the requisite strollers, dog walkers, and Mission hipsters in tight black jeans, is obviously a favorite at this neighborhood crossroads.

Laszlo Bar
2526 Mission Street; tel: 401-0810; www.laszlobar.com; Mon–Fri 6pm–2am, Sat–Sun noon–2am; bus: 14, 22, 26, 33, 49
Attached to the Foreign Cinema, Laszlo has high ceilings and a modern interior with movies continuously playing on the back wall. Its mixed crowd represents Foreign Cinema's respectability and Mission Street hipster grunginess. Small plate appetizers from next door and nightly DJ's add to the experience.

Lime
2247 Market Street; tel: 621-5256; www.lime-sf.com; Sun–Thur 5pm–midnight, Fri–Sat til 1am, kitchen closes 1 hour before close, brunch: Sat 11am–3pm, Sun 10.30am–3pm; metro: F, J, K, L, M, N, T to Castro; bus: 22, 24, 37; map p.138 B1
It is impossible to escape the feeling that you have stepped into *A Clockwork Orange* entering Lime, especially as the mini TVs scattered throughout the all white interior grow increasingly naughty as the night goes on. Tan, muscled bartenders mix cocktails heavy in rum and infused vodka with the requisite muddled lime.

Above: a Mexican lunch in the Haight.

Ritual Coffee Roasters
1026 Valencia Street; tel: 641-1024; www.ritualroasters.com; Mon–Fri 6am–10pm, Sat 7am–10pm, Sun 7am–9pm; bus: 14, 22, 33, 49, 53
From the square tables in the front to the lounge-like couches in the rear, it is usually difficult to find a seat in this epicenter of Mission hipness. Although the selection of coffee, teas, and pastries is enticement enough to give it a try. Free Wi-Fi.

Zeitgeist
199 Valencia Street; tel: 255-7505; daily 9am–2am; BART: to Van Ness; metro: F, J, K, L, M, N, T to Van Ness; bus: 14, 22, 26, 33, 49; map p.138 A2
Everyone is welcome at this punk/biker bar. Its stark interior studded with beer kegs and playing loud punk rock, gives way to a beer garden. At its long communal tables, bike messengers mix with thirtysomething punk types, twentysomething hipsters and rocker girls.

Around San Francisco

Connecticut Yankee
100 Connecticut Street; tel: 552-4440; www.theyankee.com; Mon–Sat 11am–2am, Sun 10am–2am; bus: 19, 22, 48; map p.139 D1
Built as a saloon in 1907, it has been serving Potrero Hill for 100 years. Today, locals gather in the beer garden to enjoy the bar's menu during the day, or inside where live music is played most nights.

Java Beach Café
1396 La Playa Street; tel: 665-5282; www.javabeachcafe.com; Mon–Fri 5.30am–11pm, Sat–Sun 6am–11pm; metro: N to Ocean Beach; bus: 18
Sitting on the Great Highway facing the Pacific Ocean, this small café is filled with surfers and locals who would be at home near any California beach. It is perfect for lunch or breakfast on a sunny day, or for an espresso to warm up when the fog rolls in.

Children

One of the great things about traveling with children in San Francisco is that many of the city's attractions are suitable for people of all ages. A stroll across the Golden Gate Bridge, exploring the markets of Chinatown, cresting a hill aboard a cable car, or zigzagging down legendary Lombard Street are all crowd pleasers for young and old alike. San Francisco is a very kid-friendly city with an abundance of state-of-the-art playgrounds, restaurants that offer children's menus (and often crayons), bathrooms equipped with changing tables for babies, and lots of wide open spaces for running around.

Attractions

ALCATRAZ

While older kids will appreciate the excellent audio tour, little ones might be spooked, but everyone will enjoy the ferry trip across the bay.
SEE ALSO ALCATRAZ, P.32–3

FISHERMAN'S WHARF

Pier 39 is a major tourist attraction, second only in California to Disneyland. Despite the kitsch, children will enjoy visiting the fabled sea lions on the north side of Pier 39 near K dock. For the very young, the vintage carousel delights. The following attractions found here are also popular with kids:

Aquarium of the Bay
Pier 39; tel: 623-5301; www.aquariumofthebay.com; June–Aug: daily 9am–8pm, Sept–May: Mon–Fri 10am–6pm, Sat–Sun 10am–7pm; entrance charge; metro: F to Pier 39; bus: 15, 37,49; map p.134 C4
Kids of all ages are fascinated by sharks and other marine life on display here, as moving walkways take you through clear tunnels to give you a diver's-eye view of the Bay.

***Jeremiah O'Brien* Liberty Ship**
Pier 45; tel: 544-0100; www.ssjeremiahobrien.com; daily 10am–4pm; entrance charge; metro: F to Fisherman's Wharf; bus: 10, 15, 30, 39, 47; cable car: Powell-Mason; map p.134 B4
Tour the engine room and barracks of this faithfully restored ship that saw service in World War II.

Musèe Mèchanique
Pier 45 Shed A; tel: 346-2000; www.museemechanique.org; Mon–Fri 10am–7pm, Sat–Sun 10am–8pm; free; metro: F to Fisherman's Wharf; bus: 10, 19, 30, 47; cable car: Powell-Hyde; map p.134 B4
Bring a pocket full of change to play antique penny-arcade games assembled at this quirky collection of mechanical games and toys. More than 300 relics have been assembled, including antique slot machines, hand-

Most hotels allow children to stay in parents' rooms at no additional charge (though sometimes there is an age limit) and will provide a rollaway bed or portable crib as needed.

Below: the city reflected in Zoom's facade.

Left: under the sea at the Aquarium of the Bay.

Childcare

Most hotel concierges can arrange for childcare or recommend a babysitting service. Reputable services include:

American ChildCare Service
tel: 285-2300; www.americanchildcare.com ($20 per hour; 4 hour minimum)

The Core Group
tel: 206-9046; www.thecoregroup.org ($15–$20 per hour)

Town & Country Resources
tel: 567-0956 or 800-398-8810; www.tandcr.com (call for rates)

cranked music boxes, and coin-operated pianos.

The Wax Museum
145 Jefferson Street; tel: 885-4834; www.waxmuseum.com; Mon–Fri 10am–9pm, Sat–Sun: 9am–11pm; entrance charge; metro: F to Fisherman's Wharf; bus: 10, 47; map p.134 B4
The creepy cast of characters at this Fisherman's Wharf attraction is made up of some 200 wax figures, including celebrities and political figures.

YERBA BUENA GARDENS AND CENTER FOR THE ARTS
Beautiful gardens, outdoor events, a theater, bowling alley, art gallery, vintage carousel, ice skating rink, and playground are all part of this complex that also includes:

Zeum
221 Fourth Street; tel: 820-3320; www.zeum.org; Wed–Fri 1–5pm, Sat–Sun 11am–5pm; entrance charge; BART: to Powell; metro: F, J, K, L, M, N, T to Powell; bus: 5, 7, 12, 14, 30; map p.139 D4
At this hands-on multimedia arts and technology museum, geared toward older kids and teenagers, learn about animation, digital technology, and electronic media, and create movies, music, and art. The Metreon next door houses an IMAX theatre, 15 movie screens and restaurants.
SEE ALSO PARKS AND GARDENS, P.98

AROUND SAN FRANCISCO

San Francisco Zoo
1 Zoo Road; tel: 753-7080; www.sfzoo.org; metro: daily 10am–5pm; entrance charge; L to SF Zoo; bus: 18, 23
The zoo is home to more than 1,000 animals in 125 acres on the edge of the Pacific. The African Safari and Grizzly Gulch are two of the newer habitats. The Lemur Forest and big cats remain perennial favorites. Also here is a Children's Zoo and an historic miniature steam train.

Average price for a three-course meal and a half-bottle of house wine for the parents:

$	less than $25
$$	$25–$50
$$$	$50–$100
$$$$	more than $100

Family Dining

Chow
215 Church Street; tel: 552-2469; $$; metro: F, J, K, L, M, T to Church; map p.138 A2

Park Chow
1240 Ninth Avenue; tel: 665-9912; $$; metro: N to 9th Avenue; map p.136 B1
Comfort food with a pedigree. Choose from a superb roasted chicken, pork chops, macaroni and cheese, chicken pot pie, spaghetti and meatballs, Asian-inspired noodle dishes, and tasty salads, among others. Some dishes can be ordered in smaller portions.

Below: giraffes watch their visitors at San Francisco Zoo.

Chow offers daily specials and uses local and organic ingredients. Prices are affordable and the atmosphere is cozy and welcoming. No reservations.

Giorgio's Pizzeria
151 Clement Street; tel: 668-1266; www.giorgiospizza.com; $; bus: 1, 2, 3, 4; map p.136 B4
A San Francisco favorite for pizza and (outstanding) calzones. The laidback old-school Italian atmosphere includes a trellis with plastic grapes hanging from the ceiling, red-and-white checkered vinyl tablecloths and jukebox in the back. Staff is friendly and very accustomed to dealing with children. On Wednesday from 4–6 pm, children can make their own mini pizzas with some coaching from the staff during the weekly 'Kids' Happy Hour.'

Health and Necessities

Walgreens, a discount drugstore chain, is ubiquitous in San Francisco. Here you will find everything from diapers and sweatshirts to sunscreen and film. Many also have a limited grocery selection and children's toys.

If a child accidentally swallows something that could cause harm, call the State Poison Control hotline (tel: 800-876-4766).

SEE ALSO ESSENTIALS, P.49

Museums

Cartoon Art Museum
655 Mission Street; tel: 227-8666; www.cartoonart.org; Tue–Sun 11am–5pm; entrance charge, under 6 free, 1st Tue of month 'Pay What You Wish Day'; BART: to Montgomery; metro: F, J, K ,L, M, N, T to Montgomery; bus: 7, 9, 14, 30, 45; map p.135 D1
A museum dedicated to the cartoon as art form. Exhibits range from illustrators like Edward Gorey and Charles Shultz to political satirists and local talents like Keith Knight and Paul Madonna.

SEE ALSO MUSEUMS AND GALLERIES, P.82

Exploratorium
3601 Lyon Street; tel: 561-0360; www.exploratorium.edu; Tue–Sun 10am–5pm; entrance charge, under 4 free, 1st Wed of month free; bus: 28, 30, 76; map p.133 D3
Located inside the landmark Palace of Fine Arts building, this cutting-edge museum offers more than 650 hands-on science, technology, art, nature, and human perception exhibits, including the popular Tactile Dome, a pitch-black labyrinth navigated by touch. Even kids who bore easily will find something to be mesmerized with here.

SEE ALSO MUSEUMS AND GALLERIES, P.89

Randall Museum
199 Museum Way; tel: 554-9600; www.randallmuseum.org; Tue–Sat 10am–5pm; donation suggested; metro: F, K, L, M, T to Castro; bus: 24; map p.137 E1
A small museum in spectacular Corona Heights. Appreciated by locals but often overlooked by visitors, it includes a petting zoo and drop-in arts and crafts classes. A worthwhile gem.

SEE ALSO MUSEUMS AND GALLERIES, P.89

Outdoors

The consistently mild climate in San Francisco lends itself to a myriad of outdoor activities, from flying kites at Ocean Beach, to renting bikes and discovering the treasures of Golden Gate Park, to simply taking an urban hike and conquering some of the city's renowned hills.

SEE ALSO PARKS AND GARDENS, P.98–101; WALKS AND VIEWS, P.124–9

GOLDEN GATE PARK
Bordered by Fulton Street, Lincoln Way, Great Highway and Stanyan streets; tel: 831-2700; metro: N to Irving Street and 9th Avenue; bus: 7,18, 21, 44; map p.136–7
Though they may not be particularly interested in the art collection at the de Young Museum, for kids, this 1,017-acre park is a goldmine. A vintage 1912 carousel stands adjacent to the large, recently refurbished **Koret Children's Corner** playground on the south-east side. Due west, a walking path with stone bridges and weeping willows encircles picturesque **Stow Lake** and leads to a waterfall on top of **Strawberry Hill**. At the boathouse, paddleboats can be rented for a leisurely tour of the lake, as well as bikes and inline skates.

Below: the vintage carousel at Yerba Buena Gardens.

In the north-east corner, the **Conservatory of Flowers** is a magnificent wood and glass greenhouse that houses rare tropical plants, orchids, and trees – 17,000 species – including carnivorous flora, always a hit with kids. Golden Gate Park is also home to a herd of buffalo, two windmills, **Strybing Arboretum**, an amazing 55-acre botanical garden (children love the succulent garden and the teaching garden), a chain of lakes, horse stables, tennis and bocce courts, and more.

OCEAN BEACH
Great Highway; tel: 556-8371; free; metro: N to Ocean Beach; bus: 5, 18, 31
San Francisco's largest beach, 3 miles of sand and wild coastline stretching south from Cliff House. It is not a place for swimming: tides and currents are powerfully strong and the water is very cold, but the beach is perfect for kids to run around, build sandcastles, and have picnics.

Stores

A few areas stand out when shopping for kids. In Laurel Heights, **Sacramento Street**, between Presidio Avenue and Spruce Street, is home to stylish baby boutiques as well as stores for children's furnishings, shoes, educational toys, and unique clothing. Look out for **Snippety Crickets**, a hair salon for kids. A block south on California Street, some of the big chains, such as **Gap Kids**, **Gymboree**, and **Stride Rite**, are found at Laurel Village. **Union Street** in Cow Hollow, **24th Street** in Noe Valley and **Chestnut Street** in the Marina are also good spots to find cool indie stores for kids.

> Some good Internet resources for family travel are www.familytravelforum.com, www.familytravelnetwork.com and www.travelingwithyourkids.com

Above: enjoying the playground at Golden Gate Park.

The Ark
3845 24th Street; tel: 821-1257; www.thearktoys.com; daily 10am–6pm; metro: J to Church Street & 24th Street; bus: 24, 48
3325 Sacramento Street; tel. 440-8697; daily 10am–6pm; bus 1, 2, 4, 43; map p.133 D1
Two locations of this family-owned business offer high-quality, well-crafted wooden and classic toys, games and crafts designed to spark the imagination.

Citikids
152 Clement Street; tel: 752-3837; Mon–Sat 10am–6pm, Sun 11am–5pm; bus: 2; map p.136 B4
A children's department store, geared mostly toward babies and toddlers. A large selection of gear including strollers, car seats, high-chairs, and boosters, plus clothing, furniture, books, toys, and other necessities.

Cover to Cover Booksellers
1307 Castro Street; tel: 282-8080; www.covertocoversf.com; bus: 24, 48, metro: J to Church Street & 24th Street; Mon–Sat 10am–9pm, Sun 10am–6pm
A cozy neighborhood bookstore that holds book-signings by authors such as J.K Rowling.

Gamescape
333 Divisadero Street; tel: 621-4263; Mon–Sat 10am–7pm, Sun 11am–5pm; bus: 24; map p.137 E2
An encyclopedic collection of board, card, role-playing, and miniature games, from classics to current.

Kids Only
1608 Haight Street; tel: 552-5445; Mon–Fri 10.30am–6.30pm, Sat 10am–6pm, Sun 11am–5pm; bus: 6, 7, 71; map p.137 D2
Looking for a Bob Marley onesie or a CBGB t-shirt for the newborn? This eclectic little store is full of groovy apparel.

Churches

San Francisco's religious structures and the services they host are a varied mix of the traditional and unconventional. Sts Peter and Paul Church in North Beach is an old-fashioned favorite for Roman Catholic Italian weddings, while the progressive Glide Memorial United Methodist Church attracts boisterous crowds to soul-raising Sunday Celebrations, and Buddha's Universal Church is the largest Buddhist Church is the US. Still other places of worship present intimate temples, soaring cupolas, and labyrinths for meditative walking. Check service schedules ahead of time to avoid stumbling into one in progress.

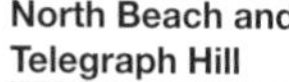

North Beach and Telegraph Hill

Sts Peter and Paul Church

666 Filbert Street; tel: 421-0809; www.stspeterpaul.sanfrancisco.ca.us/church; Sun–Fri 7.30am–4pm, Sat 7.30am–6pm; free; bus: 20, 30, 35, 41; map p.134 C3

Crowning Washington Square with its Romanesque façade and frothy twin spires, this Catholic church, built in 1924, is popular for traditional Italian weddings. Baseball legend Joe DiMaggio and Marilyn Monroe even had their wedding photos snapped here, although their ceremony actually took place at City Hall.

Chinatown

Buddha's Universal Church

720 Washington Street; tel: 982-6116; www.bucsf.com; call for public tours; free; bus: 1, 9X, 20, 41; map p.135 C2

The largest Buddhist church in the US, filled with gold leaf and mosaic tiles, an altar resembling the ship of the Dharma, and a rooftop garden and terrace.

Above: the soaring spires of Sts Peter and Paul Church.

Old St Mary's Church

660 California Street; tel: 288-3800; www.oldsaintmarys.org; Mon–Fri 7am–4.30pm, Sat 10am–6pm, Sun 8.30am–1pm; free; BART: to Montgomery; metro: F, J, K, L, M, N, T to Montgomery; bus: 1, 15, 30; cable car: California; map p.135 C2

This Paulist-led parish church was San Francisco's Catholic cathedral for most of the second half of the 19th century, until its location amidst ill-reputed neighbors (note the inscription under the clock reading 'Son Observe the Time and Fly from Evil') led to a new cathedral being built at a better-respected address.

Tien Hau Temple

125 Waverly Place; Mon–Sun 10am–4pm; donation suggested; bus: 1, 9X, 30, 45; cable car: California; map p.134 C2

Climb to the third floor to reach this historic temple dedicated to the Queen of the Heavens and Goddess of the Seven Seas (said to protect travelers, sailors, artists, and prostitutes), where red paper lanterns flood the ceiling and incense fills the air.

Union Square and Financial District

Glide Memorial Methodist Church

330 Ellis Street; tel: 674-6000; www.glide.org; service Sun 9am, 11am; free; BART: to Powell; metro: F, J, K, L, M, N, T to Powell; bus: 27, 31, 38; map p.138 C4

In the thick of the Tenderloin, Reverend Cecil Williams and his devoted staff and volunteers have cared for the poor and homeless for more than 40 years. Sunday Celebrations feature the 100-member Glide Ensemble singing jazz, blues, gospel, and spirituals.

Left: the intricate bronze doors at Grace Cathedral.

On the first Sunday of October, Sicilian parishioners from Sts Peter and Paul Church conduct a procession honoring Maria Santissima del Lume (Mary, Most Holy Mother of Light). They head along Columbus Avenue down to Fisherman's Wharf for the traditional Blessing of the Fleet.

Nob Hill

Grace Cathedral

1100 California Street; tel: 749-6300; www.gracecathedral.org; free; Mon–Fri 7am–6pm, Sat 8am–6pm, Sun 7am–7pm; free; bus: 1, 27; cable car: California, Powell-Hyde, Powell-Mason; map p.134 B1

The stately Episcopal Grace Cathedral sits on land gifted by the Charles Crocker family. Completed in 1964, the Gothic style church (resembling Paris' Notre Dame) features famed east entrance doors that are gilded bronze replicas of Lorenzo Ghiberti's 15th-century *Gates of Paradise* sculpted for the Baptistery in Florence. Two winding labyrinths, one inside of limestone, and one outside of terrazzo stone, provide paths for traditional meditative walking.

Central Neighborhoods

Cathedral of St Mary of the Assumption

1111 Gough Street; tel: 567-2020; www.stmarycathedralsf.org; Mon–Fri 6.45am–4.30pm, Sat 6.45am–5.30pm, Sun 7.30am–3.30pm, concert 3.30pm; free; bus: 2, 3, 4, 38; map p.138 A4

The architecture of this strikingly modern structure soars 19 stories heavenward, creating a cavernous, coffered cupola marked with a giant golden cross. Beneath, up to 2,400 worshippers flank three sides of the altar. Music pipes from a fine Fratelli Ruffatti organ from Padua, Italy, and above the altar a large, suspended sculpture by Richard Lippold shimmers with reflected light.

Below: the style of worship is both orthodox and unorthodox.

St John Coltrane African Orthodox Church

1286 Fillmore Street; tel: 673-7144; www.coltranechurch.org; Sun service 11.45am; free; bus: 22, 31; map p.137 E4

This church – perhaps the world's only one dedicated to a jazz musician – draws a diverse crowd of Christians, jazz lovers, and novelty-seekers to its 3 hour Sunday services, which though untraditional, express heartfelt sentiments.

Mission and Castro

Misión San Francisco de Asís (Mission Dolores)

3321 16th Street; tel: 621-8203; www.missiondolores.org; Mon–Sun 9am–4pm; donation suggested; metro: F, J, K, L, M, T to Church; bus: 22, 37; map p.138 A1

Founded in 1776 by Spanish missionary Father Junipero Serra, Misión San Francisco de Asís (commonly referred to as 'Mission Dolores') is San Francisco's oldest intact building. Carved Mexican altars stand at the front of a narrow, elongated adobe church; above, a restored ceiling is decorated with bright Ohlone Indian designs. The peaceful cemetery doubles as a blooming garden, where more than 5,000 Native Americans are buried, as well as famed namesakes of San Francisco streets, including the first Mexican governor, Luis Antonio Arguello.

Environment

With an extensive recycling program, a bike-riding population, and countless campaigns to 'green' the city by planting trees and native species on its rooftops and public spaces, San Francisco has rightly developed a reputation for being an eco-friendly city. But as much as it tries, it is also a densely populated metropolitan area that carries the inevitable environmental concerns, ranging from air quality to water shortage. San Francisco's greatest threat lies just below the surface in the network of seismic faults that occasionally jolt the city and can cost lives and millions of dollars worth of damage.

Tremors Beneath

From its plunging cliffs to its dramatic peaks and valleys, the astounding natural beauty of the Bay Area is the result of the shifting tectonic plates that ensure residents are kept on their toes. Sitting between two major fault lines, the San Andreas skirting the edge of the city and the Hayward running up the East Bay, San Francisco is continually under threat of violent earthquakes. Fortunately, better building codes, and retrofitting efforts have stabilized many bridges, highway overpasses, and downtown buildings that have suffered in previous quakes. Landfill is still an issue, however. Today builders dig deep, reaching bedrock to anchor their skyscrapers, but neighborhoods such as the Marina still illustrate what can happen to filled-in bay or wetlands: in the 1989 Loma Prieta earthquake, the posh district's ground liquefied and its million dollar homes collapsed.

Despite the threat, San Franciscans handle the subject of earthquakes with great aplomb. 'What are you going to do about it?' they will say, throwing up their hands. Still, there are basic rules every Californian school kid learns: If an earthquake occurs, stay indoors, preferably under something sturdy like a piece of furniture or in a door frame; and if outside, avoid trees, power lines, buildings, and bridges. For further instructions, the San Francisco phone book has a heavy index of information on earthquake safety.

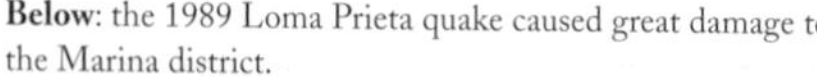

Below: the 1989 Loma Prieta quake caused great damage to the Marina district.

Catching Like Wildfire

In arid California, fire is serious business. Every summer, wildfires rip through the state and occasionally destroy homes and communities. The Oakland Hills Fire of 1991 killed 25 people, injured 150 others and caused an estimated $1.5 billion in damages. It demonstrated that even the populated Bay Area is not immune to a fire's destruction. Whenever traveling outside the cities anywhere in California, it is essential to be extremely aware of fire hazards. During

Left: bicycles and recycling bins – but is it enough?

> Anyone growing up in earthquake country will tell you that each shake is different from the last. Sometimes a rolling undulation, sharp crack, or violent shaking, they can last anywhere from a few short seconds to a couple long minutes. The earthquake exhibit at the California Academy of Sciences simulates several different types of tremors.

the dry summer and autumn months there are strict laws regarding campfires, and in some instances, they are not allowed at all. Cigarettes should never be put out on the ground or thrown from a car window.

Water Fights

Contrary to the common misconception of a lush California, much of it is, in fact, a semi-desert. Its Mediterranean climate, where 98 percent of its annual rainfall occurs between November and March, leaves it open for severe drought and fights over water. The movie *Chinatown* documented this in Southern California, but San Francisco is also known for its own dramatic battle for water. In the early 20th century, the city proposed damming the Hetch Hetchy River high above Yosemite National Park to meet its growing needs. The contest pitted the entire city of San Francisco against the legendary environmental champion, John Muir, who died shortly thereafter.

During the major drought of the mid 1980s to the early 1990s, California residents were forced to ration water; this included restaurants making water service at the table by request only. Conservation remains a hot topic, especially as global warming continues to dry out California, but the new water battle raging in San Francisco is bottled versus tap. Due to environmental concerns pertaining to waste and its resulting carbon footprint, Mayor Gavin Newsom recently signed an executive order prohibiting the city from purchasing bottled water. Instead, city workers must rely on the filtered tap flowing from the Hetch Hetchy Resevoir.

Congestion

San Francisco is the second most densely populated major city in the US, and is a part of the larger Bay Area, home to more than 7 million people. Despite large municipal transit agencies and the state of the art BART system, millions of Bay Area residents get in their cars every day to drive to work. The Bay Area is ranked second in the nation, just behind Los Angeles, for the length of its average commute and the amount of time drivers sit waiting in traffic. The air pollution caused by this congestion is blown into the South Bay and Sacramento Valley, away from San Franciscan eyes and noses. Fortunately, there are organizations such as the Bay Area Air Quality Management District working on ways to get people out of their cars. It also sponsors 'Spare the Air' days that provide free Bay Area transit on days when air pollution has a high risk of exceeding federal and state safety levels.

Below: a familiarly busy sight on the Golden Gate Bridge.

Essentials

Whatever your 'must-see' list when visiting San Francisco, needs such as posting a letter, checking your email, or finding a pharmacy, may well demand your attention at some point. The following listings give an overview of practical information for visitors to San Francisco, from entering the US to calling home, so that you can dedicate your time to getting on with the fun stuff. If you suffer any major problems, there are listings of embassies and consulates, as well as the city's main hospitals. Bear in mind too, that your hotel concierge can be a goldmine of useful information, as can the Visitor Information Center.

Baggage Restrictions

There are detailed restrictions on traveling with liquids, medicines, and dangerous items. For the latest information, refer to the US Transportation Security Administration (tel: 866-289-9673; www.tsa.gov).

File claims for damaged or missing luggage before leaving the airport. For questions and complaints, contact the Federal Aviation Administration Consumer Hotline (tel: 866-835-5322; www.faa.gov) or the Aviation Consumer Protection Division (tel: 202-366-2220; http://airconsumer.ost.dot.gov).

Climate

San Francisco weather can change significantly from hour to hour and between neighborhoods. Springs are warm and sunny (average high in April 63°F; low 50°F), while summers are cool and overcast, with the city blanketed in fog (average high in July 66°F; low 54°F). Come September and October, the summer chill is replaced with beautifully mild and sunny days (average high in September 70°F; low 56°F). Rain storms (no snow) appear in December and January, though crisp, sunny days offer breaks from the damp and dreary ones (average high in January 56°F; low 46°F).

To carry liquids, gels, and aerosols in your carry-on bag, they must be in containers 3 oz or smaller, and all the containers must be put together in one quart-size, zip-top, clear plastic bag.

Clothing

Plan ahead for varied weather and bring easy-to-layer clothes. Shorts are uncommon, and the hills hard to climb in sky-high heels. A raincoat and sturdy umbrella are vital for winter months: rain storms are no drizzle affair.

The city's casual, come-as-you-are vibe means jeans, T-shirts, and tennis shoes are ubiquitous on streets and in many restaurants and entertainment venues. However, snazzier eateries and nightclubs warrant something a bit nicer.

Above: how to identify your local cops.

Customs

Adult visitors staying longer than 72 hours may bring along the following items duty free: 1 liter of wine or liquor; 100 cigars (non-Cuban), or 3lbs of tobacco, or 200 cigarettes; and gifts valued under $100.

Absolutely no food (even in cans) or plants of any type are permissible. Visitors may also arrive and depart with up to $10,000 currency without declaration. For the most up-to-date information on what may be brought with you, refer to the US Customs and Border Protection website (www.cbp.gov).

Left: make your trip as easy as possible, so you can get on and enjoy the local attractions.

Electricity

Electricity in the US is 110 Volts, 60 Hertz AC. Outlets are generally for flat blade, two-prong plugs. Most foreign appliances require a transformer and/or plug adaptor.

Embassies and Consulates

Details for other embassies and consulates can be found in the Yellow Pages.

Australia
Tel: 536-1970; www.dfat.gov.au

Canada
Tel: 834-3180; www.sanfrancisco.gc.ca

Ireland
Tel: 392-4214; www.irelandemb.org

New Zealand
Tel: 399-1255; www.nzemb.org

South Africa
Tel: 202-232-4400; www.saembassy.org

UK
Tel: 617 1300; www.britainusa.com/sf

Emergency Numbers

Ambulance, fire, or police: dial 911 from any telephone, no coins needed

Police (non-emergency): tel: 553-0123

Health

DRUGSTORES (PHARMACIES)

Some medicines that are available over the counter in your home country may require a prescription in the US. 24-hour locations of the useful Walgreens drugstore chain (www.walgreens.com) can be found at the following locations:

498 Castro Street; tel: 861-3136; metro: F, K, L, M, T to Castro; bus: 33, 34, 35, 37.

1189 Potrero Avenue; tel: 647-1397; bus: 9, 33, 48.

3201 Divisadero Street; tel: 931-6417; bus: 28, 30, 30X, 43, 76.

Additional Walgreens and Rite Aid (www.riteaid.com) branches are open late into the evening.

Below: one of the most useful places in San Francisco.

INSURANCE AND HOSPITALS

Healthcare is private and can be very expensive, especially hospitalization. Foreign visitors should always ensure that they have full medical insurance covering their stay before traveling to the US. Below are hospitals with 24-hour emergency rooms.

California Pacific Medical Center
Castro Street at Duboce Avenue; tel: 415-600-6000; www.cpmc.org; metro: N to Duboce; bus: 24, 37; map p.137 E2

Saint Francis Memorial Hospital
900 Hyde Street; tel: 353-6300; www.saintfrancismemorial.org; bus: 1, 2, 19, 27, 31, 38AX, 38BX; map p.134 B1

San Francisco General Hospital
1001 Potrero Avenue; tel: 206-8000; www.sfdph.org; bus: 9, 33, 48

UCSF Medical Center
505 Parnassus Avenue; tel: 476-1000; www.ucsfhealth.org; metro: N to UCSF; bus: 6, 43, 66; map p.136 C1

Holidays

National US holidays are: New Year's Day (January 1); Martin Luther King Jr. Day (3rd Monday in January); President's Day (3rd Monday in February); Memorial Day (Last Monday in May); Independence Day (July 4); Labor

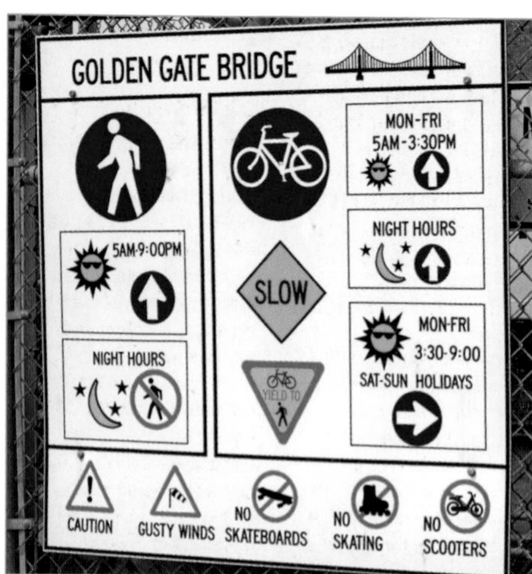

Above: before you set out on Golden Gate Bridge...

Day (1st Monday in September); Columbus Day (2nd Monday in October); Veteran's Day (November 11); Thanksgiving Day (4th Thursday in November); and Christmas Day (December 25).

Information

Visitor Information Center of San Francisco
900 Market Street; tel: 391-2000; www.onlyinsanfrancisco.com; May–Oct: Mon–Fri 9am–5pm Sat–Sun 9am–3pm; Nov–Apr: Mon–Fri 9am–5pm, Sat: 9am–3pm; BART: to Powell; metro: F, J, K, L, M, N, T to Powell; bus: 6, 7, 27, 30, 45; cable car: Powell-Hyde, Powell-Mason; map p.138 C4
The center is down the stairs near the cable car turntable at Market and Powell Streets and supplies brochures, maps, and helpful answers. Call for a listing of monthly events.

Internet

Internet cafés include:
Quetzal Internet Café
1234 Polk Street; tel: 673-4181; www.coffeeandcocoa.com; Mon–Fri 6.30am–10pm, Sat–Sun 7.30am–10pm; bus: 1, 4, 19, 27, 31; map p.134 B1
Golden Gate Perk Internet Café
401 Bush Street; tel: 362-3929; www.ggperk.com; Mon–Fri 8am–8pm, Sat 11am–6pm; BART: to Montgomery; metro: F, J, K, L, M, N, T to Montgomery; bus: 1, 2, 3, 9, 31; map p.135 C1
Also, many cafés have WiFi hotspots, and public library branches provide free Internet access (San Francisco Public Library; tel: 557-4400; http://sfpl.org)

Media

The largest regional newspaper is the *San Francisco Chronicle* (www.sfgate.com/chronicle). The Sunday 'Pink Pages' lists art, music, and entertainment events. Free alternative weeklies are found in newspaper boxes, cafés, and bars. The four main weeklies are *The San Francisco Bay Guardian* (www.sfbg.com), *SF Weekly* (www.sfweekly.com), *San Francisco Bay Times* (www.sfbaytimes.com), and *Bay Area Reporter* (BAR; www.ebar.com). The latter two are gay- and lesbian-oriented, and most easily found in and around the Castro neighborhood. The city's magazines include *San Francisco Magazine* (www.sanfran.com) and *7x7* (www.7x7sf.com). Web-based city guides include www.sfstation.com and http://sf.flavorpill.net.

Money

CURRENCY

The dollar ($) is divided into 100 cents (¢). The coins are the penny (1¢), nickel (5¢), dime (10¢), quarter (25¢), and the less-common half dollar (50¢) and $1 coin. Common banknotes are the $1, $5, $10, $20, $50, and $100 bills.

BANKS AND CURRENCY EXCHANGE

Bank hours are generally Monday through Friday, from about 9am to 5pm. Some are open Saturday mornings. ATMs can be used to obtain currency; change foreign currency at airports, major banks downtown, or American Express offices.

ATMs

ATMs are at banks, some stores, and bars, and charge usage fees. Debit card use on purchases at major grocery and drugstores allows you to get cashback; check with your bank before traveling.

CREDIT CARDS

Credit cards are accepted at most restaurants, hotels, and stores.

TRAVELER'S CHECKS

With the popularity of ATMs, credit cards, and debit cards, traveler's checks are increasingly less common. However, banks, stores, restaurants, and hotels generally accept US dollar-denominated traveler's checks. If yours are in foreign denominations, they first must be changed to dollars. Un-exchanged checks should be kept in your hotel safe. Record the checks' serial numbers in a separate place to facilitate refunds of lost or stolen checks.

SALES TAXES

In San Francisco, an 8.5 percent sales tax is added to the prices of goods and services; in surrounding cities, the sales tax is 8.25 percent. Hotels charge a 14 percent tax.

Postal Services

Post offices open at 8–9am and close at 5–6pm, Monday through Friday; the post office in the Macy's department store on Union Square (tel: 956-0131) is also open on Sunday. Use the Civic Center post office for general-delivery mail *(poste restante)*.

US Postal Service
Tel: 800-275-8777; www.usps.com

Civic Center Post Office
101 Hyde Street; tel: 563-7284; Mon–Fri 9am–5pm; BART: to Civic Center; metro: F, J, K, L, M, N, T to Civic Center; bus: 6, 7, 9, 21, 49; map p.138 B4

Telephone

Local calls are inexpensive; long distance calls are decidedly not. Public phones accept coins and credit cards, but the latter charge exorbitant rates. The San Francisco area code is 415, which you only need to dial from outside of the city; the country code is 1. Toll-free numbers begin 1-800, 1-888, 1-877, or 1-866.

Directory enquires: 411
US calls outside your area code: 1 + area code + phone number
International Calls: 011+ country code + number
Operator: 0 for assistance with local calls; 00 for international calls

Be careful where you light-up in San Francisco: the city may be blanketed in fog, but the air is quite smoke-free. Smoking laws are strict, and it is banned in many public places such as offices, shops, restaurants, and bars, and the minimum legal age for smoking is 18 years old.

Below: be aware of California's strident smoking laws.

Time Zone

San Francisco is on Pacific Standard Time. PST is 3 hours behind Eastern Standard Time (New York) and 8 hours behind Greenwich Mean Time (London).

Tipping

Restaurants: 15–20 percent. Most restaurants add a service charge automatically for parties of six or more.
Taxis: 10–15 percent
Bars: 10–15 percent, or at least $1–2 per drink
Coat check: $1–2 per coat
Doormen: $1–2 for hailing a cab or bringing in bags
Porters: $1 per bag (more if you packed bricks)
Valet parking: $2–3
Concierge: $5–10
Maids: $3–5 per day
Hairdressers and salons: 15–20 percent

Visa Information

US citizens returning to the US by air or land from Canada, Mexico, the Caribbean, and Bermuda will need a passport or other accepted identification. Under the current Visa Waiver Scheme, for nationals of 27 countries (including the UK, Australia and New Zealand) no visa is needed for US stays of less than 90 days (for business or pleasure) upon showing an individual machine-readable passport. For passports renewed or extended between October 26, 2005 and October 25, 2006 a digital photograph printed on the data page or an integrated computer chip with information from the data page (an e-Passport) is required. Passports renewed on or after October 26, 2006 must be e-Passports.

All other foreign citizens need visas. Application forms and information are available at US embassies and consulates. Plan several weeks in advance. Double check current requirements at http://travel.stage.gov.

Below: the always-handy ATM, found all over the city.

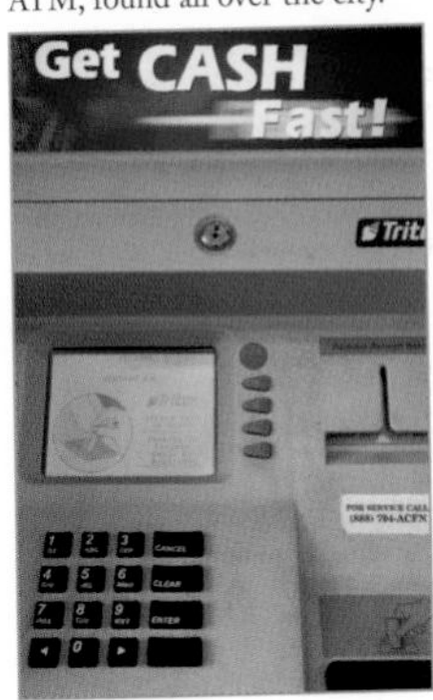

Fashion

A singular parade of styles strut San Francisco's streets, ranging from ultra-casual to edgy hipster to boho-chic. Emporiums and high-end designer outposts flood Union Square, but style hounds find more fashion fuel in boutiques and thrift stores. Hayes Valley and the Mission deliver cool, contemporary designs; Fillmore, Union, and Chestnut Streets cater largely to luxe label-addicts; the Castro and Haight specialize in funky second-hand and casuals; while North Beach is good for choice denim. Stores are generally open Monday–Saturday 11am–6pm, and Sunday noon–6pm, the listings below note exceptions.

Local Fashions and Designers

San Francisco's fashion sense is dominated by jeans, T-shirts, and sneakers, but a stylish set ups the ante with edgy, attitude-laced looks for patrolling hipster haunts, while carefully-coifed preppy and Euro-chic designer looks stroll smart neighborhoods.

If you're looking for the basics, snag San Francisco-based attire at the flagship **Levi's** store (300 Post Street, off Stockton Street; tel: 501-0100; www.levisstore.com; map p.135 C1), the company that gave birth to blue jeans in 1873. Or, if soaking in a 'shrink-to-fit' tank isn't your thing, head to behemoth Gap Inc.'s trusty trifecta (**Banana Republic**, **Gap**, and **Old Navy**; www.gap-inc.com), which was founded in San Francisco in 1969.

Excellent local independent designers include: **Dema** (1038 Valencia Street; tel: 206-0500; www.godemago.com); **House of Hengst** (924 Valencia Street; tel: 642-0841; www.houseofhengst.com); **Minnie Wilde** (3266 21st Street; tel: 642-9453; www.minniewilde.com)

Above: high-end names decorate Maiden Lane.

and **Sunhee Moon** (3167 16th Street; tel: 355-1800; www.sunheemoon.com; map p.138 A1). All four are found in the hip Mission District (BART: 16th Street; bus: 14, 22, 26, 33, 49).

Fashion also grabs the city's attention during San Francisco Fashion Week (www.fashionweek-sf.com), set up in 2004.

Major Retailers and Designers

SEE ALSO SHOPPING, P.112–4

The Union Square neighborhood is stuffed with major department stores and retail outposts. **Forever 21** (tel: 984-0380; www.forever21.com) and **H&M** (tel: 986-0156 www.hm.com) burst at the seams with of-the-moment trends. **Urban Outfitters** (tel: 989-1515; www.urbanoutfitters.com) caters to cool kids, and its upscale big sister **Anthropologie** (tel: 434-2210; www.anthropologie.com) dresses up boho-chic ladies.

The well-known, high-end designers are clustered on Post Street, Stockton Street, Grant Avenue, Geary Street, and Maiden Lane.

Apparel and Accessories

AB Fits
1519 Grant Avenue; tel: 982-5726; www.absfit.com; closed Mon; bus: 15, 20, 30, 41; map p.134 C3
Premium denim destination. Also at 40 Grant Avenue (tel: 391-3360).

Ambiance
1458 Haight Street; tel: 552-5095; www.ambiancesf.com; bus: 6, 7, 33, 71; map p.137 D2
Romantic, funky, and vintage-inspired girly goodies.

Anica
2418 Polk Street; tel: 447-2878; www.anicaboutique.com; bus: 19, 41, 47, 49, 76; map p.134 A3

Left: made in San Francisco: the flagship Levi's store.

Many streets sparkle with gorgeous jewelry, gems, and girl's best friends, but Union Square is especially dazzling. Splurge at **De Vera** (29 Maiden Lane), veteran **Shreve and Co.** (200 Post Street), or many Powell and Sutter Street offerings. Across town, **Gallery of Jewels** (2115 Fillmore Street) supplies local creations.

Finely-picked progressive line-up for sophisticated females.

Behind the Post Office
1510 Haight Street; tel: 861-2507; bus: 6, 7, 33, 44, 71; map p.137 D2
Emerging and established names for trendy, urban ladies.

Citizen Clothing
536 Castro Street; tel: 575-3560; metro: K, L, M, T to Castro; bus: 24, 33, 35, 37; map p.137 E1
Well-picked men's hip casuals.

Dylan
2146 Chestnut Street; tel: 931-8721; www.dylanboutique.com; bus: 22, 30, 43; map p.133 E3
Understated elegance for guys and gals.

My Roommate's Closet
3044 Fillmore Street; tel: 447-7703; www.myroommatescloset.com; bus: 22, 30, 43; map p.133 E2
Ever-changing racks of chic, discounted designer duds.

Ooma
1422 Grant Avenue; tel: 627-6963; www.ooma.net; bus: 15, 30, 45; map p.135 C3
Brightly-colored bastion for feminine, feisty fabulousness.

Villain's
1672 Haight Street; bus: 6, 7, 33, 71; map p.137 D2
Scores of hip, funky looks for the fellas.

Secondhand

Also look for **Crossroads Trading Company** stores (www.crossroadstrading.com).

Below: trying it on in a Mission boutique.

American Rag Cie
1305 Van Ness Avenue; tel: 474-5214; www.amrag.com; bus: 2, 3, 8, 47, 49; map p.134 B1
Pricey but trendy second-hand and vintage-inspired pieces.

Buffalo Exchange
1555 Haight Street; tel: 431-7733; www.buffaloexchange.com; bus: 6, 7, 33, 43, 71; map p.137 D2
Broken-in looks that do not break the bank. Also at 1210 Valencia Street (tel: 647-7733).

Shoes

Bulo
418 Hayes Street; tel: 864-3244; www.buloshoes.com; metro: F, J, K, L, M, N, T to Van Ness; bus: 21, 47, 49; map p.138 A3
A goldmine of posh, trendy European styles.

Gimme Shoes
416 Hayes Street; tel: 864-0691; www.gimmeshoes.com; bus: 5, 7, 42, 49, 71; map p.138 A3
Global, fashion-forward footwear. Also at 2358 Fillmore Street (tel: 441-3040).

Shoe Biz
1446 Haight Street; tel: 864-0990; www.shoebizsf.com; bus: 6, 33, 43, 71; map p.138 A2
Stylish sneakers jostle for shelf space alongside sky-high stilettos. Also at 877 Valencia Street (tel: 550-8655).

Lingerie

Alla Prima
1420 Grant Avenue; tel: 397-4077; Closed Mon; bus: 15, 30, 45; map p.134 C2
Pretty palette of European lingerie. Also at 539 Hayes Street (tel: 864-8180).

Belle Cose
2036 Polk Street; tel: 474-3494; www.bellacose.net; bus: 12, 19, 47, 49, 76; map p.134 B2
Vintage and vintage-inspired ooh-la-la glamour.

Food and Drink

It is fortunate that San Francisco has so many hills, so residents and visitors alike can quickly burn off the many culinary enticements this city has to offer. From delicate pastries at the many cafés to delectable small plates served at fashionable bars and esteemed fine dining establishments with their celebrity chefs, it is virtually impossible to abstain in the 'Paris of the West.' Blessed with thriving immigrant communities, year-round natural abundance, and a slight spirit of rebellion, San Francisco over the past 150 years has emerged as one of the culinary capitals of the world.

'Gastronomic Orgies'

Nothing has changed since Gertrude Stein made reference to San Francisco's culinary excesses. The Bay Area is known for its farmers, growing everything from rare heirloom tomatoes to raising heritage herds of beef cattle. But its original claim to fame was the sea's bounty and its inspired dishes like Chioppino, a seafood stew derived from a traditional Italian dish.

While Fisherman's Wharf is always crowded with seafood lovers, mid-November through May is particularly busy, enticing locals eager to snag the favorite Dungeness Crabs off the boats. In San Francisco, crab is enjoyed steamed, cracked, and drowned in butter, accompanied only by a loaf of San Francisco's famous sourdough.

In recent years, celebrity chefs and food artisans have turned eclectic San Francisco into the epicenter of the American sustainable food movement. Based upon the idea that food should be produced locally and from techniques derived of age-old traditions, it has given the city an impressive assortment of boutique charcuteries, cheese makers, and bakeries; farmers' markets; and cuisine that highlights the Bay Area's natural cornicopia and diverse population.

Immigrant Influences

Coming from all around the world in the mid-19th century, immigrants added vast diversity to the city's culinary character. In addition to the Mexican and American traditions already here, French, Irish, German, Basque, Spanish, Italian, and, of course, Chinese immigrants brought with them the tastes of home.

With yeast in short supply, the settlers who arrived in the Gold Rush utilized fermented dough as the basis of their bread. This technique hardly originated with this generation of gold seekers, but San Francisco is home to natural yeasts and bacteria circulating in the air that create the chewy texture and highly sour taste that define San Franciscan sourdough.

Poised at the edge of the Pacific, San Francisco boasts especially strong and diverse pan-Asian cuisine. Still to this day, immigrants continue to bring food secrets that broaden the city's palate, as in the Ethiopian, Arabian, Moroccan, Afghan, and Turkish restaurants.

Eating Out

There is something for everyone here: eateries encompass all price ranges for every type of food available. Breakfast is generally between 7am to 10am, except on the weekends when brunch service runs until 1 or 2pm. Weekday lunch is between 11.30am to 2.30pm and dinner starts around 5.30pm.

Drinking

San Franciscans pay attention to both what they eat and what washes it down. This is a drinking city. Early on, residents began brewing their own beer. Today, there are many microbreweries around the city with the strength and complexity to rival any cocktail or glass of wine, including

Left: the famed San Francisco sourdough bread.

the **Anchor Steam Brewery** on Potrero Hill which not only makes beer, but gin and rye bourbon as well.

Surrounded by excellent wine country, San Francisco is an easy access point for visiting the many acclaimed vineyards and trying an excellent selection of local wine, from traditional varietals such as Chardonnay and Cabernet, to lesser-known specialties like Gamay Beaujolais.

SEE ALSO WINE COUNTRY, P.28–9

Fisherman's Wharf

Baker's Hall at Boudin Bakery

160 Jefferson Street; tel: 928-1849; www.boudinbakery.com; daily noon–6pm; metro: F to Pier 39; bus: 10, 30, 39; map p.134 B4

In the heart of Fisherman's Wharf, the Boudin bakery hawks its original San Francisco sourdough near the site of its first bakery. From chutneys to chocolate, Baker's Hall sells locally crafted goods that compliment its famous bread.

Ghirardelli Chocolate Soda Fountain at Ghirardelli Square

900 North Point Street; tel: 771-4903; www.ghirardelli.com; daily 10am–11pm; metro: F to Fisherman's Wharf; bus: 10, 30, 39, 47; map p.134 A4

It is rumored that so much chocolate was made here that when it rains the walls ooze chocolate. But even when it is not raining, the Soda Fountain's ice cream sundaes still ooze with chocolate, caramel, and plenty of whipped cream. The store sells a wide variety of Ghirardelli's products.

Chinatown

Gourmet Delight

1045 Stockton Street; tel: 392-3288; daily 7am–7pm; bus: 1, 12, 30, 41, 45; map p.134 C2

Complete with darkly burnished poultry in the windows, this is the place for Chinese deli food. Always crowded, its counters heave with chow mein, Cantonese style deep-fried chicken, sweet and sour pork, and piles of cooked vegetables. Cash only.

Lien Hing Supermarket

1112 Stockton Street; tel: 986-8488; daily 6.30am–7pm; bus: 1, 12, 30, 41, 45; map p.134 C2

Filled with fresh produce, a butcher willing to cut or grind any size of meat, and aisles full of Chinese noodles, pickled vegetables, spices, and seasonings, anyone preparing to make Chinese food at home will find what they need.

North Beach and Telegraph Hill

Coit Liquor

585 Columbus Avenue; tel: 986-4036; www.coitliquor.com; Mon–Thur, Sun 11am–11pm, Fri–Sat til 2am; bus: 9X, 30, 39, 45, 41; map p.134 C3

Looking for that perfect bottle of wine to go with your meal? The friendly staff at this neighborhood spot will help you pick out the right thing. For the curious, Coit Liquor offers wine tasting, while behind the counter it has a generous selection of spirits.

Graffeo Coffee

735 Columbus Avenue; tel: 986-2420; www.graffeo.com; Mon–Fri 9am–6pm, Sat til 5pm; bus: 9X, 30, 39, 41, 45; map p.134 C3

This local coffee roaster peddles strictly coffee beans, not cups. However, the smell alone will lure even the most adamant tea drinker into this tiny storefront.

Molinari Delicatessen

373 Columbus Avenue; tel: 421-

Below: the food temple that is the Ferry Building.

Left: Italian specialties at Molinari's Delicatessen.

2337; Mon–Fri 9am–5.30pm, Sat 7.30am–5.30pm; bus: 9X, 30, 39, 41, 45; map p.134 C2
Cranky Italians serve up the city's best deli fare. Imported cheese, cured meats, and canned goods compliment Molinari's own selection of sausage, salamis, and raviolis made in Hunter's Point.

Liguria Bakery
1700 Stockton Street; tel: 421-3786; Mon–Fri 8am–4pm, Sat 7am–4pm, Sun 7am–noon; bus: 9X, 30, 39, 41, 45; map p.134 C3
Get here early, as the ladies at Liguria bakery quickly sell out of their melt-in-the-mouth focaccia, and once it is gone, they close the doors. Only available in a few flavors, it drips with olive oil and is easily the best focaccia in the city.

Despite the amount of home-grown wine and beer, San Francisco will never give up its cocktails. Claiming to be the home of the first martini, the city has a fine tradition of drinking hard. Scotch, gin, and vodka, all poured with minimal fuss, are particular favorites.

Trader Joe's
401 Bay Street; tel: 351-1013; www.traderjoes.com; daily 9am–9pm; bus: 10, 30, 39, 47; cable car: Powell-Mason; map p.134 B4
This small, national chain grocery store offers quality goods at reasonable prices. It is a local staple, and usually crowded.

XOX Truffles
754 Columbus Avenue; tel: 421-4814; www.xoxtruffles.com; Mon–Sat 9am–6pm, Sun 10.30am–4pm; bus: 9X, 30, 39, 41, 45; map p.134 C3
For $1, patrons can get a good cup of coffee and a chocolate truffle of their choice. Tiny and handmade, their flavors range from cognac to pistachio and everything in between.

Union Square and Financial District

Ferry Building Market
1 Ferry Building, Market and the Embarcadero; tel: 693-0996; www.ferrybuildingmarket place.com; Mon–Fri 10am–6pm, Sat 9am–6pm, Sun 11am–5pm; BART: to Embarcadero; metro: F, J, K, L, M, N, T to Embarcadero; bus 2, 14, 21, 66, 71; map p.135 E2
Recently renovated, the Ferry Building is a highlight of any trip to San Francisco. Food lovers crowd to the high temple of the Bay Area sustainable food movement, to browse local chocolatiers, olive- oil makers, produce stands, meat counters, the Acme Bakery, and the Cowgirl Creamery. There's also a wine store, Asian deli, and various excellent sit-down eateries.

Ferry Plaza Farmers' Market
1 Ferry Building, Market and the Embarcadero; tel: 291-3276; www.ferryplazafarmersmarket.com; Tue 10am–2pm, Sat 8am–2pm; BART: to Embarcadero; metro: F, J, K, L, M, N, T to Embarcadero; bus: 2, 14, 21, 66, 71; map p.135 E2
Voted one of the best farmers' markets in the country by The New York Times, the Saturday market has everything from fresh seasonal vegetables to naturally nested eggs to coffee to charcuterie to prepared food venders. Tuesday is smaller, but still bountiful.

John Walker and Co.
175 Sutter Street; tel: 986-2707; www.johnwalk.com; Mon–Fri 10am–6.30pm, Sat noon–5pm; bart: Montgomery; metro: F, J, K, L, M, N, T to Montgomery; bus: 2, 7, 14, 21, 66; map p.134 C1
In this small downtown store, you can find anything from Italian Candoli grappa, to a bottle of 1980 Opus One, to hand-crafted, single-barrel Noah's Mill Kentucky Bourbon.

SoMa and Civic Center

Blue Bottle Coffee
315 Linden Street; tel: 510-653-3394; www.bluebottlecoffee.net; Mon–Fri 7am–5pm or 6pm, Sat–Sun 8am–5pm or 6pm; BART:

Despite this city's food obsession, dining in San Francisco is rarely a fancy affair. Ease and comfort are the guiding principals in this city where locals are not shy about spending hours lingering over coffee, and rarely venture out to dinner before 7pm. Few restaurants have dress codes or serve past 10pm.

to Van Ness; metro: F, J, K, L, M, N to Van Ness; bus: 6, 21, 47, 49, 71; map p.138 A3
Perhaps no other roaster in the Bay Area has quite the same devotion to the bean as Blue Bottle. Roasted everyday, each roast is as different and complex as a varietal of wine. Come by their tiny kiosk in Hayes Valley to sample it.

Civic Center Farmers' Market
1182 Market Street; tel: 558-9455; Sun 7am–5pm, Wed 7am–5.30pm; BART: to Civic Center; metro: F, J, K, L, M, N, T to Civic Center; bus: 6, 21, 26, 47, 49; map p.138 B3
The least expensive farmers' market in the city, this market excels at fresh vegetables, particularly Asian varieties.

Central Neighborhoods

Real Food Company
2140 Polk Street; tel 673-7420; www.realfoodco.com; daily 9am–9pm; bus: 12, 19, 41, 45; map p.138 B4
This local chain has a great and affordable inventory of natural foods, local bread, a diverse cheese and meat counter, and the best produce section in the city. (Also at 3060 Fillmore Street; tel: 567-6900.)

Below: take-out pizza is popular wherever you go.

Mission and Castro

Bi-Rite Market and Creamery
3639 18th Street; tel: 241-9760; www.biritemarket.com; Mon–Fri 9am–9pm, Sat–Sun 9am–8pm; BART: 16th Street; metro: J, L, M to Church; bus: 14, 22, 33, 49; map p.138 A1
With its own creamery across the street, Bi-Rite Market is the one-stop shop for anyone looking for natural foods with a little indulgence on the side.

La Palma Mexicatessen
2884 24th Street; tel: 647-1500; www.lapalmafoods.com; daily 9am–5pm; BART: to 24th Street Mission; bus: 9, 12, 14, 27, 33
A great stop for Mexican canned and dried goods and corn tortillas hand-made daily. Two-meal burritos and fresh tacos are also available at the service counter.

Mitchell's Ice Cream
688 San Jose Avenue; tel: 648-2300; www.mitchellsicecream.com; daily 11am–11pm; bus: 14, 26, 49, 67
No matter what time it is, Mitchell's is always packed with locals satisfying a sweet tooth.

Around San Francisco

Arizmendi Bakery
1331 9th Avenue; tel: 566-3117; www.arizmendibakery.org; Tue–Fri 7am–7pm, Sat 8am–7pm, Sun 8am–4pm; metro: N to Judah Street and 9th Avenue; bus: 6, 43, 44, 66, 71L; map p.136 B1
One of four related co-ops in the Bay Area, it sells fresh bread, delicious pastries, and artisan shortbread in the inner Sunset's main drag. Many would say their pizza, a special made daily on a sourdough crust, is worth a trip across the city. Cash only.

Noe Valley Bakery and Bread Company
4073 24th Street; tel: 550-1405; www.noevalleybakery.com; Mon–Fri 7am–7pm, Sat–Sun til 6pm; metro: J to Church Street and 24th Street; bus: 24, 35, 48
For Noe Valley residents, this bakery is their daily bread, literally. Long lines form early as locals wait for the breads, cakes, and pastries.

Ruby Wine
1419 18th Street; tel: 401-7708; www.rubywinesf.com; Mon–Sat noon–8pm, Sun noon–6pm; bus: 19, 22, 48, 53; map p.136 A1
High on Potrero Hill, Ruby Wine's proprietors, all alumni from the famed Oliveto restaurant, specialize in wine and accompanying artisan food.

24th Street Cheese Company
3893 24th Street; tel: 821-6658; Mon–Fri 10am–7pm, Sat til 6pm, Sun til 5pm; metro: J to Church Street and 24th Street; bus: 24, 35, 48
This Noe Valley institution has one of the most reputable cheese counters in the Bay Area. The choice is extensive, and anything can be tasted.

Below: fresh produce at the Civic Center Farmers' Market.

Gay and Lesbian

San Francisco is internationally known as one of the world's most welcoming places for gays and lesbians. The lively hub of this thriving and politically-influential community is the Castro neighborhood, where rainbow flags flutter from brightly-colored Victorian houses. The Castro is especially popular with younger gay men, but the presence of women, families, and straights is increasing. Another hotspot is SoMa, still home to large clubs, leather bars, and specialty stores. For lesbians, Noe Valley, Bernal Heights, and Valencia Street are particularly popular neighborhoods.

Information and Resources

The best source for information on the latest shows, films, events, clubs, and gay news are two free weekly newspapers: the *Bay Area Reporter* (BAR; www.ebar.com) and the *Bay Times* (www.sfbaytimes.com). These are found in cafés, bars, bookstores, and street-corner boxes, especially in and around the Castro.

The San Francisco Bay Guardian and *SF Weekly* are two non-gay-specific alternative weeklies with useful listings and information. Further resources can be found at websites such as: www.onlyinsanfrancisco.com/gaytravel and www.advocate.com/travel.aspan and at the centers, museums, and locations listed below.

The Center (San Francisco LGBT Community Center, Charles M. Holmes Campus)
1800 Market Street; tel: 865-5555; www.sfcenter.org; Mon–Fri noon–10pm, Sat 9am–10pm; free; metro: F to Market Street and Laguna Street; bus: 6, 7, 26, 71; map p.138 A2

The Center is a vital nexus for the LCBT (lesbian, gay, bisexual and transgender) community, and supplies a general information desk, library, Internet access, community-access bulletin boards, and café.

Community United Against Violence (CUAV)
170A Capp Street; tel: 777-5500, hotline 415-333-4357; www.cuav.org; map p.138 B1
An anti-violence organization that offers a 24-hour crisis line, free counseling, and legal advocacy.

GLBT Historical Society Museum
657 Mission Street, Suite 300; tel: 777-5455; www.glbthistory.org; Tue–Sat 1–5pm; BART to Montgomery; metro: F, J, K, L, M, N, T to Montgomery; bus: 7, 14, 21, 30, 45; map p.135 D1
Engrossing, varied exhibits focus on GLBT history, art, and culture.

James C. Hormel Gay and Lesbian Center, Main Library
100 Larkin Street, Third Floor; tel: 557-4400; http://sfpl.org/librarylocations/main/glc/glc.htm; Mon 10am–6pm, Tue–

Below: the colors of gay pride decorate the Castro.

Left: gay couples are part of the mainstream in San Francisco.

Thur 9am–8pm, Fri noon–6pm, Sat 10am–6pm, Sun noon–5pm; free; BART: to Civic Center; metro: F, J, K, L, M, N, T to Civic Center; bus: 6, 7, 19, 21, 71; map p.138 B3
Books, photographs, films, and memorabilia document LGBT history and culture in this resource center, the first of its kind to be located in a public institution.

Lavender Youth Recreation and Information Center (LYRIC)
127 Collingwood Street; tel: 415-703-6150, hotline: 863-3636; www.lyric.org; metro: K, L, M to Castro; bus: 24, 33; map p.137 E1
A community center for lesbian, gay, bisexual, transgender, queer, and questioning youth.

The Women's Building
3543 18th Street; tel: 431-1180; www.womensbuilding.org; Mon–Sun 9am–5pm, additional evening hours vary; BART: 16th Street Mission; metro: J to Church Street and 18th Street; bus: 14, 22, 26, 33, 49; map p.138 A1
The beautiful *MaestraPeace* mural colorfully decorates the outside of this 'multi-ethnic, multi-cultural, multi-service center for women and girls.'

> Walking tours like the **FOOT! 'Come Out to the Castro'** tour (tel:793-5378; www.foottours.com) or the '**Cruisin' the Castro Tour**' (tel: 255-1821; www.cruisinthecastro.com) deliver fun history and culture lessons over the course of an easy stroll.

Arts and Entertainment

San Franciscans are an artsy crowd, and the gay and lesbian community is no exception. Queer comedy is supplied by **QComedy**, music by the **San Francisco Gay Men's Chorus**, and innovative performance art, comedy, musicals, and drama by **Theater Rhinoceros**, the oldest gay and lesbian theater company in the US. Another theater option is **Brava! for Women in the Arts**.

The landmark **Castro Theatre** hosts special events like the San Francisco International Gay and Lesbian Film Festival (www.frameline.org/festival), which is held in June.
SEE ALSO MOVIES, P.81

Brava! for Women in the Arts
2789 24th Street; tel: 641-7657; www.brava.org; BART: 24th Street; bus: 12, 27, 48

Qcomedy
www.qcomedy.com

San Francisco Gay Men's Chorus
Tel: 865-3650; www.sfgmc.org

Theater Rhinoceros
2926 16th Street; tel: 861-5079; BART: 16th Street Mission; bus: 14, 22, 26, 33, 49; map p.138 B1

Festivals and Events

The annual San Francisco LGBT Pride Festival (tel: 864-3733; www.sf-pride.org) each June is the world's largest, featuring a Dyke March and ever-popular Pride Parade. SoMa hosts the Up Your Alley leather and fetish fair in July (www.folsomstreetfair.com/alley) and then the Folsom Street Fair – the 'grand-daddy of all leather events' – in September (www.folsomstreetfair.com). Come October, arts and craft vendors and community groups gather at the Castro Street Fair (www.castrostreetfair.org). Aids awareness and activist events include an annual Aids Candlelight Vigil (www.aidscandlightvigil.org), Aids Walk San Francisco (www.aidswalk.net/sanfran), and various events on World Aids Day (www.artistsagainstaids.com).

Health and Fitness

Gold's Gym
2301 Market Street; tel: 626-4488; metro: F, K, L, M, T to Castro; bus: 24, 33, 35, 37; map p.137 E1
1001 Brannan Street; tel: 552-4653; bus: 19, 27; map p.139 C2

Above: flamboyant style at a Ferry Building cook-off.

The Castro and SoMa locations of Gold's Gym (www.goldsgym.com) are largely used by gay men. Call for hours and daily rates.

Magnet
4122 18th Street; tel: 581-1600; www.magnetsf.com, Tue noon–6pm, Wed–Fri 3–9pm, Sat noon–6pm; metro: F, K, L, M, T to Church; bus: 24, 33, 33, 37; map p.137 E1
Taking a holistic approach to gay men's health, Magnet provides anonymous testing, counseling, seminars, dance lessons, art shows, and other events in a friendly setting.

Stores

A Different Light Bookstore
489 Castro Street; tel: 431-0891; www.adlbooks.com; Sun–Thur 10am–10pm, Fri–Sat 10am–11pm; metro: F, K, L, M, T to Castro; bus: 33, 34, 35, 37; map p.137 E1
San Francisco's biggest gay bookstore supplies a plethora of gay and lesbian oriented books, magazines, and newspapers.

Cliff's Variety
479 Castro Street; tel: 431-5365; www.cliffsvariety.com; Mon–Fri 8.30am–8pm, Sat 9.30am–8pm, Sun 11am–6pm; metro: F, K, L, M, T to Castro station; bus: 24, 33, 35, 37; map p.137 E1
This unique hardware store sells just about everything you might need for a costume, with aisles of tools, craft supplies, fancy-dress outfits, and home décor.

Nancy Boy
347 Hayes Street; tel: 552-3802; www.nancyboy.com; Mon–Fri 11am–7pm, Sat–Sun 11am–6pm; bus: 16AX, 16BX, 21, 47, 49; map p.138 A3
'Tested on Boyfriends – Not Animals' is the playful motto of this high-end Hayes Valley boutique that specializes in skincare and beauty products for men.

Rolo Castro
2351 Market Street; tel: 431-4545; www.rolo.com; Mon–Sat 11am–8pm, Sun 11am–7pm; metro: F, K, L, M, T to Castro; bus: 24, 37; map p.137 E1
A go-to spot for edgy and very-of-the-moment designer clothing, Rolo Castro is the place to pick up top-shelf trends, generally at top-dollar prices.

Under One Roof
549 Castro Street; tel: 503-2300; www.underoneroof.org; Mon–Fri 11am–8pm, Sat 10am–8pm, Sun 11am–7pm; metro: F, K, L, M, T to Castro; bus: 24, 33, 35, 37; map p.137 E1
Profits from the sales of this store's odds and ends are donated to organizations providing HIV/Aids education and support services.

The Wild Card
3989 17th Street; tel: 626-4449; Mon–Fri 11am–8pm; metro: F, K, L, M, T to Castro; bus: 24, 33, 35, 37; map p.137 E1
A gay-themed stationery store with risqué cards and naughty novelties. Fun for gifts.

Cafés

FOR FURTHER LISTINGS, SEE BARS AND CAFÉS, P.34–9

Baghdad Café
2295 Market Street; tel: 621-4434; daily 24 hours; $; metro: F, K, L, M, T to Castro; bus: 24, 35, 37; map p.137 E1
A decent 24-hour diner, popular with post-clubbing crowds with the munchies who come for burgers and fries, meaty sandwiches, and breakfast standards.

Just for You Café
732 22nd Street; tel: 647-3033; www.justforyoucafe.com;

Average price for a three-course meal and a half-bottle of house wine:

$	less than $25
$$	$25–$50
$$$	$50–$100
$$$$	more than $100

Mon–Fri 7.30am–3pm, Sat–Sun 8am–3pm; $; metro: T to 23rd Street; bus: 48
A diverse crowd raves about the hearty, homemade breakfasts, especially the giant, powdered-sugar-dusted beignets and other New Orleans and Mexican specialties.

Samovar
498 Sanchez Street; tel: 626-4700; daily 10am–11pm; metro: F, K, L, M, T to Castro; bus: 24, 33; map p.139 A1
As a change from the area's many bars, this is a popular and relaxed spot selling a wide selection of teas, with small plates providing a further temptation to linger.

Restaurants

FOR FURTHER LISTINGS, SEE RESTAURANTS, P.102–11

2223
2223 Market Street; tel: 431-0692; www.2223restaurant.com; Mon–Sat D only, Sun Br and D; $$; metro: F, J, K, L, M, T to Church; bus: 9, 22, 37; map p.137 E1
A chic neighborhood favorite for comfort food in a fun, lively setting; also a great bet for Sunday brunch.

Catch
2362 Market Street; tel: 431-5000; www.catchsf.com; daily L and D; $$; metro: F, K, L, M, T to Castro; bus: 24, 35, 37; map p.137 E1
A casual, cozy seafood spot with a heated outdoor patio, view of Market Street, nightly live piano music, and a lively, fun atmosphere.

Home
2100 Market Street; tel: 503-0333; www.home-sf.com; daily 5pm–midnight and Sat–Sun 10am–2pm; $$; metro: F, J, K, L, M, T to Church Street; 22, 33, 37; map p.138 A2
Good value, welcoming restaurant specializing in tasty versions of American favorites and other comfort foods. Also boasts a fun patio bar.

Bars and Nightclubs

FOR FURTHER LISTINGS, SEE BARS AND CAFÉS, P.34–9; NIGHTLIFE, P.94–5; THEATER AND CABARET, P.118–9

440 Castro
440 Castro Street; tel: 621-8732; www.the440.com; Mon–Sun noon–2am; metro: F, K, L, M, T to Castro; bus: 33, 34, 35, 37; map p.137 E1
Formerly called Daddy's, 440 Castro is the 'neighborhood Levi/leather bar.' The Monday underwear parties have men boozing in boxers and briefs.

Badlands
4121 18th Street; tel: 626-9320; www.badlands-sf.com; Mon–Sun 2pm–2am; metro: F, K, L, M, T to Castro; bus: 24, 33, 35, 37; map p.137 E1
Badlands packs its dance floor to the gills with a young crowd loving the Top 40 and 80s hits. TV screens around the dance floor blast music videos.

Bar on Castro
456 Castro Street; tel: 626-7220; www.thebarsf.com; Mon–Fri 4pm–2am; Sat–Sun 2pm–2am; metro: F, K, L, M, T to Castro; bus: 33, 34, 35, 37; map p.137 E1

Below: a colorful gay pride mural in the Castro.

Above: a performer dances on Market Street at the LGBT Pride Festival.

Bar on Castro has a small dance floor jam-packed with pretty boys. Mondays are popular, with 80s music and 80 cent drink specials (house spirits only).

The Café
2369 Market Street; tel: 861-3846; www.cafesf.com; metro: F, K, L, M, T to Castro; bus: 24, 35, 37; map p.137 E1
A large, young mixed crowd (guys and girls) dance, drink, and flirt the night away to Top 40 tunes. Third Saturday of the month is for lesbians.

Below: the local bars offer something for everyone.

The Eagle Tavern
398 12th Street; tel: 626-0880; www.sfeagle.com; Mon–Sun noon–2am; bus: 9, 12, 27, 47; map p.138 B2
A leather bar with cruisey, anything-goes Beer Busts on the outdoor patio, as well as occasional mud-wrestling, and live bands.

El Rio
3158 Mission Street; tel: 282-3325; www.elriosf.com; Mar–Nov: Mon–Thur 5pm–2am, Fri 4pm–2am, Sat–Sun 3pm–2am, Dec–Feb: Sat–Thur 5pm–2am, Fri 4pm–2am (sometimes closes earlier); BART: 24th Street; bus: 12, 14, 14L, 26, 49, 67
A funky Mission bar for 'chiquitas, bananas, and mixed fruits,' El Rio draws diverse crowds with live and DJ music, film and art showings, drag, spoken word, and fundraisers. The outdoor patio and 'Salsa Sundays' are especially popular.

Lexington Club
464 19th Street; tel: 863-2052; www.lexingtonclub.com; Mon–Thur 5pm–2am, Sat–Sun 3pm–2am; bus: 14, 14L, 26, 49; map p.138 B1
One of the few real lesbian bars in the city, this Mission dive for dykes draws a chill, mostly younger (and sometimes cliquey) crowd.

Lone Star Saloon
1354 Harrison Street; tel: 863-9999; www.lonestarsaloon.com; Mon–Sun noon–2am; bus: 12, 19, 27, 47; map p.138 C2
The Lone Star Saloon was the first 'bear' bar in the US. For the smoker's den, head out to the big backyard patio, which gets especially busy for weekend Beverage Benefits.

Marlena's
488 Hayes Street; tel: 864-6672; www.marlenasbarsf.com; Mon–Fri 3pm–2am, Sat–Sun 3pm–2am; bus: 16AX, 16BX, 21; map p.138 A3
A diverse group (gay, lesbian, transgender, transvestite, and drag queens) turns out for popular weekend drag shows.

Martuni's
4 Valencia Street; tel: 241-0205; http://martunis.ypguides.net; Mon–Sun 2pm–2am; metro: F to Market Street and Gough Street; bus: 6, 7, 26, 71; map p.138 A2
A mixed crowd packs in

The Interfaith Chapel at Grace Cathedral (1100 California Street) displays patches from The **AIDS Memorial Quilt** (www.aidsquilt.org), which was begun in 1987 while the devastating epidemic ravaged San Francisco. Now, more than 91,000 victims' names are on the quilt, pieces of which are displayed across the US.

houlder-to-shoulder on veekends to this fun and riendly piano bar. The martiis are dangerously large and otent; after a few, the brave sk to sing their own tunes.

Mix

086 18th Street; tel: 431-8616; Mon–Sun 6am–2am; metro: F, K, , M, T to Castro; bus: 24, 33, 35, 7; map p.137 E1

A neighborhood hang-out hat lives up its name, with a nixed crowd that's dyke- and etero-friendly. Wednesdays re chick nights.

Moby Dick's

049 18th Street; tel: 861-199; www.mobydicksf.com; Mon–Fri 2pm–2am, Sat–Sun oon–2am; metro: F, K, L, M, T o Castro; bus: 33, 34, 35, 37; nap p.137 E1

A friendly, casual neighborood bar where you can play ool, pinball, and touchscreen trivia while enjoying laily drink specials.

Midnight Sun

067 18th Street; tel: 861-4186; www.midnightsunsf.com; Mon–Fri 2pm–2am, Sat–Sun pm–2am; metro: F, K, L, M, T to astro; bus: 33, 34, 35, 37; map .137 E1

Big-screen televisions are the draw for this video bar where ay men gather to watch a nix of popular shows like *Desperate Housewives*, *Top Chef*, and *The Simpsons*.

Pilsner Inn

225 Church Street; tel: 621-7058; www.pilsnerinn.com; Mon–Sun 10am–2pm; metro: F, J, K, L, M, T to Church Street; bus: 22, 37; map p.138 A2

Locals guys enjoy the relaxed vibe, extensive draft beer selection, pool tables and pinball machines, and the smoker-friendly heated back patio. Sometimes diners from the nearby popular restaurant, Chow, come to kill time waiting for tables.

Powerhouse

1347 Folsom Street; tel: 552-8689; www.powerhouse-sf.com; Wed–Sun noon–2am; bus: 12, 19; map p.138 C3

A popular, very cruisey SoMa bar filled with loads of hunky men and not many shirts.

The Stud

399 9th Street; tel: 863-6623; www.studsf.com; bus: 12, 14, 14L, 19, 26; map p.138 C2

Mostly gay men party here, but certain nights and events, like Tuesday's famous 'Trannyshack' drag shows, draw many other types too.

Truck

1900 Folsom Street; tel: 252-0306; www.trucksf.com; Mon–Sun 4pm–2am; bus: 12, 22, 33, 53; map p.138 B2

A young, hipster Mission spot with truckish touches. Mixed crowds stop in throughout the night for drinks, fried food, and the eye-candy on both sides of the bar.

Twin Peaks Tavern

401 Castro Street; tel: 864-9470; www.twinpeaks tavern.com; Mon–Fri noon–2am, Sat–Sun 8am–2am; metro: F, K, L, M, T to Castro; bus: 33, 34, 35, 37; map p.137 E1

A longtime Castro fixture on the corner of Castro and Market Streets, Twin Peaks Tavern was the first gay bar in the US. It is a quiet spot to chat and people-watch through the glass front.

Wild Side West

424 Cortland Avenue; tel: 647-3099; Mon–Sun 1pm–2am; bus: 24

This cozy, welcoming neighborhood bar in Bernal Heights draws a primarily lesbian and local clientele, who relax and chat in the large garden out back.

Below: entertainment of all sorts is available.

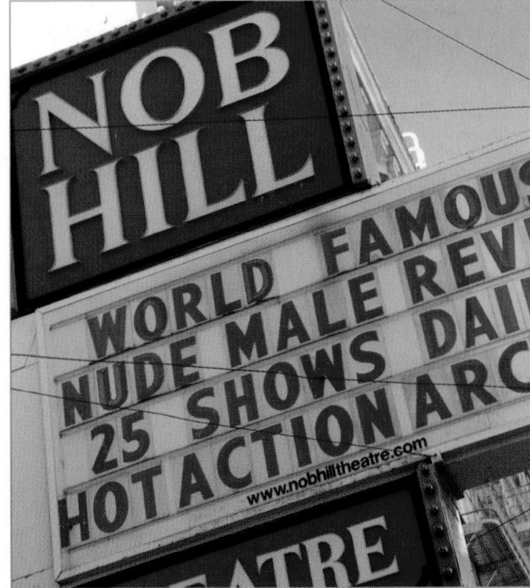

History and Architecture

BC 13000

The Farallon Islands, covered in cedar and pine forests, mark the ocean's edge and the beginning of the vast savannah that is now the San Francisco Bay.

BC 8,000

Ancestors of the Ohlone and Miwok tribes begin settling the shores of the recently filled-in bay.

1579

Sir Francis Drake lands just north of the Golden Gate, missing the bigger bay to the south presumably due to fog. At the present-day Drake's Bay, he claims the surrounding land for England, to no avail.

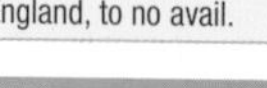

1769

Cresting Sweeney Ridge above present-day Pacifica, the governor of California, Gaspar de Portola, and his party discover the San Francisco Bay whilst looking for the port of Monterey.

1776

The Spanish arrive and build a garrison at the site of the Presidio. More than 200 years later, it retains the best array of American military architecture in the country. On the other side of the peninsula, near a lagoon called Nuestra Senora de los Dolores, the padres established the Misión San Francisco de Asís. Built with adobe in the Spanish style of its day, the mission, commonly known as the Mission Dolores, is San Francisco's oldest building and the only one left representing this era.

1822

When Mexico wins its independence from Spain, California becomes a Mexican territory and its mission system is secularized.

1835

William Richardson, an English sea captain, pitches his tent at Yerba Buena Cove and founds a settlement with the same name.

1839

Swiss settler Jean-Jacques Vioget drafts a layout for Yerba Buena based on a grid. Less than 10 years later, Jasper O'Farrell 'creates' Market Street.

1846

Early in the Mexican-American War, John Montgomery sails the USS *Portsmouth* through the Golden Gate, and raises the Stars and Stripes in the present day Portsmouth Square.

1847

Yerba Buena is renamed San Francisco.

1848

James Marshall discovers gold at John Augustus Sutter's mill in the Sierra Nevada foothills on January 24. Nine days later on February 2, the Treaty of Guadalupe Hildago is signed, making California American.

1849

The Gold Rush ignites the greatest mass migration in history, turning what was a 2,000-person town into a rugged city with a population of 20,000.

1850

The US Congress grants California statehood, skipping the intermediate stage of territory.

1855

At the corner of Pacific and Battery, a brick hotel building is constructed over the hull of a landlocked ship used as a saloon. Still called 'Old Ship Saloon,' it represents the look of the Barbary Coast era.

1859

With the discovery of the Comstock Load, a vast silver deposit in Virginia City, Nevada, San Francisco once again becomes a boomtown.

1862

The electrical telegraph is invented, linking San Francisco with the rest of the country.

1869

The Transcontinental Railroad is completed making millionaires of the 'Big Four' barons: Charles Crocker, Collis P. Huntington, Mark Hopkins, and Leland Stanford.

1870

William Hammond Hall begins the difficult task of turning the city's western sand dunes into Golden Gate Park.

1873

Cable Cars are invented, allowing for the development of San Francisco's steepest hills and outer western areas.

1875

Anti-Chinese riots raze Chinatown. The Pacific Coast Stock Exchange and the grand Palace Hotel are both built.

1882

The Chinese Exclusion Act is passed in Congress.

1886

The first brownstone west of the Mississippi is built for tycoon James Flood atop Nob Hill.

1895

The famous 'Painted Ladies' lining Alamo Square represent the city's Victorian architecture. Queen Anne's, known for their asymmetrical style and arresting turrets, are also popular at this time, as are Edwardians, distinguished by their narrow and rectangular bay windows.

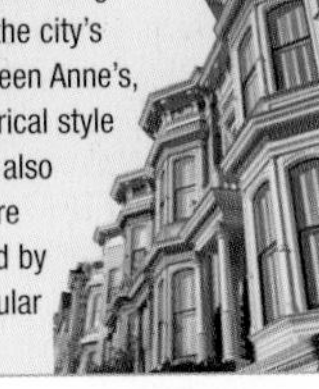

1906

At 5.12am on April 18th, an earthquake measuring an estimated 8.3 on the Richter Scale hits San Francisco. The earthquake causes considerable damage, including the destruction of City Hall, and its disruption of gas and water lines results in blazing fires all over the city that burn for three days, destroying much of San Francisco and leaving thousands of people dead or homeless.

1907

Complete with a classic copper façade, the flatiron Sentinal Building is finished, despite damage from the earthquake and fire. It represents the architectural style of San Francisco's downtown before the great quake.

1908

Chinatown is rebuilt, designed by white architects with an eye on extenuating its exotic Beijing-inspired architecture to attract tourism and tame its perceived excesses.

1910

The Angel Island Immigration Station opens. Known as 'The Ellis Island of the west' it goes on to process 175,000 Asian immigrants, often holding them for several months.

1912

The San Francisco Municipal Railway is created and becomes one of the first publicly owned transit companies in the nation.

1914

Influenced by the City Beautiful movement of the late 19th century, Arthur Brown Jr completes the new City Hall, designed in the beaux arts style.

1915

To mark the opening of the Panama Canal and the rebirth of the city, San Francisco hosts the Panama-Pacific Exposition on waterfront filled in with the refuse left from the 1906 earthquake. Afterward, it is christened the Marina and developed in the Mediterranean architectural style sweeping California in the 1920s. The only structure to remain from the Exposition is the Palace of Fine Arts.

1918

The Gothic Hallidie Building is completed during a boom in downtown development.

1926

Unique for its Romanesque and French Chateau ornamentation, the Hunter-Dulin Building opened its doors. Its most famous tenent is Dashiell Hammett's fictional Sam Spade.

1930

Diego Rivera paints murals at the Pacific Stock Exchange and the San Francisco Art Institute.

1933

The fluted Coit Tower, deeded to the city by Lilly Hitchcock Coit, is completed. Its interior is illustrated with frescoes depicting working class San Francisco.

1934

The West Coast Waterfront Strike lasts 83 days and shuts down San Francisco's port, prompting violent collisions with the police and National Guard, and inspiring a four-day general strike throughout the city.

1937

The Golden Gate Bridge opens at the cost of $35 million and the lives of 11 construction workers, six months after the Bay Bridge is completed.

1940

Known as the 'Harlem of the west', the Lower Fillmore jazz clubs begin attracting big names such as Ella Fitzgerald, Duke Ellington, Billie Holiday, Charles Mingus, and Charley Parker.

1941-5

As 1.6 million American military men pass through Fort Mason on their way to the front, Bay Area industry booms with the war effort.

1942

The US government rounds up Japanese residents, including 3rd generation citizens, and moves them to internment camps deep in the country's interior.

1945

World War II is declared over. The UN charter is signed in the War Memorial Opera House.

1955

Alan Ginsburg reads his poem *Howl* at the Gallery Six, igniting the San Francisco Poetry Renaissance.

1957

San Francisco columnist Herb Caen coins the phrase 'Beatnik' at a bar, while listening to Beat poetry the night Sputnik launched.

1951-9

In the Fillmore district, Justin Herman's controversial Urban Renewal Program demolishes African-American owned businesses and some 200 homes, replacing them with low-rise, low-income apartment blocks.

1964
On the ashes of the Crocker mansion on Nob Hill, the French Gothic inspired Grace Cathedral is completed.

1965
The Grateful Dead debut at the Fillmore Auditorium.

1967
Haight-Ashbury blossoms with the Summer of Love, launching the city and its music into the center of the counterculture.

1969
In Presidio Heights, the Zodiac killer commits his only murder in San Francisco, while continuing to taunt the SFPD and the *San Francisco Chronicle*.

1971
Inspired by the Chicano civil rights movement, artists begin a series of murals on Balmy Alley; today, there are nearly 500 murals in the Mission district. Modern Movement proponent Pietro Belluschi designs the arresting Cathedral of Saint Mary of the Assumption.

1972
The Transamerica Pyramid is finished, both redefining the skyline and initiating a boom in downtown construction. With the advent of the flexible steel corset, buildings in the earthquake-prone downtown are no longer restricted to 20 stories. Galvanizing city leaders, this begins the 'Manhattanization' of the area, which carries on for another 15 years.

1977
Harvey Milk is elected to city supervisor for the Castro district. The 'Mayor of Castro Street' is the first openly gay person ever elected to public office in the United States.

1978
In Guyana, cult leader Jim Jones and 900 members of his Bay Area's People's Temple commit mass suicide or are murdered. A few months later, the city is gripped in tragedy again as Supervisor Harvey Milk and the popular Mayor George Moscone are shot and killed at City Hall by former Supervisor Dan White.

1979
Dan White's defense in his murder trial, widely derided as the 'Twinkie Defense', delivers him seven years for manslaughter. The light sentence ignites the violent White Night Riots at City Hall.

1989
During the opening of the World Series at Candlestick Park, a 7.1 earthquake rocks the Bay Area, killing 67 people and causing billions of dollars worth of damage.

1995-2001
The 'New Economy' of the dot-com era dominates much of San Franciscan life. The optimism, inflated living costs, and get-rich mentality are reminiscent of the city's earlier boom times.

2000
The San Francisco Giants play their first season in the new Pacific Bell Park.

2002
The dot-com bubble finally bursts, leading to one of the largest crashes ever in the stock market.

2003
200,000 San Franciscans are part of the largest international anti-war demonstration in history.

2004
Mayor Gavin Newsom begins issuing marriage licenses for same-sex couples, putting this controversial issue on the national stage.

2005
The new de Young Museum opens in Golden Gate Park. Its modern architecture, synthesized with the natural landscaping, receives widespread praise.

2006
San Francisco Representative Nancy Pelosi becomes the first woman to be appointed Speaker of the House of Representatives.

2008
Ground is scheduled to break on the Transbay Terminal, the new hub of Northern Californian transportation. Plans include a high-speed rail line to Los Angeles, and a multi-use skyscraper that will be one of the tallest buildings in the US.

Hotels

There is no shortage of somewhere to lay your hat here: San Francisco possesses a dizzying array of hotels, motels, bed-and-breakfasts, and inns that range from the mundane to the dramatic. All of the major chains are well represented, but the more interesting rooms can be found in the boutique hotels. These small, amenities-rich properties are sometimes developed around a theme, such as literature, art deco architecture or the 1960s, giving the hotel a definable personality. When making reservations at the larger hotels, always inquire about special packages and discounts.

Fisherman's Wharf

Argonaut Hotel
495 Jefferson Street; tel: 563-0800, toll-free: 800-546-7866; www.argonauthotel.com; metro: F to Jones Street and Beach Street; bus: 10, 30, 47; cable car: Powell-Hyde; $$$; map p.134 B4
Directly opposite the Wharf's Hyde Street Pier, this spot boasts a maritime theme and suites with sea views, tri-pod telescopes and hot tubs.

Tuscan Inn
425 North Point Street; tel: 561-1100, toll-free: 800-780-7234; www.tuscaninn.com; metro: F to Jefferson Street and Taylor Street; bus: 10, 30, 47; cable car: Powell-Mason; $$; map p.134 B4
Of the many hotels around Fisherman's Wharf, this is by far the most pleasant. The concierge is enthusiastic and helpful, the attractive rooms are well-sized by local standards, and the location is appealing to families who wish to be near Pier 39.

Wharf Inn
2601 Mason Street; tel: 673-7411; www.wharfinn.com; metro: F to Jefferson Street and Powell Street: bus: 39, 47; cable car: Powell-Mason; $$; map p.134 B4
In the thick of the Wharf, a family-friendly gem with good service and rooms with balconies overlooking Pier 39.

North Beach and Telegraph Hill

Hotel Boheme
444 Columbus Avenue; tel: 433-9111; www.hotelboheme.com; bus: 30, 39, 41, 45; $$; map p.134 C3
A flight of narrow stairs brings you inside this delightful small hotel located in the heart of North Beach. Iron beds and brightly painted walls grace the small but lovely bedrooms, and the bathrooms are well-stocked with toiletries. The front desk staff are happy to assist with rental cars, dinner reservations, and tours. All rooms have free Wi-Fi.

San Remo Hotel
2337 Mason Street; tel: 776-8688, toll-free: 800-352-7366; www.sanremohotel.com; bus: 30,39; cable car: Powell-Mason; $; map p.134 B4
Built right after the 1906 earthquake, this originally served as a boardinghouse for sailors, poets and seniors;

Left: a smart welcome at the Four Seasons.

Left: a room with a view at the Kensington Park Hotel.

Your concierge is a treasure trove of local info. Use him for questions of every kind. You need not tip him for every tip he gives you, but if he hooks you up well, show your appreciation with a gratuity.

during Prohibition, it was a speakeasy. Today, it is a bargain, with a stellar location and immaculate rooms. Some share bathroom facilities. The penthouse is a treat and Fior d'Italia, the restaurant on the first floor, is the stuff of North Beach legend.

Washington Square Inn
1660 Stockton Street; tel: 981-4220, toll-free: 800-388-0220; www.wsisf.com; bus: 30, 39, 41; $$; map p.134 C3
A European-style bed-and-breakfast right on one of San Francisco's most scenic urban parks, Washington Square. A great place for an extended soaking in North Beach's legendary cuisine and nightlife.

Chinatown

Grant Plaza Hotel
465 Grant Avenue; tel: 434-3883, toll-free: 800-472-6899; www.grantplaza.com; bus: 30, 45; cable car: California; $; map p.135 C1
A good bet in Chinatown: immaculately clean, small rooms equipped with the basics. Location is the prime sell here, as it is ideal for the active traveler, hill walker, and dim-sum afficianado.

Royal Pacific Motor Inn
661 Broadway; tel: 781-6661, toll-free: 800-545-5575; www.royalpacific.citysearch.com; bus: 9, 14, 30, 41, 45; $; map p.135 C2
A budget motel located on the threshold of North Beach and Chinatown. Amenities include a Finnish sauna.

Union Square and Financial District

Andrews Hotel
624 Post Street; tel: 563-6877, toll-free: 800-926-3739; www.andrewshotel.com; bus: 2, 3, 27, 38, 76; $; map p.134 C1
A 1905 Victorian well-located two blocks west of Union Square. The rooms and baths are on the small side, but rates include a continental breakfast and evening wine reception. Smoking is not allowed.

Campton Place Hotel
340 Stockton Street; tel: 781-5555, toll-free: 800-235-4300; www.tajhotels.com; bus: 2, 4, 30, 45, 76; cable car: Powell-Hyde, -Mason; $$$$; map p.135 C1
Elegant, luxurious, and intimate, this is one of the most renowned and refined hotels in the city. The service is excellent, the amenities are top-notch, and the hotel restaurant consistently wins high ratings.

Cartwright Hotel
524 Sutter Street; tel: 421-2865, toll-free: 800-919-9779; www.cartwrighthotel.com; bus: 2, 3, 30, 45, 76; cable car: Powell-Hyde, -Mason; $; map p.134 C1
This genteel hotel has tastefully decorated rooms and many amenities. A continental breakfast and evening wine reception are included. Five suites are available, a plus for families, and one floor is reserved for smokers. Pets are welcome.

Chancellor Hotel
433 Powell Street; tel: 362-2004, toll-free: 800-428-4748; www.chancellorhotel.com; bus: 2, 3, 27, 38, 71; $$; map p.134 C1
The same family has owned and managed this charming hotel since 1917, which is within a stone's throw of the major department stores around Union Square. Rooms are comfortably furnished; bathrooms are small but well-stocked.

Prices per night for a standard double room, exclusive of taxes (14 percent) in high-season. Prices do not include parking or breakfast unless noted and are liable to change, so always check before you book.

$	under $150
$$	$150–225
$$$	$225–350
$$$$	$350+

Left: funky design in the lobby of Hotel Triton.

Clift Hotel
495 Geary Street; tel: 775-4700; www.clifthotel.com; bus: 2, 4, 27, 38, 76; $$$; map p.134 C1
An historic hotel recently redesigned by Philippe Starke, the Clift is a fusion of old-world elegance and contemporary hipness and home to the über-cool Asia de Cuba restaurant and the Redwood Room.

Four Seasons
757 Market Street; tel: 633-3000; www.fourseasons.com; BART: to Montgomery; metro: F, J, K, L, M, N, T to Montgomery; bus: 30, 38, 45, 76; cable car: Powell-Hyde, Powell-Mason; $$$$; map p.135 C1
With an in-house tech center, high-end stores, and two-story health club with indoor pool and Jacuzzi, in an ultra-convenient location Downtown, this recent addition to Market Street knows how to cater to its sophisticated and fairly exclusive clientele.

Prices per night for a standard double room, exclusive of taxes (14 percent) in high-season. Prices do not include parking or breakfast unless noted and are liable to change, so always check before you book.

$	under $150
$$	$150–225
$$$	$225–350
$$$$	$350+

Galleria Park Hotel
191 Sutter Street; tel: 781-3060, toll-free: 800-792-9639; www.galleriapark.com; metro: F, J, K, L, M, N, T to Montgomery; bus: 6, 30, 38, 45; cable car: Powell-Hyde, Powell-Mason; $$$; map p.135 D1
A boutique hotel with 17 suites convenient to both Union Square and the Financial District, with a comfortable, home-style ambiance. Complimentary Wi-Fi throughout the hotel and an evening wine reception.

Golden Gate Hotel
775 Bush Street; tel: 392-3702, toll-free: 800-835-1118; www.goldengatehotel.com; bus: 2, 3, 4, 76; cable car: Powell-Hyde, Powell-Mason; $; map p.134 C1
A cozy family-run hotel near Union Square and two blocks from the Chinatown Gate. The pretty rooms contain few amenities, but the hotel's rates include a continental breakfast and afternoon tea. Smoking is not allowed in the hotel. Some rooms with private bath. Pet friendly.

Handlery Union Square Hotel
351 Geary Street; tel: 781-7800, toll-free: 800-843-4343; www.handlery.com/sf; bus: 2, 4, 27, 38, 71; $$; map p.134 C1
A good choice for families, the hotel has a heated pool, morning and evening room service and even Nintendo games. Club rooms, located in an adjacent building, are large and offer dressing areas, robes, newspapers, and fresh decor.

Hotel Bijou
111 Mason Street; tel: 771-1200, toll-free: 800-771-1022; www.hotelbijou.com; BART: to Powell; metro: F, J, K, L, M, N, T to Powell; bus: 27, 31; $; map p.138 C4
A 65-room hotel dedicated to cinephiles. A 'film hotline' gives patrons the latest about local movie shoots and the walls are covered in black and white images of old cinema marquees. Nightly viewings in the mini-theater with vintage cinema seating is a quirky bonus.

Hotel Cosmo
761 Post Street; tel: 673-6040, toll-free: 800-794-6011; bus: 2, 3, 4, 27, 76; $; map p.134 B1
Big with the arty crowd due to art openings and a lobby filled with local works. The corner suites with stunning views are one of the best bargains in town.

Hotel Metropolis
25 Mason Street; tel: 775-4600, toll-free: 800-553-1900; www.hotelmetropolis.com; BART: to Powell; metro: F, J, K, L, M, N, T to Powell; bus: 27, 31; cable car: Powell-Hyde, Powell-Mason; $; map p.138 C4

Views can make or break a hotel room in SF, especially the high-rise hotels. Booking online often means you cannot request where your room faces, which might be the Golden Gate Bridge or the back alley. Booking by phone allows you to specify your view.

Eco-friendly hotel with a 'four-elements' theme and where each floor has a different color scheme. Good, centrally located bargain for families.

Hotel Monaco
501 Geary Street; tel: 292-0100, toll-free: 866-622-5284; www.monaco-sf.com; bus: 2, 3, 27, 38, 76; $$; map p.134 C1
A renovated beaux arts building with hand-painted ceiling domes and grand art nouveau murals in the common areas. Rates include morning coffee and afternoon tea, wine and cheese receptions, with neck massages and tarot readings. Rooms in this hotel are comfortable and glamorous, featuring lots of color and texture and canopied beds (some completely draped). Amenities include whirlpool tubs in most suites, yoga accessories, and L'Occitaine bath products. The Grace Slick suite, filled with original memorabilia from her Jefferson Airplane days, offers an unique slice of rock 'n' roll history. The excellent Grand Café is adjacent and provides 24-hour room service.

Hotel Nikko
222 Mason Street; tel: 394-1111, toll-free: 800-645-5687; www.hotelnikkosf.com; BART: to Powell; metro: F, J, K, L, M, N, T to Powell; bus: 27, 38; cable car: Powell-Mason, Powell-Hyde; $$$; map p.134 C1
An elegant and sophisticated Japanese hotel with decent rooms, but more importantly, one of the city's best spa facilities.

Hotel Rex
562 Sutter Street; tel: 433-4434, toll-free: 800-433-4434; www.jdvhospitality.com; bus: 2, 3, 30, 45, 76; cable car: Powell-Hyde, Powell-Mason; $; map p.134 C1
With a nod to the 1930s, the sophisticated Rex is dedicated to the literati and hosts book signings, poetry readings and jazz on Fridays in the library bar. An evening wine hour is complimentary.

Hotel Triton
342 Grant Street; tel: 394-0500, toll-free: 800-800-1299; www.hoteltriton.com; bus: 2, 3, 30, 45, 76; $$; map p.135 C1
Rock music greets patrons entering this trendy hotel just across the street from the Chinatown Dragon Gate. The wild designs and mod furniture scattered around the lobby are amusing, but do not quite compensate for the tiny bedrooms. Nevertheless, the Triton is eco-friendly and a pioneer in green hotels. They employ a sophisticated recycling program, use biodegradable cleaning products, energy efficient systems, recycled paper, and other environmentally-conscious practices.

Inn at Union Square
440 Post Street; tel: 397-3510, toll-free: 800-288-4346; www.unionsquare.com; bus: 2, 3, 27, 38, 72; $$; map p.134 C1
Some of the ways in which this hotel goes the extra distance are bottled spring water on the nightstand, early evening wine and hors d'oeuvres in front of the fireplace for guests and their associates, and overnight shoe-shining services. The nearby full-service fitness club has a heated lap pool.

Kensington Park Hotel
450 Post Street; tel: 781-5050, toll-free: 800-553-1900; www.kensingtonparkhotel.com; bus: 2, 3, 27, 38, 73; $; map p.134 C1
Opened in 1912, this British hotel champions old-fashioned rates and hospitality combined with up-to-date services. The Windsor tea room serves breakfast and afternoon tea on weekends and Winston's Bar and Lounge is open evenings and offers wine, champagne, beer and appetizers.

Mandarin Oriental
222 Sansome Street; tel/toll-free: 800-622-0404; www.mandarinoriental.com; BART: to Montgomery; metro: F, J, K, L, M, N, T to Montgomery; bus: 10, 41; cable car: California; $$$$; map p.135 D2
Extraordinary views and decadent service. Binoculars are provided in each room, and some have glass bathtubs near the windows.

Maxwell
386 Geary Street; tel: 986-2000, toll-free: 800-553-1900; www.maxwellhotel.com; bus: 2, 3, 27, 38, 71; $$; map p.134 C1
An inviting, theatrical lobby leads to art-deco-inspired guestrooms that range from small to spacious. Room service is courtesy of Max's on the Square, featuring delicious deli fare.

Ritz-Carlton
600 Stockton Street; tel: 296-7465, toll-free: 800-241-3333;

Below: breakfast in style at the Mandarin Oriental Hotel.

Above: spectacular views from the Mandarin Oriental over North Beach and the Financial District.

www.ritzcarlton.com; bus: 1, 30, 45; cable car: California; $$$$; map p.135 C1

Once a giant neoclassical corporate headquarters, now a luxury hotel catering to those with fat pocketbooks. Opened in 1991, the Ritz offers enormous rooms, a fitness center, indoor pool, fine dining restaurant, and prime service.

Serrano

405 Taylor Street; tel: 885-2500; www.serranohotel.com; bus: 27, 38; cable car: Powell-Hyde, Powell-Mason; $$; map p.134 C1

A 17-story Spanish Revival building with a Moorish-style lobby, 236 rooms and 19 suites in the heart of the Theater District. Pet and kid friendly with a good restaurant, Ponzu, downstairs.

Sir Francis Drake

450 Powell Street; tel: 392-7755, toll-free: 800-795-7124; www.sirfrancisdrake.com; bus: 2, 3, 27, 38, 74; $$$; map p.134 C1

Glide past the uniformed valets into the grand lobby of this 1928 landmark building. A recent $20 million renovation refurbished all guestrooms and public spaces. The excellent Scala's Bistro is located next door, and on the top floor there is a small fitness room and a popular nightclub with a spectacular view.

Warwick Regis

490 Geary Street; tel: 928-7900, toll-free: 800-203-3232; www.warwickhotels.com; bus: 2, 3, 27, 38, 75; $$; map p.134 C1

Guests receive all the amenities expected of a much larger hotel like twice-daily maid service, marble-tiled baths, afternoon tea and cookies, same-day laundry service and 24-hour room service. All the elegantly appointed guest rooms are quiet. The Union Square location is especially convenient for theatergoers.

Westin St Francis

335 Powell Street; tel: 397-7000, toll-free: 866-500-0338; www.westinstfrancis.com; bus: 2, 3, 4, 76; cable car: Powell-Hyde, Powell-Mason; $$$; map p.134 C1

The location, across the street from Union Square, adds to the excitement of staying at this legendary hotel. If the historic aspects interest you, reserve a room in the original building. Baths are small and guest rooms rather dark, but they are furnished with handsome reproductions and chandeliers. An on-site fitness center, room service, and chef Michael Mina's acclaimed restaurant complete the package.

York Hotel

940 Sutter Street; tel: 885-6800, toll-free: 800-552-1900; www.yorkhotel.com; bus: 2, 3, 4, 27, 76; $; map p.134 B1

The setting for Hitchcock's *Vertigo* has recently been renovated and offers a deluxe continental breakfast with the very reasonably-priced room rates. The Plush Room theater, once a prohibition-era

Prices per night for a standard double room, exclusive of taxes (14 percent) in high-season. Prices do not include parking or breakfast unless noted and are liable to change, so always check before you book.

$	under $150
$$	$150–225
$$$	$225–350
$$$$	$350+

If you will have a car in SF, be sure to find out if parking at your hotel is free, or available for a fee. Fees can easily add up to $150 for a week.

speakeasy now known for torch singers and cabaret, is located here.

SoMa and Civic Centre

Adagio Hotel
550 Geary Street; tel: 775-5000; www.thehoteladdagio.com; bus: 27, 38; $$$; map p.134 C1
Comfortable and chic, the Adagio Hotel has Aveda bath products, Internet access, and superb customer service.

Bay Bridge Inn
966 Harrison Street; tel: 397-0657; www.baybridgeinn.com; bus: 12, 27, 42; $; map p.139 C3
Nothing but the basics here, but one attraction for party animals is that the clean, motel-style rooms are convenient to the 11th Street nightclub scene in SoMa.

Phoenix Hotel
601 Eddy Street; tel: 776-1380, toll-free: 800-248-9466; www.thephoenixhotel.com; bus: 19, 31; $; map p.138 B4
Popular with touring bands and edgy celebrities, the Phoenix has funky rooms with bamboo furniture and a tropical oasis touch. The adjoining Bambuddah restaurant and bar serves Asian-themed delights while you are poolside.

Harbor Court Hotel
165 Steuart Street; tel: 882-1300, toll-free: 866-792-6283; www.harborcourthotel.com; metro: F to Don Chee Way and Steuart Street; bus: 2, 12, 14, 31, 71; $$$; map p.135 E2
Across from the Rincon Center, this 1907 building with bay views has been converted into an elegant boutique hotel with comfortable rooms and varied luxury amenities. Guests have complimentary access to the state-of-the-art fitness center next door.

Hotel Milano
55 5th Street; tel: 543-8555; toll-free: 800-398-7555; www.hotelmilanosf.com; BART: to Powell; metro: F, J, K, L, M, N, T to Powell; bus: 14, 26, 27; $$$; map p.139 C4
The location – next door to the San Francisco Centre, a few blocks from Yerba Buena Gardens and Moscone Center, and close to an underground Muni station – makes this hotel a good pick for energetic tourists who like to shop. An on-site fitness room, restaurant, and full service make up for the spare decor.

Hotel Vitale
8 Mission Street; tel: 278-3700, toll-free: 888-890-8688; www.hotelvitale.com; BART: to Embarcadero; metro: F, J, K, L, M, N, T to Embarcadero; bus: 2, 14, 21, 31, 71; $$$; map p.135 E2
The newest hotel on SF's waterfront, with a slew of amenities you will not find anywhere. Complimentary yoga classes, free car service within one mile, and many other pampering details.

Inn at the Opera
333 Fulton Street; tel: 863-8400, toll-free: 800-325-2708; www.innattheopera.com; bus: 5, 21, 47, 49; $$$; map p.138 A3
A favorite spot for the performing artists who appear nightly in San Francisco's nearby arts centers. Good for opera and symphony goers, but the surrounding neighborhood is a bit sketchy.

Below: the imposing façade of the Westin St. Francis.

InterContinental San Francisco
888 Howard Street; tel: 888-811-4273; www.intercontinentalsanfrancisco.com; bus: 14, 27; $$$; map p.139 C4
This towering green glass hotel, the latest in SoMa's skyline redesign, represents a brand new benchmark in local luxury.

Mosser
54 4th Street; tel: 986-4400; www.themosser.com; BART: Powell; metro: F, J, K, L, M, N, T to Powell; bus: 9, 30, 45; $$; map p.139 C4

Below: a deluxe room at the Hotel Adagio.

Above: the Garden Court at the Palace Hotel.

An ornate stained-glass window in the lobby, antique phone booths, and an incredibly slow elevator are quirky reminders of this hotel's past, but the good linens, latest gadgets, prime SoMa location and good rates make it an affordable choice for young sophisticates.

Palace Hotel

2 New Montgomery Street; tel: 512-1111, toll-free: 800-325-3535; www.sfpalace.com; BART: to Montgomery; metro: F, J, K, L, M, N, T to Montgomery; bus: 3, 9, 10, 45, 71; $$$$; map p.135 D1

An historical landmark just South of Market, and home of the magnificent Garden Court Restaurant. Truly one of the city's most opulent returns to a guilded age. Enjoy a cocktail under the Maxfield Parrish mural in the Pied Piper bar.

W Hotel

181 3rd Street; tel: 777-5300, toll-free: 800-946-8357; www.whotels.com; bus: 9, 14, 30, 45, 76; $$$$; map p.139 D4

Sparse elegance and minimalist design lures the hip and the wannabe's to SoMa. The delectable XYZ restaurant downstairs is top-notch. The modernity extends to the well-stocked rooms, each with CD players, 27-inch TVs, Wi-Fi and goose-down duvets.

Nob Hill

Fairmont Hotel and Tower

950 Mason Street; tel: 772-5013; toll-free: 800-527-472; www.fairmont.com; bus: 1; cable car: California; $$$; map p.134 C2

A favorite set location for filmmakers and an elegant experience, the Fairmont was about to open when the 1906 earthquake struck.

Undaunted, the hotel opened exactly a year later. Experience the opulence of turn-of-the-century SF, or take in the playful classicism of the rotunda in the Laurel Court.

Huntington Hotel

1075 California Street; tel: 474-5400, toll-free: 800-227-4683; www.huntingtonhotel.com; bus: 1; cable car: California; $$$$; map p.134 C1

A refined family-owned hotel built in 1924 at the top of Nob Hill, where publicity-shy celebrities stay in discreet luxury. Originally an apartment building, rooms are larger than average. For views, ask for a room above the eighth floor. Huntington Park is just across the street, making the location especially pleasant for families with young children. The **Nob Hill Spa** on the premises is one of the city's best.

SEE ALSO PAMPERING, P.97

Inter-Continental Mark Hopkins

1 Nob Hill; tel: 392-3434, toll-free: 800-662-4455; www.sanfrancisco.intercontinental.com; bus: 1; cable car: California; $$$; map p.134 C1

> Since San Francisco is a very popular convention and tourist town, it is imperative to make reservations well ahead of time. If you have not done so, phone SF Reservations, tel: (800) 677-1500 (toll-free in US) or 510-628-4400 or visit www.hotelres.com.

Below: fluttering flags at the Fairmont Hotel.

At the summit of Nob Hill, with grand views in all directions, this hotel offers luxury rooms on the site of the original Mark Hopkins mansion. The rooftop cocktail lounge, **Top of the Mark**, has been a city staple since 1939, and an atmosphere of quiet refinement prevails throughout.
SEE ALSO BARS AND CAFÉS, P.36

Petite Auberge
863 Bush Street; tel: 928-6000, toll-free: 866-302-0896; www.jdvhospitality.com; bus: 2, 3, 4, 76; cable car: Powell-Hyde, Powell-Mason; $; map p.134 C1
A small, cozy French-style inn. There is a pretty parlour and afternoon wine, and the room rate includes a gourmet breakfast.

Renaissance Stanford Court
905 California Street; tel: 989-3500, toll-free: 800-227-4736; www.mariott.com; bus: 1; cable car: California; $$$; map p.134 C2
An elegant renovation credited with setting the standard for San Francisco grand-hotel revivals. Great views, and you can hear the ding-dinging of the cable cars out your window.

White Swan Inn
845 Bush Street; tel: 775-1755, toll-free: 800-999-9570; www.jdvhospitality.com; bus: 2, 3, 4, 76; cable car: Powell-Hyde, Powell-Mason; $$; map p.134 C1
A cozy English-style bed-and-breakfast inn. The romantic rooms and suites all have fireplaces to combat the infamous San Francisco chill. A gourmet breakfast buffet is served daily. Afternoon tea with home-baked cookies and evening wine and hors d'oeuvres are served in the parlor.

Central Neighbourhoods

Alamo Square Inn
719 Scott Street; tel: 315-0123, toll-free: 866-515-0123; www.alamoinn.com; bus: 1, 24; $$; map p.137 E3
Bed-and-breakfast with Jacuzzi, fireplaces and complimentary wine, near the oft-photographed 'Painted Ladies' of Alamo Square.

Above: one of the elegant bathrooms at the Inter-Continental Mark Hopkins.

Chateau Tivoli
1057 Steiner Street; tel: 776-5462, toll-free: 800-228-1647; www.chateautivoli.com; bus: 21, 22; $; map p.137 E3
On Alamo Square, this plush Victorian bed-and-breakfast inn brimming with antiques and curios has 22 attractive rooms, some with fireplaces and Jacuzzis.

Hotel Del Sol
3100 Webster Street; tel: 921-5520, toll-free: 877-433-5765; www.jdvhospitality.com; bus: 22, 43, 76; $; map p.133 E3
Once a boring, ordinary motel, the Del Sol has had a radical make-over and now proves that looks are almost everything. Color is used to great effect, splashed on walls, fabrics, and mosaic tiles that decorate tabletops and walkways. Comfortable medium- to large-sized rooms surround a heated swimming pool, small lawn and hammock; suites are available.

Hotel Drisco
2901 Pacific Avenue; tel: 346-2880, toll-free: 800-634-7277; www.hoteldrisco.com; bus: 3, 24; $$; map p.133 D2
A 100 year-old hotel tucked away in a beautiful, historical residential area of Pacific Heights. Great for those who have done the downtown thing and want a bit of peace and quiet among the City's upper crust.

Hotel Majestic
1500 Sutter Street; tel: 441-1100, toll-free: 800-869-8966; www.thehotelmajestic.com; bus: 2, 3, 4, 38; $$; map p.134 A1
Constructed in 1902, the Majestic claims to be the oldest still-operating hotel in the

Prices per night for a standard double room, exclusive of taxes (14 percent) in high-season. Prices do not include parking or breakfast unless noted and are liable to change, so always check before you book.

$	under $150
$$	$150–225
$$$	$225–350
$$$$	$350+

Above: the Hotel Del Sol is a great choice for when you're traveling with children.

city. Old-world atmosphere and good special rates.

Laurel Inn
444 Presidio Avenue; tel: 567-8467; toll-free: 800-552-8735; www.jdvhospitality.com; bus: 1, 2, 4, 43; $$; map p.133 D1
Do not let the exterior fool you: this recently renovated inn has a lot to offer. Its most important feature is that each room is designed as if it was a studio apartment. While not the best choice for first-time SF visitors, it is a great option for returning tourists or extended-stay guests. Close to the semi-secret Sacramento Street shopping strip.

Marina Inn
3110 Octavia Street; tel: 928-1000, toll-free: 800-274-1420; www.marinainn.com; bus: 28, 30, 76; $; map p.134 A3
This is an inexpensive, gracious Victorian inn off Lombard Street, not far from the Golden Gate Bridge, the Presidio, and the upscale shopping on Union and Chestnut streets. The rooms are simply furnished; inside rooms are considerably quieter but do not have much natural light. A Continental breakfast is included in the price.

While many boutique hotels do not have fitness centers, most have arrangements with offsite gyms where guests can work out for free or a reduced rate.

Metro Hotel
319 Divisadero Street; tel: 861-5364; www.metrohotelsf.com; bus: 6, 7, 22, 38; $; map p.137 E2
A comfortable and ridiculously affordable hotel in the central and increasingly trendy NoPa (north of the Panhandle) location, just steps from Haight Street. Do not look for amenities here. Rooms are small and sometimes noisy, but clean. The private garden is inviting. Lots of groovy bars and inexpensive food options, including a great vegan restaurant, are nearby.

Haight-Ashbury and Golden Gate Park

Inn 1890
1890 Page Street; tel: 386-0486, toll-free: 888-466-1890; www.inn1890.com; bus: 7, 33, 37, 43, 71; $; map p.137 C2
This is a beautiful, 18-room corner Victorian bed-and-breakfast in the heart of the Upper Haight neighborhood, where the architecture survived the 1906 earthquake. Built in 1890, some rooms have their own fireplace, and you are one block from fabulous Golden Gate Park. A great alternative to the towering hotels of downtown.

Red Victorian Bed-and-Breakfast Inn
1665 Haight Street; tel: 864-1978; www.redvic.com; bus: 7, 33, 37, 66, 71; $; map p.137 D2
The Summer of Love is alive and well at this peace haven on Haight Street. Reasonably-priced 1960s-themed rooms have private baths, canopied beds, colorful quilts and tie-dyed fabrics. No televisions but plenty of good vibes. The Red Victorian is perfect for the whimsical, budget traveler. Each room reflecting a different theme, such as the Flower Child Room or the Playground, and the ambiance is friendly and casual. Book in and have fun.

Stanyan Park Hotel
750 Stanyan Street; tel: 751-1000; www.stanyanpark.com; bus: 7, 33, 43, 66, 71; $; map p.137 C2
An elegant, affordable early 20th-century boutique hotel located across the street from Golden Gate Park. Suites are large and ideal for families. Continental breakfast is included. Steps from Haight Street and the infamous Hippie Hill.

Mission and Castro

24 Henry Guesthouse and Village House
24 Henry Street; tel: 864-5686, toll-free: 800-900-5686; www.24henry.com; metro: K, L, M, T to Church; bus: 24, 37; $;

Prices per night for a standard double room, exclusive of taxes (14 percent) in high-season. Prices do not include parking or breakfast unless noted and are liable to change, so always check before you book.

$	under $150
$$	$150–225
$$$	$225–350
$$$$	$350+

Some hotels view Internet access as a cash cow, with outrageous fees for online access in your room similar to direct-dialed long-distance. If you need to be constantly checking your e-mail, try to find one with free Wi-Fi. If your hotel charges you, there is a good chance a local café will have free Wi-Fi.

map p.137 E2
Two refurbished late-1800s Victorian houses have been turned into hotels. Each has a parlour and five bedrooms, right in the heart of the Castro.

Beck's Motor Lodge
2222 Market Street; tel: 621-8212; metro: F, K, L, M, T to Castro; bus: 37; $; map p.137 E1
Quintessential American motel, complete with tacky carpets, garish furnishings, and glasses sealed in plastic. You either think Beck's is kitsch fun, or you run away screaming. Prime location in the Castro.

Noe's Nest
3973 23rd Street; tel: 821-0751; www.noesnest.com; metro: J to Church Street and 24th Street; bus: 48; $$
Tiny, five-room bed-and-breakfast inn in pretty, residential Noe Valley neighborhood beyond the Castro. Noe's nest has decks, fireplaces, a Jacuzzi, themed rooms, and a local neighborhood feel.

Parker Guesthouse
520 Church Street; tel: 621-3222, toll-free: 888-520-7275; www.parkerguestouse.com; metro: J to Church Street and 18th Street; bus: 33; $; map p.138 A1
A relaxed and welcoming guesthouse in the Castro with 21 rooms (only two with shared bathrooms) and terrycloth robes for every guest. A garden and steam room complete the package.

Oakland, Berkeley and the Bay Area

Claremont Resort and Spa
41 Tunnel Road, Berkeley; tel: 510-843-3000; toll-free: 800-551-7266; www.claremont resort.com; $$$$
Perched atop the Berkeley hills in the East Bay, the Claremont is modern in its services and amenities, but the architecture and grounds are a throwback to the golden age of Gatsby or Garbo. Truly an oasis of luxury, and with a fabulous restaurant to boot. The spa facilities are top-notch.
SEE ALSO PAMPERING, P.97

Inn Above Tide
30 El Portal, Sausalito; tel: 415-332-9535, toll-free: 800-893-8433; $$$$
Boasting that it is the only Bay Area hotel actually on the water, the Inn Above Tide is just that, perched over the Bay in Sausalito. All views include the San Francisco skyline, and you can watch the sailboats as you soak in an oversized hot tub.

Wine Country

Ledson Hotel
480 First Street East, Sonoma; tel: 707-996-9779; www.leson hotel.com; $$$$
The Ledson hotel, while less than a decade old, has become the ultimate lodging on the Sonoma Square. With only six rooms, guests truly feel indulged, and no detail is missed. The romantic restaurant downstairs serves tasty food and also features live jazz.

MacArthur Place
29 East MacArthur Street, Sonoma; tel: 707-938-2929, toll free: 800-722-1866; www.macarthurplace.com; $$$$
MacArthur Place is a sprawling, art-filled, impeccably landscaped spa for a truly special occasion. Robe-clad guests stroll the gardens on their way to spa services such as Red Wine Grapeseed Baths and Chardonnay Sugar Scrubs. Bacchus would have approved.

Sonoma Hotel
10 West Spain Street, Sonoma; tel: 707-996-2996, toll-free: 800-468-6016; www.sonoma-hotel.com; $$
A comfortable inn decorated in French-country style, in a good location within easy reach of Sonoma's wineries, shops, and restaurants. A continental breakfast and evening wine tasting are included in the rate. Rooms are simple and attractive, and all include a private bathroom.

Below: whether you prefer your surroundings to be classic (left) or quirky (right), San Francisco has hotel options to suit.

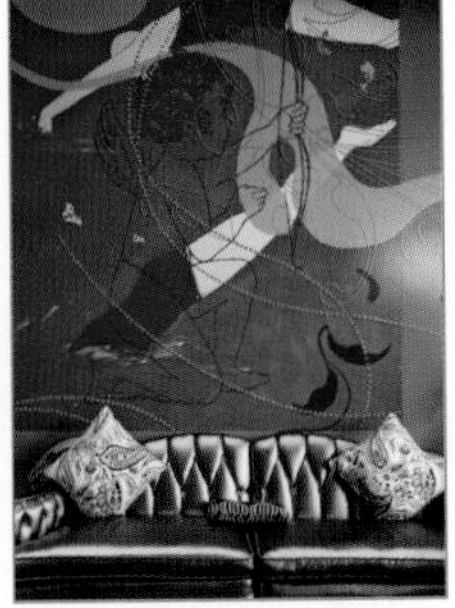

Literature

San Francisco has a remarkably rich and thriving literary tradition. From Mark Twain and Dashiell Hammett to Armistead Maupin and Amy Tan, writers of all sorts have scribbled in and about the City by the Bay, drawing inspiration from the spirited, swirling masses of colorful characters, diverse cultures, and unique cityscapes. Today, San Francisco still brims with established and would-be wordsmiths lured from all over the world, and hosts a bundle of bookstores, independent publishers, author readings, and writers' groups, often found linked to the lively café culture.

From Frogs to a Falcon

San Francisco's star-studded literary history kicked off in the Gold Rush years, with **Mark Twain** penning *The Celebrated Jumping Frog of Calaveras County*. In 1879, **Robert Louis Stevenson** lived on Bush Street, writing in Portsmouth Square. On the Oakland waterfront, 'Prince of the Oyster Pirates' **Jack London** *(The Call of the Wild)* bought his first sloop at the still-standing First and Last Chance Saloon on Jack London Square. Oakland remembers **Gertrude Stein** rather less fondly; she wrote of Oakland 'There is no there there'. Back across the Bay, **Dashiell Hammett** *(The Maltese Falcon)* spun hardboiled detectives based on his Pinkerton Detective days.

Beats and Beyond

In the mid-1950s North Beach became Beat-central, attracting **Jack Kerouac** (author of Beat manifesto *On the Road*), **Allen Ginsberg**, **Lawrence Ferlinghetti**, **Philipp Whalen** and **Michael McClure**, among others. In 1955, Ginsberg read his incendiary poem *Howl*, which resulted in an infamous obscenity trial for his publisher, Lawrence Ferlinghetti; Kerouac memorialized the epic night in *Dharma Bums*. The Merry Pranksters, led by **Ken Kesey** *(One Flew Over the Cuckoo's Nest)*, and LSD-tinged exploits followed, described in **Tom Wolfe's** *The Electric Kool-Aid Acid Test*.

Above: the Beats put the city's literary scene on the map.

Armistead Maupin's 1976 *Tales of the City* chronicled the lives of young San Franciscans (Macondray Lane will look familiar). Writers **Maxine Hong Kingston** *(The Woman Warrior)* and **Amy Tan** *(The Joy Luck Club)* wrote about the Chinese-American experience in San Francisco.

The Modern Lit Scene

San Francisco's literary scene is a busy affair. Readings, workshops, performances, and special events fill the calendar, and come October, the lively LitQuake festival (www.litquake.org) delivers several events in varied venues. Periodicals include *Zyzzyva* (www.zyzzyva.org), *Juxtapoz* (www.juxtapoz.com), **Francis Ford Coppola's** *Zoetrope: All Story* (www.zoetrope.com), *The Believer* (www.believermag.com) and *McSweeny's* (www.mcsweenys.net). The last two are produced by the independent publisher McSweeny's, founded by **Dave Eggers** *(A Heartbreaking Work of Staggering Genius)*, who also set up 826 Valencia, a youth literary center.

Further Reading: Books about San Francisco

art-SITES San Francisco: the Guide to Contemporary Art-Architecture-Design, by Sidra Sitch, art-SITES Press (2003)

Left: browsing in the iconic City Lights Bookstore.

> Spoiler alert! A sober plaque in Union Square's Burritt Alley honors Hammett's San Francisco-set *The Maltese Falcon*, but also gives away the thriller's end. Nearby, Dashiell Hammett Street is one of several honoring San Francisco literati. Another – Jack Kerouac Street – is near City Light Bookstore, the brains behind the plan.

Footsteps in the Fog: Alfred Hitchcock's San Francisco, by Jeff Kraft and Aaron Leventhal, Santa Monica Press (2002)
San Francisco Stories, edited by John Miller, Chronicle Books (1990)
Stairway Walks In San Francisco, by Adah Balalinsky, Lexicos, San Francisco (1984)
Walking San Francisco on the Barbary Coast Trail, by Daniel Bacon, Quick Silver Press (1997)

General Book Stores

Barnes & Noble

Fisherman's Wharf, 2550 Taylor Street; www.bn.com; tel: 292-6762; daily 9am–9pm; metro: F to Jefferson Street and Taylor Street; bus: 9, 10; cable car: Powell-Mason; map p.134 B4

Major national chain booksellers in Fisherman's Wharf.

Borders Books and Music

400 Post Street; tel: 399-1633; www.borders.com; Mon–Thur 8am–11pm, Fri–Sat 8am–midnight, Sun 9am–11pm; BART: to Powell; metro: F, J, K, L, M, N, T to Powell; bus: 5, 9, 21, 31; map p.135 C1

Union Square mega-chain.

City Lights Bookstore

261 Columbus Avenue; tel: 362-8193; www.citylights.com; daily 10am–midnight; bus: 12, 15, 30, 41, 45; map p.135 C2

Left-leaning Lawrence Ferlinghetti founded this 'Beatnikdom' cornerstone, which contains a first-rate poetry section and contains regular author readings.

Green Apple Books and Music

506 Clement Street; tel: 387-2272; www.greenapplebooks.com; Sun–Thur 10am–10.30pm, Fri 10am–11.30pm; bus: 1, 2, 4, 38; map p.136 B4

Well-loved and well-stocked Inner Richmond treasure trove, brimming with new and used titles.

Stacey's Bookstore

581 Market Street; tel: 800-926-6511; www.staceys.com; Mon–Fri 8.30am–7pm, Sat 11am–6.30pm; BART: to Montgomery; metro: F, J, K, L, M, N, T to Montgomery; bus: 2, 5, 6, 9, 31; map p.135 D1

Veteran of independent bookstores: both San Francisco's oldest and largest.

Specialist Book Stores

Willam Stout Architectural Books

804 Montgomery Street; tel: 391-6757; www.stoutbooks.com; Mon–Fri 10am–6.30pm, Sat 10am–5.30pm; bus: 9X, 10, 29, 30; map p.135 C2

This store ends many a quest for coffee-table titles.

Modern Times

888 Valencia Street; tel: 282-9246; www.mtbs.com; Mon–Sat 10am–9pm, Sun 11am–6pm; bus: 14, 26, 49; map p.138 B1

Politically-minded tomes.

Get Lost Travel Books

1825 Market Street; tel: 437-0529; www.getlostbooks.com; Mon–Fri 10am–7pm, Sat 10am–6pm, Sun 11am–5pm; metro: J, K, L, M, T to Church; bus: 26; map p.138 A2

Equips voyagers with travel guides and tie-ins.

Below: quirky murals adorn Green Apple Books's façade.

Movies

San Francisco is mad about movies and movies are mad about San Francisco. With its iconic views and backdrops, the city is no stranger to the silver screen; it cameos in everything from classics like Hitchcock's *Vertigo* to contemporary documentaries like *The Wild Parrots of Telegraph Hill.* A handful of local industry heavyweights also contribute to the general film frenzy. The calendar is crammed with first-rate film festivals, and the streets sparkle with neighborhood theater gems, among them rare single-screen movie theaters and utterly unique art-house theaters. In short, film-savvy San Franciscans are very well-served.

On the Silver Screen

San Francisco's unique looks and recognized landmarks have long held an allure for movie-makers. In the 1930s, Howard Hawks' *Barbary Coast* relived the city's wild Gold Rush days and W.S. Van Dyke's *San Francisco* spectacularly recreated the 1906 earthquake. In 1941, Humphrey Bogart skulked Nob Hill backways in *The Maltese Falcon*, and a decade later, Kim Novak hurtled herself into the Bay in *Vertigo*.

In following years, the city streets saw serious wear and tear, with Steve McQueen tearing across the hills in *Bullitt* in 1968 (*The Rock* followed suit nearly 30 years later), and Barbra Streisand deftly dodging cable cars in *What's Up Doc?* (1972). North Beach has seen the spotlight many times: Saints Peter and Paul Church hosted a *Dirty Harry* (1971) shoot-out, City Lights Bookstore starred in Beat-inspired *Heart Beat* (1980), and Tosca Café appeared in *Basic Instinct* (1992). More recently, San Francisco featured in the documentary *The Wild Parrots of Telegraph Hill* (2000) and Disney's *The Princess Diaries* (2001). Additionally, numerous films from all periods feature a myriad of landmark structures like the Golden Gate Bridge, Alcatraz, City Hall, and the Transamerica Pyramid.

Above: the legendary car chase scene in *Bullitt*.

Across the Bay in Emeryville, Pixar Animation Studios makes blockbuster animation, including *Toy Story* (1995), *Finding Nemo* (2003), *The Incredibles* (2004), and *Ratatouille* (2007).

The Oakland Bay Bridge's cameo in *The Graduate* (1967) gave sharp locals a good laugh. One scene shows Benjamin supposedly driving east along the bridge on his way to Berkeley, but he was mistakenly placed on the scenic upper deck, which only carries traffic west into San Francisco.

Local Names

A number of familiar film faces have set up shop in the Bay Area. After leaving Hollywood in 1969, Francis Ford Coppola built up businesses here including the American Zoetrope movie studio, and recently George Lucas, of *Star Wars* fame, moved Lucasfilm into the Presidio.

Festivals

These festivals charge admission. Check websites for screening times and locations.

Noir City
www.noircity.com; Jan
Rare, classic film noir; think dark alleys and darker motives.

Spike and Mike's Festival of Animation
tel: 858-459-8707; www.spike

Left: classic San Francisco noir in *The Maltese Falcon*.

andmike.com; Feb–Apr
Offbeat animated shorts.

San Francisco International Asian American Film Festival
tel: 863-0814; www.naatanet.org/festival; Mar
The country's largest showcase of new Asian and Asian-American films.

San Francisco International Film Festival
tel: 561-5000; www.sfiff.org; Apr–May
Renowned showcase of nearly 200 new features, documentaries, and shorts.

San Francisco International LGBT Film Festival
tel: 703-8650; www.frameline.org; June
The world's premier LGBT (Lesbian, Gay, Bisexual, Transgender) film festival.

San Francisco Silent Film Festival
tel: 777-4908; www.silentfilm.org; July
Classic and rare silents accompanied by live music.

San Francisco Jewish Film Festival
tel: 621-0556; www.sfjff.org; July–Aug
The first and largest of its kind.

Movie Theaters

AMC Theaters at the Metreon
101 4th Street; tel: 369-6201; www.westfield.com/metreon; BART: to Powell; metro: F, J, K, L, M, N, T to Powell; bus: 5, 9X, 14, 30, 45; map p.139 C4
Fifteen theaters covering recent releases and an IMAX screen.

Castro Theatre
429 Castro Street; tel: 621-6120; www.castrotheatre.com; metro: F, K, L, M, T to Castro; bus: 24, 33, 35, 37; map p.137 E1
One of the most beloved movie theaters in San Francisco, showing a repertory of the classic and avante-garde.

4 Star
2200 Clement Street; tel: 666-3488; www.hkinsf.com/4star; bus: 1, 2, 28, 29, 38
Catch alternative world movies plus first-run Hong Kong flicks.

Landmark Clay
2261 Fillmore Street; tel: 267-4893; www.landmarktheatres.com; bus: 1, 3, 12, 22; map p.133 E1
One of five Landmark theaters in the city, this single-screen, comfy, former nickelodeon now hosts independents and popular midnight movies.

Red Vic Movie House
1727 Haight Street; tel: 668-3994; www.redvicmoviehouse.com; metro: N to Carl Street and Cole Street; bus: 6, 7, 33, 37, 71; map p.137 C2
A Haight favorite supplying classics and unfamiliar fringe titles, and comfy couches.

Roxie
3117 16th Street; tel: 863-1087; www.roxy.com; BART: 16th Street; bus: 14, 22, 33, 49, 53; map p.138 A1
A popular Mission art-house theater with a risk-taking reputation and a documentary-heavy program.

Sundance Cinema Kabuki
1881 Post Street; tel: 929-4650; www.sundancecinemas.com/kabuki.html; bus: 1, 4, 22, 31, 38; map p.137 E4
Recently remodeled Japantown movie theater shows independents and blockbusters, as well as much of the San Francisco Film Festival.

Victoria Theatre
2961 16th Street; tel: 863-7576; www.victoriatheatre.org; movie days vary; BART: 16th Street; bus: 14, 22, 49, 43; map p.138 B1
The city's oldest operating theater is an ornate former vaudeville house dating from 1908.

Below: the Castro theatre.

Museums and Galleries

San Francisco is home to diverse art, history, and science museums. The majority are clustered downtown and in the SoMa district, but a number are also strewn about outlying neighborhoods. Prominent fine art collections are displayed at the San Francisco Museum of Modern Art and the M.H. de Young Memorial Museum among others, not to mention the world-class Asian Art Museum. Alongside these, a raft of museums celebrate San Francisco's history, as well as its ethnically diverse population.

Art Museums

Asian Art Museum

200 Larkin Street; tel: 581-3500; www.asianart.org; Tue–Wed 10am–5pm, Thur 10am–9pm, Fri–Sun 10am–5pm; entrance charge, under 13 free, 1st Tue of month free; BART: to Civic Center; metro: F, J, K, L, M, N, T to Civic Center; bus: 5, 19, 21, 47, 49; map p.138 B4

With 17,000 artworks spanning 6,000 years of history, this museum houses one of the world's most comprehensive collections of Asian art. After decades in Golden Gate Park, the museum moved in 2003 to new Civic Center quarters – formerly the city's main library building – which were redesigned by Gae Aulenti. Now, instead of books, the historic, beaux-arts building houses paintings, sculptures, ceramics, stoneware, basketry, puppets, weaponry, and textiles.

Special rotating exhibits are shown on the first floor, while the second and third floors showcase around 2,500 pieces from the permanent collection in regionally-grouped galleries covering China, Japan, Korea, India, Iran, the Himalayas, and Southeast Asia. Among the many treasures, look for a bronze Buddha on the third floor dated AD 388; it is the oldest dated Chinese Buddha known in the world. It is also one of some 7,700 objects donated by Avery Brundage, the Chicago industrialist whose endowment in the 1960s sparked the museum's creation.

Above: Chinese sculpture of a tomb guardian, at the Asian Art Museum.

Bi-monthly tea ceremony demonstrations (reservations recommended and extra charge required) are also held on-site. The museum store supplies an array of unique, Asian-themed merchandise, and Café Asia provides a casual spot for a quick bite.

Cartoon Art Museum

655 Mission Street; tel: 227-8666; www.cartoonart.org; Tue–Sun 11am–5pm; entrance charge, under 6 free, 1st Tue of month 'Pay What You Wish Day'; BART: to Montgomery; metro: F, J, K ,L, M, N, T to Montgomery; bus: 7, 9, 14, 30, 45; map p.135 D1

Original cartoons and animation art – of both underground and mainstream varieties – are showcased at this notable museum endowed by *Peanuts* creator Charles M. Schulz. Rotating exhibits draw from a 6,000-piece permanent collection that ranges from graphic novels and comic strips to political and advertising cartoons.

Contemporary Jewish Museum of San Francisco

Mission Street between 3rd and 4th Streets; tel: 344-8800; www.jmsf.org; check website for new hours and charges; BART: to Montgomery; metro: F, J, K, L, M, N, T to Montgomery; bus: 5, 6, 9,

Left: the striking exterior of the de Young Museum.

On the first Thursday of each month, the San Francisco tradition of 'First Thursdays' turns typically calm galleries into lively, wine-sipping social events. This is when many galleries schedule their openings and then keep their doors open late.

12, 21, 30, 45; map p.139 C4
Jewish art and culture are the focus of this museum slated to reopen in June 2008. The new facility, designed by Daniel Libeskind (architect of New York City's Freedom Tower), will incorporate the historic Jessie Street Power Substation.

M.H. de Young Memorial Museum
50 Hagiwara Tea Garden Drive; tel: 750-3600; www.deyoungmuseum.org; Tue–Thur 9.30am–5.15pm, Fri 9.30am–8.45pm, Sat–Sun 9.30am–5.15pm; entrance charge, under 13 free, 1st Tue of month free; metro: N to Irving Street and 9th Avenue; bus: 5, 21, 44; map p.136 B2
In 2005, the M.H. de Young Memorial Museum *(see floorplan, p.84)* reopened in Golden Gate Park in a bold facility that replaced the one severely damaged by the 1989 Loma Prieta earthquake. The controversial design features a copper-clad exterior that will green to patina over time and a 144-ft observation tower that stands out (literally and figuratively) in the natural park setting.

Several fine collections are displayed in the spacious, light-filled interior: American art from the 17th through the 20th centuries; art from Africa, the Americas, and the Pacific; and a range of textiles. The concourse level hosts 20th-century and contemporary art (including works by Georgia O'Keeffe, Edward Hopper, and Grant Wood), art from the Americas, Native American art, and a room of murals. Upstairs, rare works from Africa, Oceania, and New Guinea are shown, as well as early American artworks and separate textile and photography exhibits.

The museum also mounts special exhibitions on the first floor and has a sculpture garden, museum store, café, and panoramic views from its nine-story observation tower, which are particularly stunning on a clear day.

Below: modern art at the M.H. de Young Memorial Museum.

Museo Italo-Americano
204C Bay Street; tel: 673-2200; www.museoitaloamericano.org; Mon by appointment, Tue–Sun noon–4pm; free; metro: F to the Embarcadero and Stockton Street; bus: 10, 15; map p.134 C4
This small permanent collection features paintings, sculptures, photographs, and works on paper by prominent Italian and Italian-American artists.

Palace of the Legion of Honor
34th Avenue and Clement Street; tel: 750-3600; www.thinker.org; Tue–Sun 9.30am–5.15pm; entrance charge, under 13 free, 1st Tue of month free; bus: 1, 2, 18, 38
Built to commemorate the California soldiers who died during World War I, the Legion of Honor reproduces an 18th-century Parisian palace on a three-quarter scale. Within the beautiful beaux-arts building is a rich collection of ancient and European art that spans 4,000 years and includes more than 80 Rodin sculptures.

Upper level

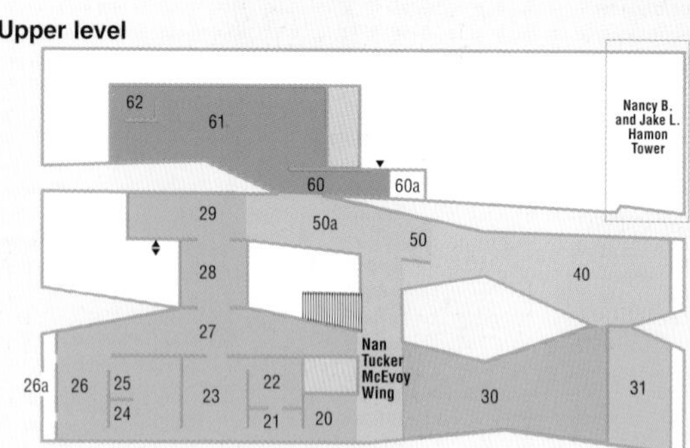

Concourse level

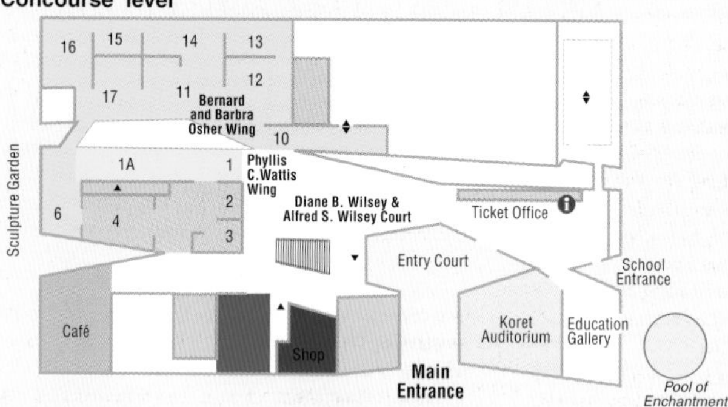

Exhibition level

Herbst Special Exhibition Galleries

Ticket Office

Shop

Media Room

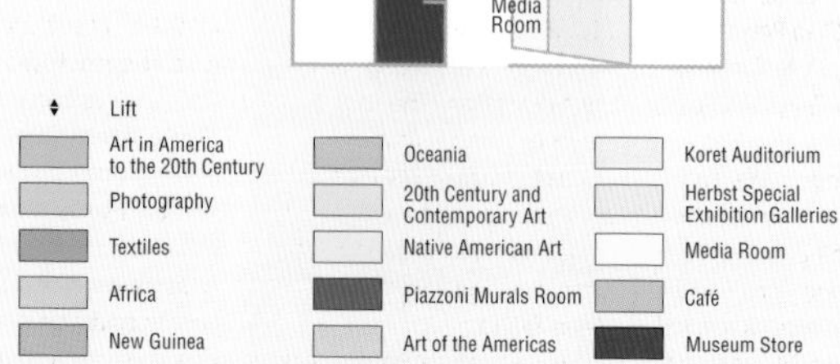

An original cast of Rodin's *hinker* poses in the outdoor ourt of Honor. Inside, the ‹y-lit terrace level displays n array of antiquities from ireece, Rome, Egypt, ssyria, and Mesopotamia, ıcluding pottery, sculpture, nd metalwork. The terrace evel also displays European orcelain and works on paper.

European art from the 4th–20th centuries is shown n the upper level, including aintings, sculpture, tapes-ries, and decorative arts. aintings include works from nany European masters, such s Fra Angelico, El Greco, Rembrandt, Rubens, Watteau, Gainsborough, Cézanne, Renoir, Degas, Matisse, Monet, and Picasso. One ighlight among the European lecorative arts is the collec-ion of French Baroque inlaid urniture. The three sculpture alleries include two devoted ntirely to Rodin; look for amous Rodin works like *The Three Shades*, *Eve*, *The Kiss*, and *The Prodigal Son*.

After a tour of the galleries, echarge at the Legion Café and enjoy the breathtaking views of the ocean, Golden Gate Bridge, and Marin Head-ands afforded by the museum's Lincoln Park perch.

San Francisco Craft and Folk Art Museum

51 Yerba Buena Lane; tel: 227-4888; www.mocfa.org; Tue–Fri 11am–6pm, Sat–Sun 11am–5pm; entrance charge, 18 and under free; BART: to Powell; metro: F, J, K, L, M, N, T to Powell; bus: 5, 9, 21, 30, 38; map p.139 C4

On an appealing pedestrian lane of stores and cafés, this museum exhibits traditional and contemporary craft and folk art from all over the world.

San Francisco Museum of Modern Art

151 Third Street; tel: 357-4000; www.sfmoma.org; Labor Day–Memorial Day: Mon–Tue 11am–5.45pm, Thur 11am–8.45pm, Fri–Sun 11am–5.45pm; Memorial Day–Labor Day: Mon–Tue 10am–5.45pm, Thur 10am–8.45pm, Fri–Sun 10am–5.45pm; entrance charge, under 13 free, Thur 6–9pm free, 1st Tue of month free; BART: to Powell; metro: F, J, K, L, M, N, T to Powell; bus: 9, 30, 31, 45, 71; map p.139 D4

The San Francisco Museum of Modern Art celebrated its 60th anniversary in 1995 by moving into a striking new SoMa location. The modernist building – marked by a truncated tower with black and white bands – was designed by internationally-renowned Swiss architect Mario Botta.

Inside, natural light pours into an airy atrium and four floors of galleries. In them, a permanent collection strong in American Abstract Expressionism, Fauvism, and German Expressionism is displayed. Paintings and sculptures include Henri Matisse's seminal *Femme au Chapeau* (Woman with the Hat), painted in 1905, as well as works by Jackson Pollock, Paul Klee, Piet Mondrian, Pablo Picasso, Andy Warhol, Marcel Duchamp, Diego Rivera, and Georgia O'Keeffe. The museum also has a fine photography collection, including works by Alfred Stieglitz, Edward Weston, Ansel Adams, Dorthea Lange, Robert Frank, and William Klein.

Cutting-edge design objects and contemporary art books are among the quality offerings at the museum store. Nearby,

Above: Rodin's *The Thinker* dominates the courtyard at the Palace of the Legion of Honor.

Caffe Museo's Mediterranean-style menu is a popular bet for lunch breaks.
SEE ALSO BARS AND CAFÉS, P.36

University of California, Berkeley Art Museum
2626 Bancroft Way; tel: 510-642-0808; www.bampfa.berkeley.edu; Wed 11am–5pm, Thur 11am–7pm, Fri–Sun 11am–5pm; entrance charge, under 13 free, 1st Thur of month free; BART: Downtown Berkeley; AC Transit bus: 7, 51

This collection of more than 13,000 artworks (the largest university art museum in the US) includes works by Mark Rothko, Jackson Pollock, and Albert Bierstadt. Across the street, the Pacific Film Archive offers daily screenings of movies pulled from a pool of 10,000 films that includes international classics, Soviet silents, rare animation, and the largest collection of Japanese films outside of Japan.

Yerba Buena Center for the Arts
3rd Street between Mission and Howard; tel: 978-2787; www.ybca.org; gallery hours: Tue–Wed noon–5pm, Thur noon–5pm, Fri–Sun: noon–5pm; entrance charge, 1st Tue of month free; BART: to Montgomery; metro: F, J, K, L, M, N, T to Montgomery; bus: 5, 7, 12, 14, 30; map p.139 D4

In a two-building complex, the YBCA exhibits contemporary art and community-based work, and presents contemporary dance, theater, and music performances.

Art Galleries

San Francisco has art galleries galore, showing and selling works from both emerging talent and internationally-known names. For a handy guide containing maps, addresses, and details of specific shows and special events, pop into a gallery and pick up a copy of the *Art Now Gallery Guide – West Coast*, or the *San Francisco Bay Area Gallery Guide*.

The classy crowd of established commercial dealers is densest near Union Square, but SoMa and the Mission also host a growing crop of galleries. A particularly popular address is 49 Geary Street: among others, the Stephen Wirtz, Jack Fisher, and photography-focused Robert Koch, Shapiro, and Fraenkel galleries share this high-rise. A small sampling of other notable galleries follows.

Catharine Clark Gallery
150 Minna Street; tel: 399-1439; www.cclarkgallery.com; Tue–Fri 10.30am–5.30pm, Sat 11am–5.30pm; free; BART: to Montgomery; metro: F, J, K, L , M, N to Montgomery; bus: 9, 14, 15, 30, 45; map p.135 D1

A dedicated video project room is one of the draws of this top-notch gallery, which features sculpture, painting, and mixed-media works from local, national, and international contemporary artists.

Crown Point Press
20 Hawthorne Street; tel: 974-6273; www.crownpoint.com; Tue–Sat 10am–6pm; free; BART: to Montgomery; metro: F, J, K, L, M, N, T to Montgomery; bus: 6, 9, 10, 30, 45; map p.139 D4

Born as a print workshop in 1962, the press displays a range of etchings, engravings, aquatints, photogravure, and intaglio prints in its public gallery.

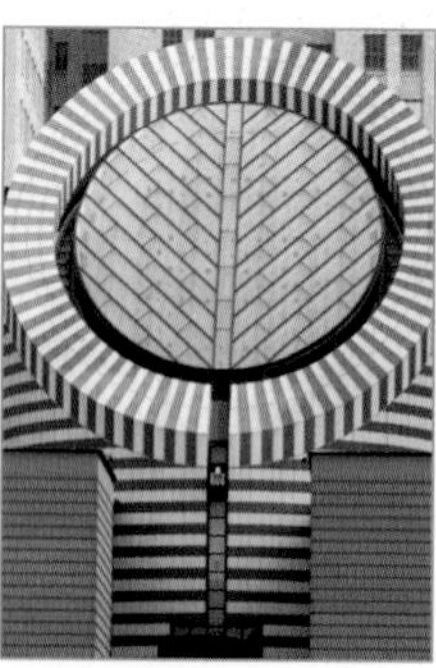

Left: the San Francisco Museum of Modern Art has a eye-catching interior, exterior, and collection, including Jasper Johns' *Flag*.

ackett-Freedman ìallery
50 Sutter Street, Suite 400; tel: 62-7152; www.hackett eedman.com; Tue–Fri 0.30am–5.30pm, Sat 11am–pm; free; BART: to Powell; etro: F, J, K, L, M, N, T to Pow-l; bus: 5, 15, 30, 38, 45; map 135 C1
his reputable gallery spe-ializes in works by 20th-entury modern masters nd postwar American and alifornian art. It is not nely for arty company, with ne Dolby Chadwick and aldwell Snyder galleries ıst down the road.

ian Francisco Museum of Modern Art Gallery
ort Mason Building A; tel: 441-777; www.sfmoma.org; Tue–at 11.30am–5.30pm; free; bus: 0, 19, 30, 47, 49; map p.134 A4
his lofty, light-filled space hows sculpture, paintings, hotography, and mixed-nedia work from Northern alifornian artists. In addi-ion, it offers an innovative art ental program.

The Shooting Gallery
39 Larkin Street; tel: 931-8035; www.shootinggallerysf.com; ue–Sat noon–7pm; free; bus: 9, 38; map p.134 B1
his un-intimidating gallery in he Tenderloin district pecializes in exhibits of Low-Brow' artwork.

ialería de la Raza
857 24th Street; tel: 826-8009; www.galeriadelaraza.org; Ved–Sat noon–6pm; free; BART: 4th Street; bus: 14, 48, 49
his Mission gallery, founded n 1970, celebrates Chicano nd Latino art and culture, nd is a mixed space for art nd activism.

Kanadu Gallery
40 Maiden Lane; tel: 392-9999; www.folkartintl.com; call for ours; free; BART: to Powell; netro: F, J, K, L, M, N, T to Powell; us: 5, 6, 7, 21,38; map p.135 C1

> The Mission neighborhood is literally a colorful one: its streets (Balmy Alley for example) are decorated with over 200 murals. Guided tours of these artworks are given by the knowledgeable **Precita Eyes Mural Arts and Visitor Center** (tel: 285-2287; www.precitaeyes.org), founded in 1977. *(See also Walks and Views, p.124.)*

Just off Union Square, San Francisco's only building designed by Frank Lloyd Wright (echoing his Guggenheim Museum in New York) houses a gallery of artwork, textiles, jewelry, and artifacts from around the world.

History Museums

Cable Car Museum
1201 Mason Street; tel: 474-1887; www.cablecarmuseum.org; Apr–Sept: Mon–Sun 10am–6pm, Oct–Mar: Mon–Sun 10am–5pm; free; bus: 1, 12; cable car: Powell-Hyde, Powell-Mason; map p.134 C2
This historic cable car barn and powerhouse displays antique cable cars, engines, winding wheels, and other mechanical devices that help the beloved moving monuments run smoothly.

California Historical Society Museum
678 Mission Street; tel: 357-1848; www.californiahistorical society.org; Wed–Sat noon–4.30pm; entrance charge, under 5 free; BART: to Montgomery; metro: F, J, K, L M, N, T to Montgomery; bus: 7, 9X, 14, 30, 45; map p.135 D1
Early Californian history is chronicled by 5,000 oil paintings, drawings, costumes, lithographs, and decorative arts. A fine collection of 500,000 photographs includes works by Eadweard Muybridge and

Above: one of the vibrantly colored murals in the Mission.

Ansel Adams.

Chinese Historical Society of America Museum
965 Clay Street; tel: 391-1188; www.chsa.org; Tue–Fri noon–5pm, Sat 11am–4pm; entrance charge, under 6 free, 1st Thur of month free; bus: 1, 30; cable car: Powell-Hyde, Powell-Mason; map p.134 C2
Small displays in the historic Julia Morgan Chinatown YWCA explore Chinese history and culture in the US, including how Chinese contributions fueled the development of American West industries.

Hyde Street Pier Historic Ships Collection
Hyde Street on Jefferson Street; tel: 447-5000; www.maritime.org; Memorial Day–Sept: Mon–Sun 9.30am–5.30pm, Oct–Memorial Day: Mon–Sun 9.30am–5pm; entrance charge, under 16 free; bus: 19, 32; cable car: Powell-Hyde; map p.134 B4
Moored here are six vintage vessels built in the late 19th and early 20th centuries. Tour below decks of the *Eureka* steam ferryboat, see how to set the topsail and staysail on-board the *Balclutha* square-rigger, or raise your voice to the tune of sailor

songs at the monthly chantey sing (tel: 561-7171; 1st Saturday of month; reservations required). The other historic ships on-site are two schooners, a steam tug, and a paddle-wheel tug.

Museum of the African Diaspora
685 Mission Street; tel: 358-7200; www.moadsf.org; Wed–Sat 11am–6pm, Sun noon–5pm; entrance charge, under 13 free; BART: to Montgomery; metro: F, J, K, L, M, N, T to Montgomery; bus: 5, 14, 15, 30, 45; map p.135 D1
Artwork and artifacts focus on the global, uniting influence of the art, culture, and history of Africa. Permanent displays on rituals and ceremony, slavery passages, music, theater, adornment, and culinary traditions are supplemented with varied rotating exhibits.

North Beach Museum
1435 Stockton Street; tel: 391-6210 (ask for museum); Mon–Thur 9am–4pm, Fri 9am–6pm; free; bus: 15, 41; map p.134 C3
Artifacts and vintage photographs celebrate the history and culture of the vibrant North Beach neighborhood in this small museum tucked away in a bank building.

Oakland Museum of California
1000 Oak Street, Oakland; tel: 510-238-2200; www.museumca.org; Wed–Sat 10am–5pm; Sun noon–5pm; entrance charge, under 6 free, 2nd Sun of month free; BART: Lake Merritt
Three-tiers of spacious galleries and gardens provide an inviting backdrop for engrossing exhibits on the art, history, and environment of California.

Pacific Heritage Museum
608 Commercial Street; tel: 399-1124; www.ibankunited.com/phm; Tue–Sat 10am–4pm; free; BART: to Montgomery; metro: F, J, K, L, M, N, T to Montgomery; bus: 1, 10, 15, 41; map p.135 D2
This small museum housed in the historic US Subtreasury Building (on the site of the original US Branch Mint) focuses on Pacific Rim cultural, artistic, and economic achievements.

San Francisco National Maritime Museum
900 Beach Street; tel: 561-7100; www.maritime.org; Mon–Sun 10am–5pm; free; bus: 19, 31; cable car: Powell-Hyde; map p.134 A4
This ship-shaped museum celebrates San Francisco's colorful maritime heritage and houses interactive exhibits, intricate models, muralist Hilaire Hiler's expressionist vision of Atlantis, oral history re-creations, and scores of seafaring memorabilia. Until it reopens in 2009, visit the Maritime Park's Visitor Center (499 Jefferson Street, at Hyde Street) for helpful information.

Society of California Pioneers Museum
300 4th Street; tel: 957-1849; www.californiapioneers.org; Wed–Fri and 1st Sat of month 10am–4pm; entrance charge; BART: to Powell; metro: F, J, K, L, M, N, T to Powell; bus: 9X, 30, 45, 76; map p.139 D4
A sizeable collection of paintings, photographs, works on paper, silverware, and mining artifacts vividly chronicles California's history from the Gold Rush era to the 1940s.

Wells Fargo Museum
420 Montgomery Street; tel: 396-2619; www.wellsfargohistory.com; Mon–Fri 9am–5pm; free; BART: to Montgomery; metro: F, J, K, L, M, N, T to Montgomery; bus: 6, 9, 10, 15, 30X; cable car: California; map p.135 D2
An authentic, yellow-wheeled Concord Coach from the 1860s stands in this downtown lobby museum, on the site where Wells Fargo opened in 1852. Gold dust is displayed, and exhibits tell of dangerous stagecoach robbers and the 1906 earthquake.

Science Museums

California Academy of Sciences
875 Howard Street; tel: 321-8000; www.calacademy.org; Mon–Sun 10am–5pm; entrance charge, 3 and under free, first Wed of month free; BART: to Powell; metro: F, J, K, L, M, N, T to

Below: San Francisco's varied ethnic heritage is celebrated in art at the Museum of the African Diaspora (left) and at the Pacific Heritage Museum (right).

Left: sculpture at the Oakland Museum of California.

Powell; bus: 9, 12, 14, 27, 30; map p.139 C4
This interactive natural history museum houses a collection of 18 million scientific specimens, including plants, animals, fossils, and artifacts. The Steinhart Aquarium contains a bright array of exotic fish and other swimming and slithering species. Also on site are a live coral reef and a large collection from the Galapagos Islands. In 2008, the Academy will move from its temporary Howard Street home back to Golden Gate Park.

Chabot Space and Science Center
10000 Skyline Boulevard, Oakland; tel: 510-336-7300; www.chabotspace.org; Sept 15–July 4: Wed–Thur 10am–5pm, Fri–Sat 10am–10pm, Sun 11am–5pm; July 10–Sept 2: Tue–Thur 10am–5pm, Fri–Sat 10am–10pm, Sun 11am–5pm; entrance charge, under 3 free
High in the Oakland hills both children and adults can have fun learning about the planet and universe at this center, which features interactive exhibits, an observatory, a planetarium, special star-gazing events, and beautiful views of the Bay Area. Please note that the center is pretty much only accessible by car.

Exploratorium
3601 Lyon Street; tel: 561-0360; www.exploratorium.edu; Tue–Sun 10am–5pm; entrance charge, under 4 free, 1st Wed of month free; bus: 28, 30, 76; map p.133 D3
Hundreds of fascinating, hands-on exhibits are found at this museum of science, art, and human perception conceived by Frank Oppenheimer. The varied topics explored include physics, computers, biology, visual perception, listening, language, and memory. In the bizarre Tactile Dome exhibit (extra charge; reservation recommended) visitors must crawl, climb, squeeze, and grope through a pitch-black maze of materials, honing in dramatically on their sense of touch.
SEE ALSO CHILDREN, P.42

Randall Museum
199 Museum Way; tel: 554-9600; www.randallmuseum.org; Tue–Sat 10am–5pm; donation suggested; metro: F, K, L, M, T to Castro; bus: 24; map p.137 E1
This hands-on, kid-friendly arts and science museum hosts a live animal exhibit as well as a woodshop, greenhouse, gardens, lapidary workshop, and arts and ceramic studios.
SEE ALSO CHILDREN, P.42

Other Museums

Ripley's Believe It or Not! Museum
175 Jefferson Street; tel: 771-6188; www.ripleysf.com; June–Sept: Sun–Thur 9am–11pm, Fri–Sat 9am–midnight; Sept–May: Sun–Thur 10am–10pm, Fri–Sat 10am–midnight; entrance charge; metro: F to Fisherman's Wharf; bus: 10, 47; map p.134 B4
Bizarre attractions include a cable car model made of 270,836 matchsticks.

> To get in tune with the environment, head to the Exploratorium's Wave Organ – a wave-activated acoustic sculpture created by Peter Richards and George Gonzales in 1986. On a concrete and marble jetty, 25 organ pipes emit subtle tones (best heard at high-tide) as seawater swells in and out of them.

Music and Dance

San Francisco is vividly alive with music and dance, delivering rhythms sure to get shoes tapping and dance performance that showcase the fancy footwork of others. Operatic arias and symphonic melodies fill concert halls, chamber quintets perform in peaceful churches, jazz bands sizzle in intimate clubs, and hot rock, pop, and alternative bands jam on small stages and in spacious arenas alike, while in the San Francisco 1960s tradition, parks often become concert venues in the summer. Dance is not short on attention either, with varied traditional and experimental performances gracing the city's stages.

Classical

MAIN VENUES

Louise M. Davies Symphony Hall
201 Van Ness Avenue; tel: 864-6000; www.sfsymphony.org; BART: Civic Center; metro: F, J, K, L, M, N, T to Van Ness; bus: 5, 21, 47, 49; map p.138 B3
This elegant hall houses the acclaimed San Francisco Symphony Orchestra. Its main season runs from September to July.

War Memorial Opera House
301 Van Ness Avenue; tel: 864-3330; www.sfopera.com; BART: Civic Center; metro: F, J, K, L, M, N, T to Van Ness; bus: 5, 21, 47, 49; map p.138 B3
The glamorous beaux arts War Memorial Opera House is regularly filled with those keen to hear the San Francisco opera company perform. The fall season generally lasts September to November, and the summer season May to July.

Aria-admirers turn out in droves to Golden Gate Park each fall for a relaxed, cultured afternoon of Free Opera in the Park

OTHER COMPANIES AND VENUES

Chanticleer
tel: 252-8589; www.chanticleer.org

Donald Pippen's Pocket Opera
tel: 928-8930; www.pocketopera.org

Kronos Quartet
tel: 731-3533; www.kronosquartet.org

Philharmonic Baroque Orchestra
tel: 252-1288; www.philharmonia.org

Below: performing at the War Memorial Opera House.

San Francisco Contemporary Music Players
tel: 978-2787, www.sfcmp.org

San Francisco Performances
tel: 398-6449; www.performances.org
Common venues for hearing these excellent musical offerings include the Yerba Buena Center for the Arts *(see Museums and Galleries, p.86)*, the Florence Gould Theater in the California Palace of the Legion of Honor *(see Museums and Galleries, p.83)*, in addition to:

Herbst Theater
War Memorial Veterans Building, 401 Van Ness Avenue; tel: 392-4400; http://sfwmpac.org; BART: to Civic Center; metro: F, J, K, L, M, N, T to Van Ness; bus: 5, 21, 47, 49; map p.138 B3

CHAMBER MUSIC

For chamber music, two common venues are:

Old First Presbyterian Church
1751 Sacramento Street; tel: 474-1608; www.oldfirstconcerts.org; bus: 1, 19, 47, 49; cable car: California; map p.134 B1

Left: live jazz is popular in San Francisco.

20, 30, 41, 45; map p.135 C2
A jazzy gem with an intimate, 1930s speakeasy vibe supplies Big Bands early in the week and national and international acts heading into the weekend.

Saloon
1232 Grant Street; tel: 989-7666; www.sfblues.net/Saloon.html; Mon–Sun 9.30pm; bus: 12, 20, 30, 41, 45; map p.135 C3
North Beach dive (the oldest bar in San Francisco) dishes out blues nightly.

Yoshi's
1330 Fillmore Street; tel: 655-5600; www.yoshis.com/sf; Mon–Sun 8pm and 10pm; bus: 22, 31; map p.137 E4
A newly-opened outpost of the world-renowned Jack London Square jazz club (510 Embarcadero West, Oakland; tel: 510-238-9200), supplies big names and Japanese cuisine.
SEE ALSO RESTAURANTS, P.111

St John's Presbyterian Church
2727 College Avenue, Berkeley; tel: 753-2792; www.chambermusicsundaes.org; Sun 3pm; BART: Rockridge; bus: AC Transit 51

Jazz

FESTIVALS

San Francisco buzzes with jazz events in summer and fall:

Fillmore Street Jazz Festival
www.fillmorejazzfestival.com; July; free

North Beach Jazz Festival
http://nbjazzfest.com; July; entrance charge varies

San Francisco Jazz Festival
www.sfjazz.org; Oct–Nov; entrance charge

SF Jazz Summerfest
www.sfjazz.org; June–Oct; free

VENUES

(see also 'Contemporary', right)

Biscuits and Blues
401 Mason Street; tel: 292-2583; www.biscuitsandblues.com; Tue–Thur 8pm, Fri–Sat 8pm and 10pm, Sun 8pm, some additional 10pm shows; BART: to Powell; metro: F, J, K, L, M, N, T to Powell; bus: 38; cable car: Powell-Hyde, Powell-Mason; map p.134 C1
A Bay Area standard, this casual supper-club west of Union Square teams a Southern-style menu with soulful blues and blues-based rock.

Boom Boom Room
1601 Fillmore Street; tel: 673-8000; www.boomboomblues.com; Tue–Sat 8pm; bus: 22, 38; map p.137 E4
Live blues – plus boogie, groove, and soul – keep this fun Fillmore joint hopping.

Jazz at Pearl's
256 Columbus Avenue; tel: 291-8255; www.jazzatpearls.com; Mon–Sun 8pm and 10pm; bus:

Contemporary

San Francisco has a star-studded musical legacy and current culture. **The Grateful Dead**, **Jefferson Airplane** and **Janis Joplin** staged concerts in Golden Gate Park, and at the Fillmore and Avalon ballrooms (where concerts

Below: all sorts make up the thriving music scene.

Left: the city is well stocked with record stores.

and light shows set world standards). **Carlos Santana** grew up in the Mission, **Credence Clearwater Revival** came from the East Bay's El Cerrito, and **Green Day** and **Counting Crows** hail from Berkeley. Now, the Bay Area's eclectic music scene includes everything from hip hop to indie to electronica.

FESTIVALS

Hardly Strictly Bluegrass Festival
www.strictlybluegrass.com; Oct; free

Mission Creek Music and Arts Festival
www.mcmf.org; June; entrance charge

Noise Pop
www.noisepop.com; Feb; entrance charge

San Francisco Bluegrass and Old-Time Festival
www.sfbluegrass.org; Feb; entrance charge

San Francisco Blues Festival
www.sfblues.com; Sept; entrance charge

Stern Grove Festival
www.sterngrove.org; June–Aug; free

> The intimate, legendary Fillmore Auditorium – where Bill Graham famously launched his empire in the 1960s – remains one of the city's best music venues. The venue's history lives on in photos, posters, and in one of Graham's classic, homey touches: a bowl of free apples for concert-goers to enjoy.

VENUES

Bimbo's 365 Club
1025 Columbus Avenue; tel: 474-0365; www.bimbos365club.com; days and show times vary; bus: 30; cable car: Powell-Mason; map p.134 B3
Swank 1930s throwback nightclub with art deco detailing, showcasing acts ranging from rock to jazz.

Bottom of the Hill
1233 17th Street; tel: 621-4455; www.bottomofthehill.com; Mon–Sun 8.30pm show; bus: 19, 22; map p.139 D1
Great hard rockin' dive for punk, alternative, rockabilly, and more.

Elbo Room
647 Valencia Street; tel: 552-7788; www.elboroom.com; Sun–Thur 9pm, Fri–Sat 10pm; BART: 16th Street; bus: 14, 22, 26, 33, 49; map p.138 B1
Mission hipster destination, both for the chill bar downstairs and the happening music scene upstairs: live and DJ-delivered jazz, hip-hop, funk, soul, indie-rock, and more.

Fillmore Auditorium
1805 Geary Boulevard; tel: 346-6000; www.thefillmore.com; Mon–Sun show times vary; bus: 2, 3, 22, 38; map p.137 E4
Major headlining acts in a historic 1960s venue.

Great American Music Hall
859 O'Farrell Street; tel: 885-0750; www.musichallsf.com; show times vary; bus: 2, 3, 27, 38; map p.138 B4
A former Barbary Coast bordello now lures international performers, playing rock, blues, folk, and more.

Hemlock Tavern
1131 Polk Street; tel: 923-0925; www.hemlocktavern.com; show times vary; bus: 2, 19, 38, 47, 49; map p.134 B1
Hipsters chill in the bar up front and open-air smoking room, and underground rock bands light up the intimate back.

Independent
628 Divisadero Street; tel: 771-1421; www.theindependentsf.com; show times vary; bus: 21, 24; map p.137 E3
Supplier of popular live rock, punk, folk, hip-hop, and more.

Masonic Center
1111 California Street; tel: 776-

702; show times vary; bus: 1; cable car: California, Powell-Hyde, Powell-Mason; map p.134 C1
Comfortable, sit-down auditorium with excellent acoustics hosts varied performances ranging from Van Morrison to jazz concerts to comedians.

Slim's
333 11th Street; tel: 255-0333; www.slif-sf.com; show times vary; bus: 12, 19, 47; map p.138 B2
Jam-packed SoMa spot for live national touring acts, with a motley mix of rootsy music: blues, R&B, and alternative.

Thee Parkside
1600 17th Street; tel: 503-0393; www.theeparkside.com; show times vary; bus: 22; map p.139 D1
Potrero neighborhood rock 'n' roll joint, with special It's a Free Country Sunday concerts of rockabilly, country, and bluegrass (Sunday 4pm; free).

MUSIC STORES
Gold mines for vinyl-lovers:

Groove Merchant
687 Haight Street; tel: 252-5766; Tue–Sat noon–7pm, Sun noon–6pm; bus: 6, 22, 71; map p.137 E2
For the hippest of the hip.

Rooky Ricardo's
448 Haight Street; tel: 864-7526; Mon–Sun noon–6pm; bus: 6, 7, 22; map p.138 A2
Boasts LPs and 45s from all genres and generations.

Jack's Record Cellar
254 Scott Street; tel: 431-3047; call for hours; bus: 6, 7, 22, 71; map p.137 E2
The oldest record shop in the city, this historic place is a great stop-off for dusty 78s.

Ritmo Latino
2401 Mission Street; tel: 824-8556; www.ritmolatino.com; call for hours; BART: 24th Street; bus: 14, 26, 33, 49; map p.138 B1
For mariachi, *conjunto*, Latin jazz, and more.

Amoeba Music
1855 Haight Street; tel: 831-1200; www.amoebamusic.com; Mon–Sat 10.30am–10pm; Sun 11am–9pm; bus: 7, 33, 43, 71; map p.137 C2
An independent institution in a converted-bowling alley.

Aquarius Records
1055 Valencia Street; tel: 647-2272; www.aquariusrecords.com; Mon–Wed 10am–9pm, Thur–Sun 10am–10pm; BART: 24th Street station; bus: 14, 26, 33, 49
Boutique-like independent.

Rasputin Music
69 Powell Street; tel: 800-350-8700; www.rasputinmusic.com; Mon–Thur 10.30am–8pm, Fri–Sat 10.30am–9pm, Sun noon–7pm; BART: to Powell; metro: F, J, K, L, M, N, T to Powell; bus: 27, 31; map p.138 C4
A good choice for browsing the latest releases.

Dance

FESTIVALS

Ethnic Dance Festival
Tel: 474-3914; www.worldartswest.org/edf; June; entrance charge
Brings together soloists and companies, professionals and students, varied classical, sacred, social, and folk dance styles from all over the world.

COMPANIES

Alonzo King's Lines Ballet
Yerba Buena Center for the Arts, 700 Howard Street; tel: 863-3040 (info), 978-2787 (box office); www.linesballet.org; BART: to Montgomery; metro: F, J, K, L, M, N, T to Montgomery; bus: 7, 9X, 14, 30, 45; map p.139 D4
This top-notch contemporary ballet company performs at the Yerba Buena Center for the Arts, and tours all over the world.

ODC Dance
3153 17th Street; tel: 863-6606; www.odcdance.org; show times vary; BART: 16th Street; map p.138 B1
This modern dance company, known nationally for its entrepreneurial savvy and artistic innovation, performs a variety of contemporary dance recitals, and puts on a well-loved annual production of The Velveteen Rabbit.

San Francisco Ballet
War Memorial Opera House, 301 Van Ness Avenue; tel: 865-2000; www.sfballet.org; BART: Civic Center; metro: F, J, K, L, M, N, T to Van Ness; bus: 5, 21, 47, 49; map p.138 B3
The San Francisco Ballet takes the stage at the Opera House for its main season during February through April, presenting traditional full-length ballets and contemporary pieces. The annual *Nutcracker* production in December is very popular.

For an entertainingly alternative take on the classic *Nutcracker* ballet each winter, San Franciscans of all ages don their best sugar plum fairy tutus and pirouette over to the celebrated, offbeat, and fantastically-fun **Dance-Along Nutcracker**, presented by the San Francisco Lesbian/Gay Freedom Band (tel: 255-1355; www.sflgfb.org).

Below: dancers from the San Francisco Ballet Company.

Nightlife

San Francisco has nightlife options across the board, with international and local DJ's spinning for varied tastes, and live bands and comedy clubs spicing up the mix. Bear in mind, most dance clubs are 21 and over (ID required at the door) and entrance charges may be cash only. Slick venues have dress codes, but generally the diverse crowds are fittingly diversely-dressed. Many nightspots are hybrid affairs, decidedly blurring the lines between bars, lounges, and clubs, so for more suggestions see also 'Bars and Cafés', 'Gay and Lesbian', and 'Music and Dance'.

Nightclubs

1015 Folsom
1015 Folsom Street; tel: 431-7444; www.1015.com; Fri 10pm–4am, Sat 10pm–7am, additional hours vary; bus: 12, 27; map p.139 C3
A mega-club delivering solid house and trance from top-notch DJ's to a young crowd.

111 Minna
111 Minna Street; tel: 974-1719; www.111minna gallery.com; Tue–Fri noon–9pm, Fri–Sat 9pm–2am; BART: to Montgomery; metro: F, J, K, L, M, N, T to Montgomery; bus: 5, 14, 15, 45, 76; map p.135 D1
During the day, this space is an art gallery, but when the sun goes down, it slips on a nightclub vibe to host happy hours and an eclectic mix of artists, movie screenings, DJ's, and live performances.

222 Club
222 Hyde Street; tel: 440-0222; www.222club.net; hours vary; bus: 16AX, 16BX, 19, 31; map p.138 B4
Hipsters brave gritty Tenderloin streets for packed basement dancing at this DJ bar with a back-alley feel.

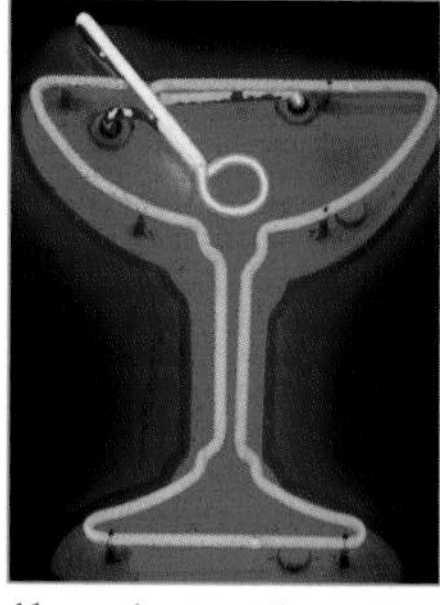

Above: always a welcome sign.

Dolce
440 Broadway Street; tel: 989-3434; www.dolcesf.com; Fri–Sat 9pm–2am; bus: 9AX, 9BX, 10, 12, 41; map p.135 C2
A North Beach nightclub with a young, sexy crowd dancing to mash-ups of Top 40, hip-hop, and 80s hits.

DNA Lounge
375 11th Street; tel: 626-1409; www.dnalounge.com; hours vary; bus: 9, 12, 27, 47; map p.138 B2
Solid sound and lighting systems for a Goth and generally alternative crowd that comes to dance. There are also special DJ nights and live acts performing regularly.

The End Up
401 6th Street; tel: 646-0999; www.theendup.com; Thur 10pm–4am, Fri 11pm–Sat 1pm, Sat 10pm–Mon 4am; bus: 9X, 12, 19, 27, 47; map p.139 C3
A diverse, hard-partying crowd carouses til dawn and beyond.

Harry Denton's Starlight Room
450 Powell Street; tel: 395-8595; www.harrydenton.com; daily 6pm–2am; BART: to Powell; metro: F, J, K, L, M, N, T to Powell; bus: 2, 9, 30, 38, 45; map p.134 C1
Live jazz, Big Band, and Motown hits performed high above Union Square.

Mezzanine
444 Jessie Street; tel: 625-8880; www.mezzaninesf.com; hours vary; BART: to Powell; metro: F, J, K, L, M, N, T to Powell; bus: 6, 7, 14, 21, 26; map p.139 C4
Mixed masses dance to live and electronic sounds from both international and hot new talents.

Mighty
119 Utah Street; tel: 762-0151, info line: 626-7001; hours vary; bus: 9, 9X, 9BX, 22, 53; map p.139 C2

For the latest bulletin on which buzz bands are playing and which DJ's are spinning, check out online guides like SFStation (www.sfstation.com), Flavorpill (http://sf.flavorpill.net), Metro Wize (www.metrowize.com), and Nitevibe (www.nitevibe.com).

\n unpretentious crowd hikes ›ut to this warehouse-type ›enue for good beats and ›reaks.

Ruby Skye

·20 Mason Street; tel: 693-0777; www.rubyskye.com; Thur–Sat ›pm–4am; BART: to Powell; metro: F, J, K, L, M, N, T to Powell; bus: 2, 3, 7, 21, 38; map ›.134 C1

Big DJ names draw big dancing crowds to this massive Union Square club.

Slide

·30 Mason Street; tel: 421-·916; www.slidesf.com; hours vary; BART: to Powell; metro: F, J, K, L, M, N, T to Powell; bus: 2, 3, 9, 21, 76; map p.134 C1

Get dolled up to get in, then slide (watch those elbows and stilettos) into a slick downstairs nightclub.

Comedy Clubs

Cobb's Comedy Club

915 Columbus Avenue; tel: 928-4320; www.cobbscomedy club.com; Thur–Sun show 8pm, Fri–Sat show 10.15pm too; bus: 30; map p.134 B3

Big name bookings include familiar faces from television.

The Punchline

444 Battery Street; tel: 397-7573; www.punchlinecomedyclub.com; daily show 8pm, Fri–Sat show 10pm too; BART: to Embarcadero; metro: F, J, K, L, M, N, T to Embarcadero; bus: 1, 5, 10, 30, 41; map p.135 D2

National and local talents crack up crowds every night of the week. Alumni include Robin Williams, Ellen DeGeneres and Chris Rock, so you never know when you might catch the next big thing.

Purple Onion

140 Columbus Avenue; tel: 956-1653; www.purpleonion comedy.com; hours vary; bus: 9AX, 9BX, 12, 20, 41; map p.135 C2

An intimate, well-loved North Beach venue and a real neighborhood spot that books both comedy and music acts.

Left: tearing up the dancefloor.

Late-night Food

In addition to the post-club craving solutions below, Mexican taquerias in the Mission and Mel's Drive-In diners (www.melsdrive-in.com) are other good bets.

Bob's Donut and Pastry Shop

1621 Polk Street; tel: 776-3141; www.bobsdonuts.com; Daily 24 hours; $; bus: 1, 19, 38, 47, 49; map p.134 B1

Old-fashioned satisfaction from mouthwatering glazeds and apple fritters.

Osha Thai Noodle

696 Geary Street; tel: 673-2368; www.oshathai.com; Sun–Thur 11am–1am, Fri–Sat 11am–3am; $; bus: 2, 4, 27, 38; map p.134 B1

Pack in and debrief the night's adventures over Pad Thai.

Tommy's Joynt

1101 Geary Boulevard; tel: 775-4216; www.tommysjoynt.com; Daily 11am–1.45am; $; bus: 2, 3, 38, 47, 76; map p.138 A4

Hearty comfort food in a friendly, 'Hofbrau' style setting.

Transport Home

The Muni Owl Service runs from 1–5am on the Metro L and N lines and the 5, 14, 22, 24, 38, 90, 91, and 108 bus lines (www.sfmta.com). BART runs until around midnight. For more details, see http://transit.511.org/providers/night.

SEE ALSO TRANSPORTATION, P.121–2

Below: enjoying a cocktail.

Pampering

San Francisco has a plethora of plush pampering solutions to satisfy beauty product junkies, spa-addicts, and anyone merely craving a mean massage. A bevy of stores, from major international retailers to unique boutiques and pharmacies, supply the latest lotions and potions for skin, hair, and body, as well as high-end cosmetics and fragrances. Union Square, in particular, is happy hunting ground. Meanwhile, tranquil spas whisk stressed-out city-dwellers away from the noisy, hustling crowds and deliver deluxe facials, massages, and special signature treatments to sooth and rejuvenate body, mind, and spirit.

Stores

SEE ALSO GAY AND LESBIAN, P.60

Church Street Apothecary
1767 Church Street; tel: 970-9828; www.churchapothecary.com; Mon–Sat 11am–7pm, Sun 11am–5pm; metro: J to Church Street and Day Street; bus: 24, 26
Quaint Noe Valley's source for high-end holistic, organic beauty products, homeopathic remedies, and housewares for the whole family.

Diptyque
171 Maiden Lane; tel: 402-0600; www.diptyqueusa.com; Mon–Sat 10am–6pm, Sun noon–5pm; BART: to Powell; metro: F, J, K, L, M, N, T to Powell; bus: 2, 4, 38, 45, 76; cable car: Powell-Hyde, Powell-Mason; map p.135 C1
Ah-inducing aromas like the best-selling blackcurrant and Bulgarian rose Baies scent waft from this rare outpost of the elite Paris-based candle-purveyor, which also concocts soaps and eaux de toilette.

Fresh
301 Sutter Street; tel: 248-0210; www.fresh.com; Mon–Wed 10am–7pm, Thur 10am–8pm, Fri–Sat 10am–7pm, Sun 11am–6pm; BART: to Powell; metro: F, J, K, L, M, N, T to Powell; bus: 2, 3, 4, 30, 45; map p.135 C1
Product junkies rejoiced at the recent opening of this outpost Boston-based purveyor of posh cosmetics, skincare, and bodycare, which include a signature Sugar line.

Above: a salesgirl tests the latest lip colour.

MadKat Beauty
915 Cole Street; tel: 665-8448; Mon–Fri 10am–8pm, Sat 10am–7pm, Sun 10am–6pm; metro: N to Carl Street and Cole Street; bus: 6, 33, 47; map p.137 C1
Finely-edited selection of beauty products, including exclusive, international brands. Also at 1418 Grant Avenue (tel: 391-3841).

Pharmaca Integrative Pharmacy
925 Cole Street; tel: 661-1216; www.pharmaca.com; Mon–Fri 8am–8pm, Sat–Sun 9am–8pm; metro: N to Carl Street & Cole Street; bus: 6, 71; map p.137 D1
Homeopathic remedies, nutritional and botanical dietary supplements, aromatherapy, bath products, and conventional medications are found at this unique pharmacy.

Spas

Barber Lounge
854 Folsom Street; tel: 934-0411; www.barberlounge.com; Tue–Fri 10am–8pm, Sat 9am–6pm; BART: to Powell; metro: F, J, K, L, M, N, T to Powell; bus: 5, 12, 27, 45, 76; map p.139 D4
Recently-opened modern salon-spa-barbershop hybrid caters to both genders with its full service menu, complete with hot-towel shaves and deep tissue massages.

Bliss San Francisco
181 3rd Street; tel: 281-0990; www.blissworld.com; Mon–Sun 9am–9pm; BART: to Montgomery metro: F, J, K, L, M , N, T to Montgomery; bus: 5, 21, 45, 76; map p.139 D4

Left: San Francisco's spas offer high-quality relaxation.

The San Francisco Shopping Center (Shopping chapter) hosts Bare Escentuals (www.bareescentuals.com), Bath & Body Works (www.bathandbodyworks.com), The Body Shop (www.bodyshop.com), Kiehl's (www.kiehls.com), and Lush (www.lush.com). Plus, Sephora (www.sephora.com) is found just across Market Street.

Chic, spacious W Hotel day spa pampers with movie-while-you-manicure stations, men's and women's lounges, nine treatment rooms, and a brownie buffet.

Branchar and Lewis Accessories and Day Spa
3303 Buchanan Street; tel: 440-3303; www.brancharlewis.com; Mon–Fri 11am–8pm, Sat–Sun 10am–7pm; bus: 22, 28, 30, 43; map p.133 E3
Cow Hollow ladies and gents enjoy massages, manicures, hot towel shaves, and Thalgo facials, all in private rooms.

Burke Williams
845 Market Street; tel: 278-9740; www.burkewilliamsspa.com; Mon–Sun 8am–10pm; BART: to Powell; metro: F, J, K, L, M, N, T to Powell; bus: 3, 9, 14, 30, 38; cable car: Powell-Hyde, Powell-Mason; map p.138 C4
Lavish source of whirlpools, saunas, massages, facials, seaweed body wraps, and signature exfoliating and moisturizing treatments.

Claremont Resort and Spa
41 Tunnel Road, Berkeley; tel: 510-843-3000; www.claremontresort.com; BART: to Rockridge or Downtown Berkeley, then AC Transit bus: 7
Pure luxury at this Berkeley landmark, where facilities include a hydrotherapy circuit, two floatation tanks, an Aroma Spritz Bar, two swimming pools, and four saunas. A myriad of treatments are available.

Below: laps and luxury at one of the Claremont's pools.

International Orange
2044 Fillmore Street; tel: 888-894-8811; www.internationalorange.com; Mon–Fri 11am–9pm, Sat–Sun 9am–7pm; bus: 1, 2, 3, 4, 22; map p.133 E1
Fresh-feeling day spa and yoga studio (named for the Golden Gate Bridge's eye-popping paint color) supplies sumptuous treatments and yoga classes. There is also a relaxing redwood sundeck.

Kabuki Springs and Spa
1750 Geary Boulevard; tel: 922-6000; www.kabukisprings.com; Mon–Sun 10am–9.45pm; bus: 2, 3, 4, 22, 38; map p.137 E4
Serene setting for facials, acupuncture, massages, and traditional communal baths.

Nob Hill Spa
1075 California Street; tel: 345-2888; www.huntingtonhotel.com; Mon–Sun 8am–8pm; bus: 1; cable car: California; map p.134 C1
Luxurious sanctuary hidden in the Huntington Hotel delivers deluxe pampering, an indoor pool with stunning views, and spa cuisine.
SEE ALSO HOTELS, P.74

Therapeia Massage
1801 Bush Street; tel: 885-4450; www.therapeiaspa.com; Mon–Fri 10am–9pm, Sat–Sun 9am–8pm; bus: 1, 2, 3, 4; map p.134 A1
Day spa serves hot stone massage, endermologie, acupuncture, and more.

Tre Balm
3255 Sacramento Street; tel: 292-5129; www.trebalm.com; Mon–Fri 11am–7pm, Sat 9am–5pm, Sun noon–5pm; bus: 1, 2, 3, 4, 43; map p.133 D1
Elegant Laurel Heights beauty boutique and skin care studio, with coveted world-class products.

Parks and Gardens

With sprawling parks, blooming botanical gardens, and neighborhood patches of green, San Francisco is full of open spaces perfect for whiling away time out of doors. Spend a day exploring the extensive grounds of Golden Gate Park, relax for a leisurely picnic in one of many sunlit squares, or pause for a few serene moments while enjoying a gorgeous view. Unless otherwise noted, these urban oases are open around the clock; however, though delightful by day, they are generally not safe places for star-gazing after dark.

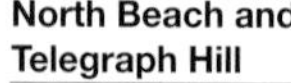

North Beach and Telegraph Hill

Ina Coolbrith Park

Taylor and Vallejo Streets; bus: 41, 45; cable car: Powell-Mason; map p.134 B2

Dedicated to California's first Poet Laureate, this steep series of steps and terraces climbs high up Russian Hill to a small lookout with picturesque views of North Beach and the Bay Bridge.

Washington Square

Bordered by Union, Stockton, Filbert, and Powell streets; bus: 15, 39, 41, 45; map p.134 C3

Prime people-watching can be had at this park overlooked by Saints Peter and Paul Catholic Church *(see Churches, p.44)*, where a rainbow of types (elderly Italians, Tai Chi devotees, sunbathers, Frisbee-tossers) escape from North Beach's congested streets.

Chinatown

Portsmouth Square

Bordered by Walter Lum Place and Clay, Washington, and Kearny streets; BART: to Montgomery; metro: F, J, K, L, M, N, T to Montgomery; bus: 1, 9X, 15, 30; map p.135 C2

Bordering the financial district, this Chinatown square hosts morning Tai Chi sessions, Chinese chess tables and benches, neighborly chatting, and youngsters clambering on jungle gyms.

Above: a frisbee-player in Mission Dolores Park.

Union Square and Financial District

Justin Herman Plaza

End of Market Street at Embarcadero; BART: to Embarcadero; metro: F, J, K, L, M, N, T to Embarcadero; bus: 5, 9, 21, 41; map p.135 D2

Opposite the Ferry Building, this lively plaza space is shared by financial district workers on lunch break, performers, skateboarders, and (in winter) ice-skaters.

SoMa and Civic Center

Yerba Buena Gardens

Bordered by Mission, Folsom, 3rd, and 4th streets; www.yerbabuena.org; Mon–Sun 6am–10pm; BART: to Powell; metro: F, J, K, L, M, N, T to Powell; bus: 5, 6,14, 21; map p.139 D4

This urban oasis features grassy landscaping, fountains, cafés, public artwork, a waterfall memorial to Dr Martin Luther King, Jr, a carousel, an ice-skating rink, bowling center, and the kid-friendly **Zeum** museum.

SEE ALSO CHILDREN, P.41

Nob Hill

Huntington Park

Bordered by California, Sacramento, Taylor and Cushman streets; bus: 1; cable car: California; map p.134 B2

Across the street from Grace Cathedral on Nob Hill, this well-maintained, bench-lined splash of green

Left: the serene view from Alta Plaza Park.

In addition to her Poet Laureate claim to fame, Oakland librarian Ina Coolbrith is also remembered for mentoring a young Jack London and entertaining other literary greats at her home on Macondray Lane. Additionally, she was the niece of Mormon founder Joseph Smith Jr.

is a pleasant place to lounge and browse the occasional art show. The square's centerpiece is a replica of the Roman Tartarughe Fountain, minus the tortoises.

Central Neighbourhoods

Alamo Square

Bordered by Steiner, Hayes, Fulton, and Scott streets; bus: 5, 21, 22, 24; map p.137 E1

Six brightly-colored Victorian homes known as the Painted Ladies line this grassy square. Often called Postcard Row, the picturesque prospect is completed by a city skyline backdrop, and is one of San Francisco's most photographed sights.

Alta Plaza Park

Bordered by Clay, Steiner, Jackson, and Scott streets; bus: 1, 3, 12, 24; map p.133 E1

Designed by John McLaren, this Pacific Heights park boasts grassy terraces, basketball and tennis courts, a playground, and sweeping views of the city.

Lafayette Park

Bordered by Laguna, Gough, Sacramento, and Washington streets; bus: 1, 12; map p.134 A1

In the midst of Pacific Heights mansions, this four-block park supplies tennis courts, excellent views, and a popular spot for local pups to play.

Haight-Ashbury

Buena Vista Park

Bordered by Haight Street and Buena Vista East and West avenues; metro: N to Duboce Street; bus: 6, 7, 71; map p.137 D2

This steeply-sloped, wooded park (which, dating from 1867, is the city's oldest) delivers on the good views promised by its name, particularly with its northern prospects of the Golden Gate Bridge and Marin Headlands.

Golden Gate Park

Bordered by Fulton Street, Lincoln Way, Great Highway and Stanyan streets; tel: 831-2700; metro: N to Irving Street and 9th Avenue; bus: 7,18, 21, 44; map p.136

Where rolling sand dunes once could be seen, Golden Gate Park's grassy hills now carpet more than 1,000 acres stretching from Haight-Ashbury to the Pacific Ocean. Inside the enormous park filled with copious gardens and groves, it is easy to forget about the city's hustle and bustle, especially on Sundays, when John F. Kennedy Drive is closed to car traffic. Scores of athletes are attracted by

Below: the Presidio's beach is just one of the many attractions of this expansive park.

Above: a sunny day entices locals to hit 'Dolores Beach'.

the many fields and miles of trails, not to mention the golf course, polo field, tennis courts, horseshoe pits, archery field, pétanque courts, and fly-fishing pond. Others come to enjoy less strenuous diversions, making use of picnic tables and barbeque pits, or simply napping on the lawns. The park has plenty of character, housing prominent museums like the **de Young** and the **California Academy of Sciences** (reopening its park location in 2008), as well as the historic Beach Chalet, a large Music Concourse, a hippie-beloved hill, a rose garden, and live bison.

SEE ALSO MUSEUMS AND GALLERIES, P.83, 88

ADDITIONAL HIGHLIGHTS:

Conservatory of Flowers

John F. Kennedy Drive at Conservatory Drive; tel: 666-7001; www.conservatoryofflowers.org; Tue–Sun 9am–4.30pm; entrance charge, under 5 free, first Tue of month free; bus: 5, 7, 33, 71

Built in the late 1870s, this dramatic, glass-domed structure was modeled after the Palm House at the Royal Botanical Gardens in Kew, England. Vibrantly-colored tropical flowers are the main focus of nearly 2,000 plant species. Outside, the Dahlia Garden decorates the eastern side of the conservatory, while a little way west, 850 varieties of colorful rhododendron bloom every year in early summer in the McLaren Memorial Rhododendron Dell.

Dutch and Murphy Windmills

John F. Kennedy Drive; free; bus: 5, 18, 31, 38

Dating from the early 1900s, the windmills looming in the park's north-west corner once pumped water to the Strawberry Hill reservoir. Fittingly, a colorful spread of tulips blooms each spring near the Dutch Windmill.

Garden of Shakespeare's Flowers

Martin Luther King Jr Drive and Middle Drive East; free; bus: 44

Visitors play name that flower in this lush garden where flowers and herbs mentioned in poems and plays penned by the famous bard decorate either side of a brick path.

Japanese Tea Garden

Tea Garden Drive; tel: 752-1171; www.sfpt.org; Mon–Sun 9am–6pm; entrance charge; bus: 21, 44

This peaceful setting of cherry blossoms, bonsai conifers, carp ponds, and wooden bridges is the oldest public Japanese-style garden in the country. It tends to be a popular destination, so expect company while strolling and then snacking on tea and cookies.

Koret Children's Quarter

Kezar Drive; free; bus: 71

Formerly known as the Children's Playground, this public playground built in 1887 is the country's oldest. Nearby, youngsters ride on colorful, carved animals at the historic Herschell-Spillman carousel, which dates from 1912.

National AIDS Memorial Grove

Between Middle Drive East and Bowling Green Drive; tel: 750-8340; www.aidsmemorial.org; free; bus: 5, 21, 71, 73

This peaceful grove is a living tribute to those whose lives have been affected by AIDS.

Portals of the Past

Between JFK Drive and Crossover Drive; free; bus: 5, 28, 29

At Lloyd Lake, six stately columns known as the Portals of the Past stand as the city's only public memorial to the 1906 earthquake and

It is no accident that statues in Golden Gate Park are hidden by dense foliage. Uncle John McLaren, the park superintendent for a period of 53 years (1890–1943), notoriously detested statuary. Ironically, a prominent statue of the Scotsman himself now stands in the the McLaren Memorial Rhododendron Dell.

fire. Before the disaster, the white marble pillars formed the portico of the Towne mansion on Nob Hill.

San Francisco Botanical Garden, at Strybing Arboretum
9th Avenue and Lincoln Way; tel: 661-1316; www.sfbotanical garden.org; Mon–Fri 8am–4.30pm, Sat–Sun 10am–5pm; free; bus: 44, 71
Mediterranean, mild temperate, and tropical cloud-forest plants are among the 7,500 diverse species from all over the world found on these 55 acres of gardens. A 'Garden of Fragrance' is one of several specialty gardens.

Stow Lake
John F. Kennedy Drive; tel: 752-0347; charge for boat rentals; bus: 5, 28, 29
At this lake, the largest of the park's 11, rowboat and pedalo rentals are offered, making for a leisurely afternoon gliding around with the turtles. At the lake's center, **Strawberry Hill** supplies the park's highest promontory.
SEE ALSO WALKS AND VIEWS, P.125

Mission and Castro

Mission Dolores Park
Bordered by Dolores, Church, 18th, and 20th streets; BART: to 16th Street; metro: J to Church Street & 18th Street; bus: 33; map p.138 A1
Frisky dogs and energetic ballplayers get their exercise in the lower part of this popular Mission park; higher up, picnickers enjoy the views and sun themselves on what has been dubbed 'Dolores Beach'.
SEE ALSO WALKS AND VIEWS, P.128

Around San Francisco

Lincoln Park
34th Avenue and Clement Street; bus: 1, 2, 18, 38
Wind-battered bluffs rim this 275-acre park, where a golf course, the grand **Palace of the Legion of Honor**, and the Land's End lookout all reward visitors with great views.
SEE ALSO MUSEUMS AND GALLERIES, P.83

The Presidio
Bordered by Lyon Street and West Pacific Avenue; tel: 561-4323; www.nps.gov/prsf; bus: 28, 29, 43, 82X; map p.132
A military post for more than 200 years, this 1,491-acre shoreline park encompasses beaches, cliffs, woods, historical sites, a golf course, a lake, 14 miles of paved roads (making biking a popular way to explore), and 11 miles of hiking trails. A popular spot is Crissy Field, the restored tidal marshland along the Presidio's northern shore. Relaxing picnickers enjoy the great views, and walkers and bikers cruise the **Golden Gate Promenade** – a nice break from the city's typically hilly terrain.

For other sweeping vistas, head to the rocky, mile-long shore of **Baker Beach** (where swimming should be avoided) or the windswept bluffs above, along which abandoned defensive gun batteries are scattered. Other Presidio possibilities include relaxing at Mountain Lake, visiting the San Francisco National Military Cemetery (or the nearby pet cemetery), and checking out Fort Point (tours Fri–Sun 10am–5pm), a historical defense fortification below the Golden Gate Bridge.

Sigmund Stern Recreation Grove
Sloat Boulevard and 19th Avenue; metro: K, M to West Portal Avenue & Sloat Boulevard; bus: 23, 28
This peaceful, 33-acre park encompasses meadows, playgrounds, horseshoe pits, tennis courts, and the natural Pine Lake. However, Stern Grove is best known for the free, outdoor summer concerts it has offered since 1938.

Sutro Heights Park
48th Avenue and Point Lobos Avenue; free; bus: 18, 38
When clear skies permit, this never-crowded former estate of one-time San Francisco mayor Adolph Sutro serves up a scenic view of the Cliff House, Ocean Beach, and the Pacific Ocean.

Below: some of Golden Gate Park's many highlights.

Restaurants

San Franciscans are serious about food. With thousands of restaurants to choose from, the best ones are not secret for long, and the boring, tasteless, or tacky are left to die on the vine. Not only is San Francisco an international hub of fine food, with groundbreaking Californian and exciting fusion cuisine, but the adventurous eater can seek out ethnic food from virtually every culture in the world. Diverse neighborhoods such as the Inner Richmond and Tenderloin offer a vast array from which to choose. Whether for brunch, lunch, or dinner, the options in San Francisco are both extensive and tasty.

Fisherman's Wharf

AMERICAN

Buena Vista Café,
2765 Hyde Street; tel: 474-5044; daily B, L and D; $$; bus: 10, 19, 30, 47; cable car: Powell-Hyde; map p.138 B4
A San Francisco institution and home of legendary Irish Coffee, a delicious elixir made with Irish whiskey, frothed cream and coffee.

Eagle Café
Pier 39; tel: 433-3689; daily B, L and D; $; metro: F to Embarcadero and Stockton Street; bus: 10, 39; map p.134 C4
A great alternative to the many overpriced Wharf restaurants, the Eagle is a lively institution known for large portions, hearty breakfasts, stiff cocktails and stellar views.

CALIFORNIAN

McCormick and Kuleto's
900 North Point Street, Ghirardelli Square; tel: 929-1730; daily L and D; $$$; bus: 10, 19, 30, 47; cable car: Powell-Hyde; map p.134 A4
Ghirardelli Square seafood spot popular for fabulous views and its huge variety of fresh, imaginative seafood dishes, as well as other tasty American fare.

Above: grab some crab and a beer on Fisherman's Wharf.

ITALIAN

Albona
545 Francisco Street; tel: 441-1040; daily L and D; $$; bus: 30, 39; map p.134 B3
This Istrian restaurant serves Northern Italian dishes influenced by the flavors of Central and Eastern Europe, such as pan-fried gnocchi in a cumin-spiced sirloin sauce. Owner Bruno makes you feel like you are in his own private living room.

Alioto's
8 Fisherman's Wharf; tel: 673-0183; daily L and D; $$; metro: F to Jefferson Street and Taylor Street; bus: 39; map p.134 B4
The Alioto name stands for politics, feuds, family and fine food in San Francisco. For generations, this family-owned establishment has ruled the Wharf with fresh, local seafood dishes and Sicilian preparations.

Scoma's
Pier 47; tel: 771-4383; daily L and D; $$$; metro: F to Jefferson Street and Taylor Street; map p.134 B4
For a glimpse of the working man's Wharf, dine right on the pier at this old-school Italian that has been serving seafood, pasta and their acclaimed chowder for 40 years.

SOUTHEAST ASIAN

Ana Mandara
891 Beach Street, Ghirardelli Square; tel: 771-8600; daily L and D; $$$; metro: F to Jones Street and Beach Street; bus: 19; map p.134 A4
French-Vietnamese inspired fare at this place, maybe a little upscale for Fisherman's

Left: San Francisco has many restaurants serving exquisite gourmet food.

Average price for a three-course meal and a half-bottle of house wine:	
$	less than $25
$$	$25–$50
$$$	$50–$100
$$$$	more than $100

Wharf. Starters include crispy rolls with crab, striped bass ceviche, and seared lobster with ginger rice.

North Beach and Telegraph Hill

AMERICAN

Washington Square Bar and Grill

1707 Powell Street; tel: 982-8123; Mon–Fri L and D, Sat–Sun Br, L and D; $$$; bus: 30, 41, 45; cable car: Powell-Mason; map p.134 C3

On Washington Square, and celebrated in countless San Francisco Chronicle columns, the 'Washbag' has had a culinary revival of late to equal its legendary atmosphere. Jazz and good times nightly.

EAST ASIAN

Sushi on North Beach

745 Columbus Avenue; tel: 788-8050; daily L and D; $$$; bus: 30, 41, 45; cable car: Powell-Mason; map p.134 C3

This family-run Asian establishment is a real find in the middle of Italian North Beach. Unique rolls, good-size pieces of fresh fish, and a fantastic miso soup set it apart from the rest.

EUROPEAN

O'Reilly's

622 Green Street; tel: 989-6222; daily B, L and D; $; bus: 30, 41, 45; map p.143 C3

This Irish pub is a cozy place for a hearty brunch, eaten either in the cool, stoneworked interior, or on the pleasant sidewalk tables. Be sure to try the Guinness-battered fish and chips.

Below: very fresh seafood...

Zarzuela

2000 Hyde Street; tel: 346-0800; daily D; $$; bus: 41, 45; cable car: Powell-Hyde; map p.134 B3

A sophisticated Spanish restaurant on the top of Russian Hill along the cable car route. This is a great place to drink sangria and share tapas or steaming plates of flavorful paella with a group of hungry friends.

ITALIAN

Firenze by Night

1429 Stockton Street; tel: 392-8485; daily D; $$; bus: 30, 41, 45; map p.134 C3

A traditional Northern Italian restaurant in North Beach on the edge of Chinatown. Famous for the outstanding pillowy-soft gnocci, tender calamari, and the pappardelle pasta Toscana with rabbit. Treat yourself to a glass of housemade limoncello with dessert.

Tipping in the US is different from many other places in the world. Most waitstaff and bartenders make minimum wage and depend on tips for survival. 10 percent means you were unsatisfied with the service. 15 percent is standard, but not great. 20 percent means you were happy with both service and food. Tipping nothing means you are a jerk. Percentages are calculated pre-tax. A quick way of calculating is to just double the tax (8.5 percent) and round up or down depending on level of satisfaction.

Above: from upmarket bacon and eggs to classic dim sum, San Franciscans have varied eating options.

Franchino's
347 Columbus Avenue; tel: 982-2157; Tue–Sun D; $$; bus: 30, 41, 45; map p.135 C2
Family owned and operated, friendly Franchino's serves huge portions of classic Italian dishes at reasonable prices.

Golden Boy Pizza
542 Green Street; tel: 982-9738; daily L and D; $; bus: 30, 41, 45; map p.134 C3
Golden Boy's Sicilian-style pan pizza is a favorite of North Beach bar-goers, and usually ordered by the slice. Look in the window and choose what whets the appetite.

L'Osteria del Forno
519 Columbus Avenue; tel: 982-1124; daily L and D; $; bus: 30, 41, 45; map p134 C3
For casual but satisfying Italian food, including marvelous antipasti, thin-crusted pizzas, a daily pasta dish, and a fine roast pork loin simmered in a milky broth. This treasure is a kid pleaser as well. Cash only.

Average price for a three-course meal and a half-bottle of house wine:

$	less than $25
$$	$25–$50
$$$	$50–$100
$$$$	more than $100

North Beach Restaurant
1512 Stockton Street; tel: 392-1700; daily L and D; $$$; bus: 30, 41, 45; map p.134 C3
This venerable institution serves hearty Tuscan cuisine featuring homemade pastas, house-cured proscuitto and a dizzyingly comprehensive wine list.

LATIN AMERICAN

Pena Pacha Mama
1630 Powell Street; tel: 646-0018; Wed–Mon D only; $$; bus: 30, 41, 45; map p.134 C3
Experience the Bolivian hospitality of the Navia family and the robust organic flavors from their native country. Live traditional music most nights makes for an unforgettable experience.

MIDDLE EASTERN

Helmand
430 Broadway; tel: 362-0641; daily D only; $$; bus: 12, 30, 41, 83; map p.135 C2
Afghani cuisine bursting with flavor and spice. Try the *bowlawni* – pastry shells stuffed with potato and leeks.

Chinatown

CALIFORNIAN

Bix
56 Gold Street; tel: 433-6300; daily D; $$$; bus: 12, 41; map p.135 D2
San Francisco's renewed taste for martinis requires swank digs and upscale munchables. Bix is a revival of the 1920s supper club, with tasty bites and live jazz.

EAST ASIAN

Empress of China
838 Grant Avenue; tel: 434-1345; daily L and D; $; bus: 1, 30, 45; map p.135 C2
The only restaurant in Chinatown with a truly spectacular view gives diners a very good perspective on the neighborhood. The cocktail lounge overlooks Grant Street, while the dining room towers above Portsmouth Square. If you do not eat here, at least stop by for a drink and enjoy the ambience.

Far East Café
631 Grant Avenue; tel: 982-3245; daily L and D; $; bus: 1, 30, 45; map p.135 C2
Food is good but not amazing, with all the standards of a Chinese restaurant. But the atmosphere is one of the best in Chi-town, with private booths, and century-old chandeliers.

House of Nanking
919 Kearny Street; tel: 421-

Parking in San Francisco, especially downtown, can be brutal. If you do not want to pay the exorbitant lot rates, arrive at least 20 minutes early to find street parking, more in North Beach. Always read street signs and curbs for parking restrictions.

1429; daily L and D; $; bus: 12, 41; map p.135 C2
Grungy and crowded, the reason for the lengthy line at nearly all hours is because this wildly popular spot, a locals' favorite, serves outstanding, inexpensive, adventurous Chinese food. The no-nonsense owners/staff will tell you what' is good tonight. Listen to them. Avoid weekends.

Union Square and Financial District

AMERICAN

Sam's Grill
374 Bush Street; tel: 421-0594; Mon–Fri L only; $$$; bus: 45, 76; map p.135 C1
Although the three-martini business lunch may be a thing of the past, this old-school grill is still going strong after 125 years. Choose either the high-ceiling dining room or a private booth, and enjoy American cuisine free from pretension and impervious to change.

Tadich Grill
240 California Street; tel: 391-1849; Mon–Sat L and D; $$$; bus: 10, 30X, 41; cable car: California; map p.135 D2
Tadich is a venerable institution that has been around in various incarnations since the Gold Rush, with wooden booths, white linen, and waiters as crusty as the sourdough. The menu of classics, includes lobster Newburg, crab Louis, and sand dabs. The cognoscenti order whatever fresh fish is available, grilled. Sidle up to the original mahogany bar, order a gin fizz and soak in old school San Francisco ambiance.

Taylor's Refresher
1 Ferry Building #6; tel: 328-3663; daily L and D; $; metro: F to the Embaracdero and Ferry Building; bus: 2, 14, 31, 71; cable car: California; map p.135 E2
High-end diner fare with a gourmet flourish. Taylor's is famous for their burgers – patties are ⅓ lb. fresh ground, all-natural beef from Golden Gate Meats – as well as their decadent milkshakes, but you will also find mouthwatering grilled chicken sandwiches, über-fresh salads, sweet potato fries and other diner faves.

CALIFORNIAN

Aqua
252 California Street; tel: 956-9662; daily D only; $$$$; bus: 1, 12, 41, 42; cable car: California; map p.135 D2
Reservations are required at this seafood restaurant that is consistently rated as the best in San Francisco. The presentation and service are top-notch and chefs from around the world vie for opportunities to work here.

EUROPEAN

Kokkari
200 Jackson Street; tel: 981-0983; daily L and D; $$$$; bus: 1, 12, 42, 83; map p.135 D2
An Aristotle Onassis–sort of Greek taverna with beamed ceilings, a massive fireplace, Oriental carpets, and huge dishes of rich food. (Do not expect to see anyone intentionally smash a plate.) The crowd exudes a robust sense of well-being. Reservations advisable.

FRENCH

Fleur de Lys
777 Sutter Street; tel: 673-7779; daily D; $$$$; bus: 2, 3, 27, 76; map p.134 C1
The premier French restaurant, with an elegant dining room and superior service.

Plouf
40 Belden Place; tel: 986-6491; Mon–Fri L and D, Sat D only; $$$; bus: 2, 4, 5; map p.135 C1
There are a number of good café-restaurants with outdoor seating on Belden Place, a charming, brick alley off Bush and Kearney streets. Plouf specializes in delicious seafood prepared with a French accent and the waiters also give the impression you have arrived in the Paris of the west.

FUSION

Cortez
550 Geary Street; tel: 292-6360; Mon–Fri D only, Sat–Sun

Below: the city's proximity to the ocean results in fantastic seafood.

Br and D; $$$; bus: 27, 38; map p.134 C1
This restaurant in the Hotel Adagio, has in a few short years become one of the most celebrated in SF, holding its own against Union Square's best. Creative, exquisite, oft-organic small plates will thrill.

INDIAN
Shalimar
532 Jones Street; tel: 928-0333; daily L and D; $; bus: 27, 38; map p.134 B1
Consistently rated one of the best Indian restaurants in the city, this spot serves traditional and tasty Indian and Pakistani food. No alcohol. Cash only.

SOUTHEAST ASIAN
Slanted Door
1 Ferry Building #3; tel: 861-8032; daily L and D; $$$; metro: F to the Embarcadero and Ferry Building; bus: 2, 21, 31, 71; cable car: California; map p.135 E2
When it opened in the 1990s, this place instantly became one of the premier restaurants in the city, serving wholesome, flavorful Vietnamese food. Make reservations long before you come to San Francisco.

SoMa and Civic Center

AMERICAN
Town Hall
342 Howard Street; tel: 908-3900; daily L and D; $$$; bus: 12, 30, 45, 76; map p.135 D1
Regional American classics like New Orleans-style smoked chicken gumbo are served up nicely in this remodeled, historic building in SoMa. Try the shrimp *etouffée* or the San Francisco favorite, *cioppino* (a type of fish stew).

Average price for a three-course meal and a half-bottle of house wine:

$	less than $25
$$	$25–$50
$$$	$50–$100
$$$$	more than $100

Above: tucking in at a Japantown restaurant.

CALIFORNIAN
Zuni Café
1658 Market Street; tel: 552-2522; Mon–Sat L and D, Sun Br, L and D; $$; BART: to Van Ness; metro: F, J, K, L, M, N, T to Van Ness; bus: 6, 7, 66, 71; map p.138 B3
Make reservations and elbow your way past the crowded copper bar for the best roasted chicken and bread salad (for two) imaginable. The burger with shoestring potatoes has a cult following. Actually, everything on the California-cuisine based menu is going to be great.

XYZ
181 3rd Street; tel: 817-7836; daily B, L and D; $$$$; bus: 12,14, 30, 45, 76; map p.139 D4
A popular spot with directors, actors, and wannabes. The excellent, creative dishes combine fine local and seasonal vegetables, plus meat and fish in modern Californian style. There is also superb service and a wine list featuring over 500 different varieties.

EAST ASIAN
Yank Sing
101 Spear Street; tel: 957-9300; Mon–Fri 11am–3pm, Sat–Sun 10am–4pm; $$; BART: to Montgomery; metro: F, J, K, L, M, N, T to Montgomery; bus: 1, 2, 6, 7, 21, 31, 71; map p.135 D2
Dim sum place using fresh ingredients in a sparkling clean interior. Great dumplings. Perfect for dim sum first-timers.

FRENCH
Le Charm
315 5th Street; tel: 546-6128; Tue–Fri L and D, Sat–Sun D only; $$; bus: 12, 27, 30, 45, 76; map p.139 D3

Below: vegetarian specialities are common too.

French food's greatest hits, reasonably priced. Ratatouille, escargot, duck confit, crème brûlée, and classic French onion soup all share this comfortable, unpretentious stage.

SOUTHEAST ASIAN
Tu Lan
8 6th Street; tel: 626-0927; daily L and D; $; BART: to Powell; metro: F, J, K, L, M, N, T to Powell; bus: 6, 14, 21, 71; map p.138 C4
This Vietnamese hot spot is known for its cramped and sketchy location. It is a hole in the wall, but people love it, waiting patiently for memorably tasty noodle dishes.

VEGETARIAN
Ananda Fuara
1298 Market Street; tel: 621-1994; daily L and D; $; BART: to Civic Center metro: F, J, K, L, M, N, T to Civic Center; bus: 5, 7, 9, 71; map p.138 B3
Inexpensive and delicious, this is the perfect change of pace for vegetarians tired of veggie burritos and Caesar salads. There is much to order here, from meatless meatloaf to mushroom ravioli.

Nob Hill

AMERICAN
Big 4
1075 California Street; tel: 771-1140; Mon–Fri B, L and D, Sat–Sun Br, L and D; $$$; bus: 1; cable car: California; map p.134 C1
The Big 4 is a manly place, named after the four robber baron railroad tycoons whose photos and memorabilia line the walls. Dark wood paneling adds to the men's-club ambiance and the menu is suitably heavy on meat and game – from filet mignon and rack of lamb to wild boar chops. Eat heartily and enjoy.

> Some neighborhoods are known for a certain cuisine – burritos in the Mission, dim sum on Stockton Street and Broadway in Chinatown, Italian in North Beach, and Indian and Vietnamese in the Tenderloin.

ITALIAN
Nob Hill Café
1152 Taylor Street; tel: 776-6500; daily L and D; $$; bus: 1; cable car: California; map p.134 C2
A cozy bistro, tucked in a quiet Nob Hill neighborhood, featuring delicious Northern Italian cuisine. Loved by locals for great wine, ambience and the ethereal tiramisu. No reservations, so get there early.

Central Neighborhoods

AMERICAN
Elite Café
2049 Fillmore Street; tel: 346-8668; Mon–Fri D only, Sat–Sun Br and D; $$; bus: 1, 3, 22; map p.133 E1
This tried-and-true locals' fave serves Cajun and Creole inspired seafood dishes in a cheery atmosphere. An excellent raw bar beckons, as does the Cajun brunch, with perfectly seasoned Bloody Marys.

> Conventional wisdom says that in San Francisco there are more medical marijuana dispensaries than McDonald's restaurants.

EAST ASIAN
Seoul Garden
22 Peace Plaza (at Laguna); tel: 563-7664; daily L and D; $; bus: 2, 3, 22, 38; map p.138 A4
Savory meats cooked right at your table, with successful but unobtrusive flair. The meat is tender and succulent, but the spiciness is up to you. Never tried Korean? This is the place to start.

EUROPEAN
Suppenkuche
601 Hayes Street; tel: 252-9289; Mon–Sat D only, Sun Br and D; $; bus: 21; map p.138 A3
At one of the few German restaurants in the city, updated German classics –

Below: hard-at-work chefs prepare yet more tasty dishes.

Above: in the distinctive Haight tacqueria, Zona Rose.

spaetzle, shnitzel, potato pancakes and wonderful, hearty soups – are served to diners sitting family style on long spartan benches. Around 20 beers (mostly German) on tap. Huge portions.

Holy Grail
1233 Polk Street; tel: 928-1233; daily D; $$; bus: 19, 38; map p.138 B4
A Cal-Irish restaurant featuring great fresh seafood and modern takes on Irish cuisine such as stews and braises. An overwhelmingly opulent dcor and live music complete the experience.

FRENCH
Chez Maman
2223 Union Street; tel: 771-7771; Mon–Sat L and D, Sun Br, L and D; $$; bus: 2, 41, 45; map p.133 E2
A French bistro without attitude. Chez Maman has in just two short years become a favorite for locals, who love the simple, tasty, inexpensive cuisine. The rule is that you must finish your plate, not that you'll mind.

FUSION
Betelnut
2030 Union Street; tel: 929-8855; Tue–Sun L and D; $$; bus: 22, 41, 45; map p.133 E2
A pan-Asian bar specializing in dumplings and noodle bowls with bold, exciting flavors.

Pres a Vi
One Letterman Drive, Building D Suite 150; tel: 409-3000; Mon–Fri L and D, Sat–Sun Br, L and D; $$$; bus: 41, 43, 45; map p.133 D2
Stellar global cuisine from a galaxy not so far away: the George Lucas compound in the Presidio. A unique location is no crutch for scrumptious small-plate seafood and savory specials.

VEGETARIAN
Greens
Building A, Fort Mason; tel: 771-6222; Mon–Sat L and D, Sun Br, L and D; $$$; bus: 28; map p.134 A3
In a one-time army warehouse on the bay, an airy upscale vegetarian restaurant that even non-veggies rave about. The Saturday evening prix fixe is a relative bargain and comes with lovely bay views. Reservations are essential. Its takeout counter, Greens to Go, is open all day.

Average price for a three-course meal and a half-bottle of house wine:

$	less than $25
$$	$25–$50
$$$	$50–$100
$$$$	more than $100

Haight-Ashbury and Golden Gate Park

AMERICAN
PJ's Oyster Bed
737 Irving Street; tel: 566-7775; daily L and D; $$; bus: 6, 43, 44, 66; map p.136 B1
A delicious and fun seafood restaurant in the heart of the Inner Sunset neighborhood, where an open kitchen and occasional Mardi-Gras nights keep the place hopping. No gimmicks here, just fresh and flavorful food.

CARRIBEAN
Cha Cha Cha
1801 Haight Street; tel: 386-5758; daily L and D; $; bus: 7, 37, 43, 71; map p.137 C2
Smack dab in the middle of Haight-Ashbury, Cha Cha Cha is a fun place for tapas, Caribbean-inspired entrees and sangria. The crowd is young, hip and noisy.

INDIAN
Naan 'n' Curry
642 Irving Street; tel: 664-7225; daily L and D; $; metro: N to Irving Street and 7th Avenue; bus: 6, 43; map p.136 B1
So much flavor for so little cash. This Inner Sunset location is one of several Indian/Pakistani eateries known for its delicious food and low prices. Short on decor but long on spiciness, the chicken vindaloo, tikka masala and tandoori all hit the mark.

LATIN AMERICAN
Zona Rose
1797 Haight Street; tel: 668-7717; daily L and D; $; bus: 7, 33, 37, 43, 71; map p.137 C2
Craving a burrito but don't want to go all the way over to the Mission? This groovy tacqueria is good for a quick

'California Cuisine' is typified by seasonal, local produce, usually organic. Flavor combinations accentuate freshness, subtlety, and texture. Meat is not always the focal point.

bite in a quirky setting. Vegetarian options are particularly popular.

MIDDLE EASTERN
Kan Zaman
1793 Haight Street; tel: 751-9656; daily D only; $; bus: 7, 33, 37, 43, 71; map p.137 C2
A perennial favorite with locals. Expect a loud, fun night with belly dancers (Thur–Sat) and hookahs filled with apple-scented treats to smoke at the tables, while sitting on floor cushions and sipping spiced wine.

Mission and Castro

AFRICAN
Bissap Baobab
2323 Mission Street; tel: 826-9287; daily D only; $$; bus: 14, 33, 49
A funky, international spot with a diverse clientele, serving West African fare and refreshing but potent cocktails made from homemade juice. Standout dishes include the spinach pastele pastry, the mafe with tofu in a peanut sauce, and the oniony chicken dibi with couscous.

CALIFORNIAN
Foreign Cinema
2534 Mission Street; tel: 648-7600; daily D; $$$; bus: 14, 49
Dinner and a movie gets a new spin at this popular, industrial-chic eatery. Diners can choose to sit inside to enjoy the innovative California cuisine, or better yet, dine on the heated outdoor courtyard where films are screened nightly on a concrete wall.

EAST ASIAN
Blowfish Sushi To Die For
2170 Bryant Street; tel: 285-3848; daily D and L; $$$; bus: 27; map p.138 B1
An unconventional sushi restaurant catering to a western palate, (you will find appetizers and rolls made with sirloin, in addition to the standard nigiri selections), Blowfish Sushi has tasty and whimsical sake cocktails served in a swank atmosphere. It is loud, and fun. For fugu fans, the restaurant is licensed to serve the Northern Pufferfish.

FUSION
Panchita's
3115 22nd Street; tel: 821-6660; daily L and D; $$; bus: 12, 14, 49
Enjoy this mix of California and Salvadorian semi-fine dining. A great place for small groups or intimate, off-the-beaten path romantic dinners.

LATIN AMERICAN
Espetus
1686 Market Street; tel: 552-8792; daily L and D; $$$; metro: F, J, K, L, M to Van Ness; bus: 6, 7, 71; map p.135 D1
Leave the vegetarians out of this one. Espetus is a Brazilian steakhouse in the South American Churrascaria style, in which various and copious meats are brought to and carved at your table on the skewers they were cooked on. A prix fixe menu means you eat 'til you burst

Above: all-night joints are popular in the clubbing areas, such as this one in the Castro.

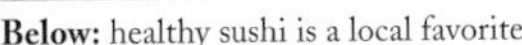
Below: healthy sushi is a local favorite.

Average price for a three-course meal and a half-bottle of house wine:

$	less than $25
$$	$25–$50
$$$	$50–$100
$$$$	more than $100

Pancho Villa
3071 16th Street; tel 864-8840; daily L and D; $; BART: to 16th Street; bus: 14, 27, 49; map p.138 B1
Here it is: the world renowned San Francisco burrito. Better than in Mexico and bigger than any in Los Angeles, and Pancho Villa creates the perfect specimen. It is counter service only, and incredibly inexpensive. Have a late lunch and you will not need dinner. As with most taquerias, pass on the refried beans and go with whole or black ones; you will appreciate the flavors and texture much better.

Puerto Alegre
546 Valencia Street; tel: 255-8201; daily L and D; $; BART: to 16th Street; bus: 14, 26, 33, 49; map p.138 B1
One of the few table-service Mexican restaurants in the Mission, this is a great place for a group of friends to get well-fed, a bit loud, and a little loopy from their infamous Margaritas. Fine dining? No. Fun dining? Si.

Above: haute cuisine in the Wine Country.

VEGETARIAN

Café Gratitude
2400 Harrison Street; tel: 824-4652; daily B, L and D; $; bus: 27, 41
Vegan, vegetarian and raw food is served here, including soups, salads, pizzas, smoothies, and organic coffee made with the finest ingredients. The setting is comfortable and easy-going. Occasional live music and a friendly staff make this off-the-beaten-path gem a perfect spot any time of the day.

Around San Francisco

CALIFORNIAN

Sutro's at the Cliff House
1090 Point Lobos, Ocean Beach; tel: 386-3330; daily L and D; $$$; metro: N to Ocean Beach; bus: 5, 18, 31
Incredible views over the Golden Gate Bay, the Marin headlands and the ocean make this well-designed, smart Cal-cuisine restaurant a truly desirable lunching location. Food is seasonal.

ITALIAN

Aziza
5800 Geary Boulevard, Richmond; tel: 752-2222; daily D; $$$; bus: 38
It takes a lot to get SF food-

Below: the food at Sutro's, in the Cliff House, comes second to the great view over Ocean Beach.

ies to outer Richmond, but Aziza delivers with its Moroccan-influenced cuisine.

MIDDLE EASTERN

Al-Masri

4031 Balboa Street, Richmond; tel: 876-2300; Thur–Sun D; $$; bus: 31, 38

Dinner at Al-Masri is an all-evening affair of unique Egyptian dishes and belly dancers, all in a fantasy courtyard atmosphere.

SOUTHEAST ASIAN

Angkor Wat

4217 Geary Boulevard, Richmond; tel: 221-7887; daily L and D; $$; bus: 38, 44; map p.136 B4

Beautiful carvings of the Buddha abound, and the waitstaff are truly gracious. Cambodian food in a clean and exotic atmosphere.

Khan Toke

5937 Geary Boulevard, Richmond; tel: 668-6654; daily D; $; bus: 2, 29, 38

This restaurant is reminiscent of a Bangkok temple, with low tables and an orchid garden. Some of the best Thai food in the city is worth the trip to Richmond.

Oakland, Berkeley and the Bay Area

CALIFORNIAN

Bay Wolf Café

3853 Piedmont Avenue, Oakland; tel: 510-655-6004; Mon–Fri L and D, Sat–Sun D only; $$$; AC Transit bus: 51, 57, 59

A pioneer of California-style nouvelle cuisine which maintains enviable quality, offsetting seasonal delights with a well-chosen wine list.

Chez Panisse

1517 Shattuck Avenue, Berkeley; tel: 510-548-5525; www.chezpanisse.com; Mon–Sat D only; $$$; BART: to Downtown Berkeley

This is the birthplace of Californian cuisine, and founder Alice Waters is its mother, pioneering the use of local, seasonal produce. Courses are fixed by the chef, with two seatings a night. There is also a café that serves lunch.

EAST ASIAN

Yoshi's

510 Embarcadero West, Jack London Square, Oakland; tel: 510-238-9200; daily D only; $$–$$$; BART: to Oakland 12th Street, then bus: 72, 58, 58X, 301

Modern Japanese cuisine at this renowned jazz club, considered one of the best in California. The food ranges from well-executed standards to more creative adventures in sashimi and nigiri. There is also a lively sushi bar. There is another Yoshi's in the Fillmore (1330 Fillmore Street; tel: 655-560).

SEE ALSO MUSIC AND DANCE, P.91

Wine Country

CALIFORNIAN

Martini House

1245 Spring Street, St Helena; tel: 707-963-2233; Mon–Thur D only, Fri–Sun L and D; $$$

Newly Michelin-starred restaurant that makes full use of local bounty with adventurous, Cal-cuisine, served in beautifully designed surrounds influenced by the region's Native American and wine-making history. The chef's tasting menu paired with wine is a particular treat, as is the special Mushroom tasting menu.

FRENCH

Bistro Jeanty

6510 Washington Street, Yountville; tel: 707-944-0103; daily L and D; $$$

Excellent flagship restaurant from chef-owner Philippe Jeanty, with a seasonal menu of homey dishes such as Coq au Vin and cassoulet, served on the outdoor patio or in the attractive dining room. The satisfying food makes you look forward to returning.

French Laundry

6640 Washington Street, Yountville; tel: 707-944-2380; Mon–Thur D only, Fri–Sun L and D; $$$$

Consistently voted the number one restaurant in the US, Chef Thomas Keller serves a masterful prix fixe menu (at $240 per head) to those lucky and smart enough to reserve a table months in advance. The nine-course dinner utilizes the finest ingredients with virtuoso preparation. Dress code.

LATIN AMERICAN

Ana's Cantina

1205 Main Street, St Helena; tel: 707-963-4921; daily L and D; $–$$

This well-priced Mex-Cal restaurant offers fresh fare and a fun atmosphere. It is a good spot for a tasty lunch, in the evenings there is often live music, and the margaritas are famous. Hosts occasional karaoke evenings.

> The markup on wine by restaurants can be astronomical. Consider buying a bottle at a corner store or supermarket and paying 'corkage', a fee typically around $20 for the house to open your wine.

Above: enjoying a lunch out.

Shopping

With San Francisco's colorful cosmopolitan array of stores, shopping in the city is a true joy. Large modern shopping centers and old-fashioned, boutique-lined neighborhoods enticingly display designer fashions, artwork and crafts, gorgeous antiques, gourmet foods, brimming bookstores, and utterly unique and offbeat gift shops, delighting throngs of window-shopping enthusiasts and deep-pocketed purchasers alike. Note that entries for other stores can be found under 'Children', 'Essentials', 'Fashion', 'Food and Drink', 'Literature', 'Music and Dance', and 'Pampering'.

Whirlwind Neighborhood Shopping Tour

To feel the city's shopping pulse beating most wildly, head to **Union Square**, where streets are stacked with elegant emporiums and retail chains, and lanes are lined with high-end designer stores.

Close by is another bustling bazaar, **Chinatown**. **Grant Avenue** especially is awash with porcelain, paper parasols, and tea-selling apothecaries. If souvenir-hunting here somehow manages to be unsuccessful, turn to **Fisherman's Wharf** and Ghirardelli Square for more truckloads of trinkets. For hippie-inspired paraphernalia though, head to **Haight Street**, a jumble of independent music, secondhand clothing, and head shops.

Hip **Mission** boutiques also serve offbeat fare, from ethnic threads to mod furniture to pirate supplies, while **Hayes Valley** delivers a cool composition of art galleries, contemporary boutiques, and handsome, unique home furnishings. Slightly edgy style is also found on **Polk Street** as it leaves posh Russian Hill for the gritty Tenderloin, with vintage and new wares for varied budgets.

More solely sophisticated clusters of beauty outlets, boutiques, and restaurants stretch along Union and Chestnut Streets. **Fillmore** and **Sacramento Streets** also present a stroll-worthy menu of deluxe delicacies ranging from Florentine soaps and vintage French furnishings to high-end European shoes.

European flavor is also found in **North Beach**, where contemporary clothing shops cozy up to dens of quaint curios and antique maps.

San Francisco's sport shop team includes **Niketown** (278 Post Street; tel: 392-6453) for swooshes; **Sports Basement** (610 Mason Street; tel: 437-0100) for gigantic bargains; **Lululemon** (327 Grant Avenue; tel: 402-0914) for cool apparel; and **North Face** (180 Post Street; tel: 433-3223) and **REI** (840 Brannan Street; tel: 934-1938) for outdoorsy adventurers.

Shopping Centers

The Cannery

2801 Leavenworth Street; tel: 771-3112; www.thecannery.com; Mon–Sat 10am–6pm, Sun 11am–6pm; metro: F to Jones Street and Beach Street; bus: 10, 19, 30, 47; cable car: Powell-Hyde, Powell-Mason; map p.134 B4

The former Del Monte fruit cannery now attracts tourists with collectibles, live courtyard entertainment, and a new Steve and Barry's outpost.

Crocker Galleria

50 Post Street; tel: 393-1505; www.shopatgalleria.com; Mon–Fri 10am–6pm, Sat 10am–5pm; BART: to Montgomery; metro: F, J, K, L, M, N, T to Montgomery; bus: 3, 10, 30, 76; map p.135 D1

Airy glass-arched pavilion, prettily-lined with galleries and specialty boutiques.

Embarcadero Center

Sacramento between Battery and Drumm Streets; tel: 772-0700; www.embarcaderocenter.com; Mon–Fri 10am–7pm, Sat 10am–6pm, Sun noon–5pm; BART: to Embarcadero; metro: F, J, K, L, M, N, T to Embarcadero;

Left: retail heaven, near Union Square.

bus: 1, 5, 6, 21; map p.135 D2
Four Financial District towers supply flower-potted patios, wide walkways, eateries, and familiar retail faces of the Banana Republic flavor.

Japantown Center
Post Street, between Fillmore and Laguna Streets; www.sfjapantown.org; bus: 2, 3, 22, 38; map p.137 E4
Captivating cluster of Japanese restaurants and boutiques, including elegant clothing and home decor at Sakura Sakura (tel: 922-9744), vintage silk kimonos at Shige Nishiguchi Kimonos (tel: 346-5567), and trendy apparel at Orange Tree (tel: 409-7890).

Westfield San Francisco Shopping Center
865 Market Street; tel: 512-6776; http://westfield.com/uscentres; Mon–Sat 9.30am–9pm, Sun 10am–7pm; BART: to Powell; metro: F, J, K, L, M, N, T to Powell; bus: 3, 6, 38, 45; cable car: Powell-Hyde, Powell-Mason; map p.138 C4
Escalators spiral up a nine-story atrium past a mish-mash of mall regulars, with Nordstrom's departments on the top five levels. A recently-added lateral expansion leads to Bloomingdale's, affordable imports such as Zara and H&M, and a dash of designer outposts, including Furla and Juicy Couture.

Department Stores

Barney's New York
77 O'Farrell Street; tel: 268-3500; www.barneys.com; Mon–Wed and Fri–Sat 10am–7pm, Thur 10am–8pm, Sun 11am–6pm; BART: to Powell; metro: F, J, K, L, M, N, T to Powell; bus: 4, 14, 27, 38; cable car: Powell-Hyde, Powell-Mason; map p.134 C1
Big Apple-based emporium dripping with fashionable, decadent designs.

Gump's
135 Post Street; tel: 800-766-7628; www.gumps.com; Mon–Sat 10am–6pm, Sun noon–5pm; BART: to Powell; metro: F, J, K, L, M, N, T to Powell; bus: 4, 14, 27, 38; cable car: Powell-Hyde, Powell-Mason; map p.134 C1
Sumptuous San Francisco institution reels in well-heeled gift-givers with refined jewelry and home adornments.

Bloomingdale's
845 Market Street; tel: 856-5300; www.bloomingdales.com; Mon–Sat 9.30am–9pm, Sun 10am–7pm; BART: to Powell; metro: F, J, K, L, M, N, T to Powell; bus: 4, 14, 27, 38; cable car: Powell-Hyde, Powell-Mason; map p.134 C1
Recent upscale addition to the Market Street mall, well-stocked with gleaming designer displays.

Macy's
170 O'Farrell Street; tel: 397-3333; www.macys.com; Mon–Sat 10am–9pm, Sun 11am–7pm; BART: to Powell; metro: F, J, K, L, M, N, T to Powell; bus: 4, 14, 27, 38; cable car: Powell-Hyde, Powell-Mason; map p.134 C1
Abiding, affordable department store standard, capped

Below: fine writing materials at Paper Source.

Left: taking a breather from shopping in Union Square.

with the ever-crowded Cheesecake Factory restaurant. Cross Stockton Street for the men's store.

Neiman Marcus
150 Stockton Street; tel: 362-3900; www.neimanmarcus.com; Mon–Wed and Fri–Sat 10am–7pm, Thur 10am–8pm, Sun noon–6pm; BART: to Powell; metro: F, J, K, L, M, N, T to Powell; bus: 4, 14, 27, 38; cable car: Powell-Hyde, Powell-Mason; map p.134 C1
Puffed-up purveyor (nicknamed 'Needless Markup') of glam and luxe labels.

Nordstrom
San Francisco Centre, 865 Market Street; tel: 243-8500; www.nordstrom.com; Mon–Sat 9am–9pm, Sun 9am–7pm; BART: to Powell; metro: F, J, K, L, M, N, T to Powell; bus: 4, 14, 27, 38; cable car: Powell-Hyde, Powell-Mason; map p.134 C1
Five classy tiers of varying affordability, with a notable shoe selection and unbeatable return policy.

Saks Fifth Avenue
384 Post Street; tel: 986-4300; www.saksfifthavenue.com; Mon–Wed and Fri–Sat 10am–7pm, Thur 10am–8pm, Sun 11am–6pm; BART: to Powell; metro: F, J, K, L, M, N, T to Powell; bus: 4, 14, 27, 38; cable car: Powell-Hyde, Powell-Mason; map p.134 C1
Fashionable trendy labels and trusty designer standbys. The men's store is just down the block.

Stores

ANTIQUES AND CURIOS

African Outlet
524 Octavia Street; tel: 864-3576; http://theafricaoutlet.net; Mon–Sun 10am–8pm; bus: 21, 47, 49; map p.138 A3
Bright fabrics, sculptures, instruments, and jewelry.

Aria
1522 Grant Avenue; tel: 433-0219; Mon–Sat 11am–6pm, Sun noon–5pm; bus: 20, 30, 39, 45; map p.135 C3
Fantastical French flea market flair, from photographs and letters to anatomical drawings. Hours vary unexpectedly: call first.

Evelyn's Antique Chinese Furniture
381 Hayes Street; tel: 255-1815; www.evelynantique.com; Mon–Sat 10.30am–6.30pm; metro: F to Van Ness; bus: 6, 47, 49, 71; map p.138 A3
Chinese furniture and collectibles from the 18th and 19th centuries.

Jackson Square
Tel: 398-8155; www.jacksonsquaresf.com; bus: 10, 15, 30X, 41; map p.135 D2
The most concentrated source for old objects of desire is undoubtedly this historic square, where a variety of traders have outlets.

Past Perfect
2224 Union Street; tel: 929-7651; Daily 11.30–7pm; bus: 22, 41, 45; map p.133 E2
Intriguing spread of mid-20th century vintage furniture, lighting, home accessories, clothes, and artwork.

Schein & Schein
1435 Grant Avenue; tel: 399-8882; www.scheinandschein.com; Wed–Sat noon–7pm, Sun noon–5pm; bus: 12, 20, 30, 41, 45; map p.135 C3
Thousands of compelling antique maps and prints from the 14th to 19th centuries.

> Union Square cooks up several trusty recipes for happy homemakers. Gourmet cookware and gadgets are served by ever-charming **Sur la Table** (77 Maiden Lane; tel: 732-7900) and luxurious linens – from high thread count sheets to towels and table runners – by San Francisco institution **Scheuer Linens** (340 Sutter Street, tel: 800-762-3950).

ARTS AND CRAFTS

Adolph Gasser

181 2nd Street; tel: 495-3852; www.gassers.com; Mon–Fri 9am–6pm, Sat 10am–5pm; BART: to Montgomery; metro: F, J, K, L, M, N, T to Montgomery; bus: 7, 9, 10, 76; map p.135 D1

Photo nirvana for professionals and hobbyists alike.

Britex Fabrics

146 Geary Street; tel: 392-2910; www.britexfabrics.com; Mon–Sat 10am–6pm, Sun noon–5pm; BART: to Powell; metro: F, J, K, L, M, N, T to Powell; bus: 2, 30, 38, 76; cable car: Powell-Hyde, Powell-Mason; map p.135 C1

Four-floors teeming with brocades and silks, 30,000 button styles, and bargain remnants.

Noe Knit

3957 24th Street; tel: 970-9750; www.noeknit.com; Mon–Thur 11am–8pm, Fri 11am–6pm, Sat–Sun 11am–6pm; metro: J to Church Street and 24th Street; bus: 48

This spot is the place to find a nifty stash of fine yarns, needles, and books.

Paper Source

2061 Chestnut Street; tel: 614-1585; www.papersource.com; Mon–Fri 10am–7pm, Sat 10am–6pm, Sun 11am–5pm; bus: 22, 28, 30, 43; map p.133 E3

Handmade papers, leather goods, bookbinding tools, and other superb selections. Also at 1925 Fillmore Street (tel: 409-7710).

HOMEWARES

Alabaster

597 Hayes Street; tel: 558-0482; www.alabastersf.com; Tue–Sat 11am–6pm, Sun noon–5pm; BART: to Civic Center; metro: F, J, K, L, M, N, T to Civic Center; bus: 5, 21, 47, 49; map p.138 A3

Creamy alabaster lamps, silk lanterns, shadow-boxed bright blue butterflies, vintage opera glasses, and other elegant home ornaments.

Cookin': Recycled Gourmet Appurtenances

339 Divisadero Street; tel: 861-1854; Tue–Sat noon–6.30, Sun 1–5pm; bus: 6, 7, 24, 71; map p.137 E3

Precariously-piled old cookware treasures.

The Gardener

1 Ferry Building; tel: 981-8181; www.thegardener.com; Mon–Fri 10am–6pm; Sat 8am–6pm, Sun 10am–5pm; BART: to Embarcadero; metro: F, J, K, L, M, N, T to Embarcadero; bus: 1, 7, 12, 41; map p.135 E2

The place to find gardening gloves, rosewood bowls, and other charmingly rustic home tools and accessories.

Nest

2300 Fillmore Street; tel: 292-6199; Mon–Sat 10.30am–6.30pm, Sun 11am–6pm; bus: 1, 3, 22, 24; map p.137 E3

Whimsical, Parisian-flavored bedspreads, baubles, and other shabby-chic home goods.

Below: Asian design from Gump's (left) and Chinatown (right).

TOYS AND TREASURES

Chinatown Kite Shop

717 Grant Avenue; tel: 989-5182; www.chinatownkite.com; bus: 1, 9X, 30, 45; cable car: California, Powell-Hyde, Powell-Mason; map p.135 C2

Parafoils, windwheels and a rainbow of kite kinds – from appliqués and airplanes to deltas and dragon – send spirits soaring.

Kidrobot

1512 Haight Street; tel: 864-0818; www.kidrobot.com; Daily 11am–7pm; bus 6, 33, 37, 71; map p.137 D2

Limited edition urban art toys, from plastic to plush to vinyl.

Paxton Gate

824 Valencia Street; tel: 824-1872; www.paxton-gate.com; Mon–Fri noon–7pm, Sat–Sun 11am–7pm; bus: 14, 26, 33, 49; map p.138 B1

Unconventional collection of items inspired by the garden and natural sciences, including tools, taxidermy, and tea.

PlanetWeavers Treasure Store

518A Castro Street; tel: 575-0240; www.planetweavers.com; Sun–Thur 10am–9.30pm, Fri–Sat 10am–10.30pm; metro: F, K, L, M, T to Castro; bus: 24, 33, 35, 37; map p.137 E1

New-age hodgepodge of aromatherapy, yoga books, and Buddha statues.

OTHER

Flight 001

525 Hayes Street; tel: 487-1001; www.flight001.com; Mon–Sat 11am–7pm, Sun 11am–6pm; bus: 6, 7, 47, 49; map p.138 A3

Zestfully-colored silk eye-masks, mod clocks, sleek bags, passport holders, and other cool jet-setting gear.

Sport

San Francisco teems with wide-ranging athletic opportunities, from hang-gliding to hiking, and from bicycling to boating. Runners, joggers, and walkers are especially plentiful, patrolling flat stretches like the Golden Gate Promenade and ambitiously climbing terrifically steep hills. Only swimming can be problematic: beaches present stunning vistas, but also host treacherous tides, cold water, and frequent fog. The mild climate encourages athletes to keep moving year round, but spectators also have many choices in rooting for professional sports teams, both in San Francisco and across the Bay.

Participant Sports

The Recreation and Park Department (tel: 831-2700; www.parks.sfgov.org) oversees over 200 parks, playgrounds, and open spaces, including a vast array of free facilities. Also, consider a trip north: Napa and Sonoma counties offer horseback riding, and whale-watching is popular in Monterey and Mendocino.

BOATING/WATER SPORTS

As far as water sports go in the Bay Area, pretty much whatever floats your boat is possible. Know that the Bay's currents and winds challenge even experienced sailors.

Kite Wind Surf
tel: 877-521-9463
Equipment rentals and lessons are available for sailboats and power boats, and windsurfing novices can take lessons.

Blue and Gold fleet
Tel: 773-1188; www.blueandgoldfleet.com

The Ruby
Tel: 861-2165

Hornblower Dining Cruises and Events
Tel: 788-8866; www.hornblower.com

Above: windsurfing in the Bay.

These charter firms supply bay boating, including trips to Alcatraz and Angel Island.

CYCLING

Cycling is a popular way to explore the city. Try pedaling through Golden Gate Park to the Great Highway, or from the southern part of the city to the Golden Gate Bridge. For rentals look alongside the park and at Fisherman's Wharf. For rules of the road, city bike lanes, maps and routes, see http://bicycling.511.org or www.sfbike.org (the latter also outlines how avoid the steepest hills).

SEE ALSO TRANSPORTATION, P.122

FISHING

Sport-fishing charter boats set out from Fisherman's Wharf (www.sfsportfishing.com). If seasickness is a problem, consider casting a line from Municipal Pier in Aquatic Park.

Miss Farallones
tel: 346-2399
One of the most popular fishing trips.

Lake Merced Boating and Fishing Company
1 Harding Road; tel: 753-1101
Freshwater trout fishing is found south of the city. This company supplies boats, licenses, bait, and tackle.

GOLF

San Francisco boasts beautiful municipal golf courses. Reservations recommended.

68 Lincoln Park
34th Avenue and Clement Street; tel: 221-9911; www.playlincoln.com; bus: 1, 2, 18, 38
An 18-hole, 5,149yd beauty.

Presidio Golf Course
300 Finley Road; tel: 561-4653; www.presidiogolf.com; bus: 1, 2, 3, 4, 33; map p.132 B1
Historic, scenic spot to tee up.

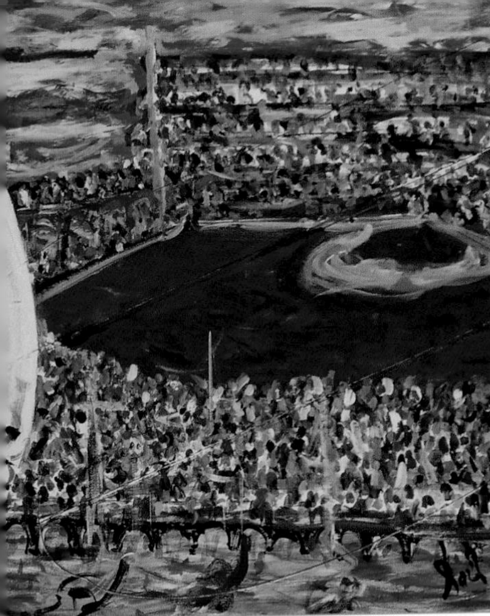

Left: passion takes on mural form at AT&T Ballpark.

Skates on Haight
1818 Haight Street; tel: 752-8376

Friday Night Skate (Midnight Rollers)
Bryant Street and Embarcadero; www.sfskaters.org; 9pm
Hundreds of social skaters gather for a 12.5 mile course.

Spectator sports

Check the websites for game schedules and ticket availability; note that tickets can be hard to snag for the Giants' and '49ers' games.

BASEBALL

The San Francisco Giants
AT&T Ballpark, 24 Willie Mays Plaza; www.sfgiants.com; metro: J, T to 2nd and King; bus: 10, 30, 45, 47; map p.139 E3
The city's beloved local team take the field at a new stadium with an old-time feel and breathtaking views.

Oakland A's
McAfee Coliseum, 7000 Coliseum Way, Oakland; http://oakland.athletics.mlb.com; BART: Coliseum
Oakland's premier team.

BASKETBALL

The Golden State Warriors
Oracle Arena, 7000 Coliseum Way, Oakland; tel: 888-479-4667; www.nba.com/warriors; BART: Coliseum
This complex is home to the NBA's local great hopes.

FOOTBALL

'49ers
Monster Park, 602 Jamestown Avenue; tel: 656-4900; www.sf49ers.com; bus: 9X, 28X, 47X
From August to December, the home team play here.

Oakland Raiders
McAfee Coliseum, 7000 Coliseum Way, Oakland; tel: 800-724-3377; www.raiders.com; BART: Coliseum
A better bet for tickets.

> With its penchant for holistic living, it is no surprise that San Francisco overflows with yoga schools of all kinds. With five locations, **Yoga Tree** (www.yogatreesf.com) is a common choice, offering classes in many styles, plus workshops and retreats.

HANG GLIDING

Consistently good coastal winds delight hang-gliders. Computerized, up-to-the-minute wind info for Fort Funston is available (tel: 333-0100).

The San Francisco Hang Gliding Center
Tel: 510-528-2300; www.sfhanggliding.com
Specializes in tandem hang-gliding, launching from Marin's Mt Tamalpais.

HIKING

To the North, Mt Tamalpais provides beautiful hiking trails. Within city limits, the challenging Coastal Trail from Fort Point to the Cliff House affords spectacular views (but make sure you avoid the unstable cliffs).
SEE ALSO WALKS AND VIEWS, P.124–9

JOGGING

The annual Bay to Breakers Run (www.baytobreakers.com) in May attracts outrageously-costumed joggers; the San Francisco Marathon (www.runsfm.com) draws serious runners. Trails wrap through Golden Gate Park, Marina Green, and Crissy Field.

INLINE SKATING

The vehicle-free roads of Golden Gate Park on Sundays are very skate-friendly, as are flat Marina and Embarcadero stretches. Rent skates at:

Golden Gate Park Skate and Bike
3038 Fulton Street; tel: 668-1117

Below: jogging in the Presidio.

Theater and Cabaret

San Franciscans have a brilliant spectrum of theatrical flavors to enjoy. Performances range from classical to contemporary, traditional to cutting-edge, and just about everything in between. Major commercial theaters stage Broadway hits, while non-profit theaters push new pieces and playwrights. The theater district's heartbeat thumps most vigorously on Geary Boulevard, just west of Union Square, but stages are sprinkled about other districts as well, and avid theater-goers fill neighborhoods all over town.

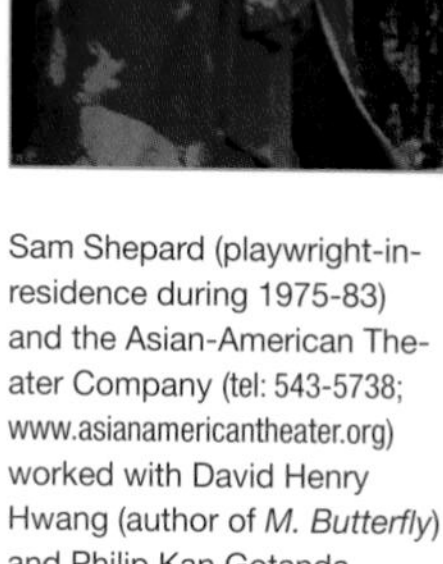

Theater Information

For the city's current theatrical menu, peruse the pink-colored Sunday 'Datebook' section of the *San Francisco Chronicle*, or free alternative weeklies including the *SF Weekly* or *Bay Guardian*, found in cafés, bookstores, and newspaper boxes. Their websites (www.sfgate.com/eguide, www.sfweekly.com, and www.sfbg.com) and online city guides such as www.sfstation.com are also useful.

Where to Buy Tickets

TIX Bay Area
Union Square; tel: 433-7827; www.tixbayarea.com; Tue–Thur 11am–6pm, Fri 11am–7pm, Sat 10am–7pm, Sun 10am–3pm; BART: to Powell; metro: F, J, K, L, M, N, T to Powell; bus: 5, 9, 21, 30, 76; map p.134 C1
Sells half-price performance-day tickets beginning at 11am.

THIRD-PARTY TICKET AGENTS
These agencies will add a booking fee.

Tickets.com
Tel: 800-955-5566; www.tickets.com

Ticketmaster
Tel: 512-7770; www.ticketmaster.com

Tickco.com
Tel: 800-279-4444; www.tickco.com

City Box Office
Tel: 392-4400; www.cityboxoffice.com

Free **Shakespeare in the Park** (tel: 800-988-7529; www.sfshakes.org) spotlights the Bard each summer, and the San Francisco Fringe Festival (www.sffringe.org) serves up untraditional and uncensored fare come fall.

History

San Francisco's early theater tradition started with a proliferation of melodeons (theater-bar-music halls) but more 'serious' theater picked up at the turn of the 20th century. In 1967, the American Conservatory Theater, led by Bill Ball, had its San Francisco premiere, soon becoming a nationally-reputed regional theater. The Magic Theater has premiered early works by major playwrights such as Sam Shepard (playwright-in-residence during 1975-83) and the Asian-American Theater Company (tel: 543-5738; www.asianamericantheater.org) worked with David Henry Hwang (author of *M. Butterfly*) and Philip Kan Gotanda.

Major Theaters

American Conservatory Theater
415 Geary Boulevard; tel: 749-2228; www.act-sf.org; Tue–Fri 8pm, Sat–Sun 2pm and 8pm; bus: 2, 4, 9, 27, 38; cable car: Powell-Hyde, Powell-Mason; map p.136 B4
A highly-reputable, Tony Award-winning regional theater that consistently delivers solid classical and contemporary fare.

Berkeley Repertory Theatre
2025 Addison Street, Berkeley; tel: 510-647-2900, 510-647-2949; www.berkeleyrep.org; Tue 8pm, Wed 7pm, Thur–Sat 8pm (some Thur and Sat 2pm), Sun 2pm and 7pm; BART: Downtown Berkeley
A renowned Berkeley theater that delivers an adventurous, diverse program.

Left: San Francisco is a popular launchpad for big plays.

Silent spectacle is not the goal of the Tony Award-winning **San Francisco Mime Troupe** (tel: 285-1717; www.sfmt.org; July–Sept; free). Instead, they use 'mime' in the ancient sense of mimic and mockery, offering satirical, very left-wing performances in San Francisco and other Bay Area parks.

Curran Theater
445 Geary Boulevard; tel: 551-2000; www.shnsf.com; show times vary; BART: to Powell; metro: F, J, K, L, M, N, T to Powell; bus: 3, 27, 38, 76; cable car: Powell-Hyde, Powell-Mason; map p.136 B4
An elegant, historic theater staging Broadway tryouts and favorites including *Wicked* and *Jersey Boys*.

Magic Theatre
204 Bay Street; tel: 441-8822; www.magictheatre.org; show times vary; bus: 10, 22, 28, 30; map p.134 C4
A dedication to new works makes for an impressive list of plays premiered here.

Orpheum Theatre
1192 Market Street; tel: 551-2000; www.shnsf.com; show times vary; BART: to Powell; metro: F, J, K, L, M, N, T to Powell; bus: 3, 27, 38; cable car: Powell-Hyde, Powell-Mason; map p.138 B3
A grand San Francisco Historical Landmark presents large-scale Broadway productions.

Fringe Theaters

New, quirky and experimental works can be found here:

Exit Theatre
tel: 673-3847; www.sffringe.org

Intersection for the Arts
tel: 626-2787; www.theintersection.org

The Marsh
tel: 800-838-3006; www.themarsh.org

Below: Beach Blanket Babylon.

New Conservatory Theatre Center
tel: 861-8972; www.nctcsf.org

Project Artaud Theatre
tel: 626-4370, 392-4400; www.artaud.org

Cabaret

Asia SF
201 9th Street; tel: 255-2742; www.asiasf.com; Tue–Wed 6.30–8.30pm, Thur 6–9pm, Fri 7–8.30pm, Sat 5–9.45pm, Sun 6–9pm; BART: to Civic Center; metro: F, J, K, L, M, N, T to Civic Center; bus: 12, 14, 19, 26; map p.138 B3
'Gender illusionists' serve Cal-Asian cuisine and saucy entertainment. Reservations required.

Beach Blanket Babylon
Club Fugazi, 678 Green Street; tel: 421-4222; Wed–Thur 8pm, Fri–Sat 7pm and 10pm; Sun 2pm and 5pm; bus: 12, 15, 30, 45; map p.134 C3
A legendary experience, this is a gloriously campy and continually updated pop-culture spoof. Buy tickets in advance and arrive early. Adults-only except for Sunday matinees.

Empire Plush Room
York Hotel, 940 Sutter Street; tel: 866-468-3399; www.theempireplushroom.com; show times vary; bus: 1, 2, 3, 4, 27; map p.134 B1
Sultry torch singers light up the stage in this plush, former 1920s speakeasy, now serving up quality cabaret.

Teatro ZinZanni
Pier 29; tel: 438-2668; http://love.zinzanni.org; Jan–Nov: Wed–Sat 6.55pm, Sun 5.55pm; Dec: Tue–Sat 6.55pm, Sun 5.55pm; metro: F to Embarcadero and Sansome St; bus: 10; map p.135 D4
Cabaret, cirque, and spectacle make for over-the-top diversion, delivered over a fine, five-course dinner.

Transportation

A major hub for flights from all over the world, San Francisco is easily reached by air, while visitors from other parts of the United States can opt to travel by rail or bus. Once here, the city and its outlying areas are comfortably navigable by public transportation. In San Francisco, a car is not generally necessary to see the sights, and can prove to be something of a hassle, especially when you can get such great views while riding a cable car to the tops of the city's hills. Efficient, affordable and comprehensive, San Francisco's public transportation network makes it easy to be green.

Getting to San Francisco

BY AIR

San Francisco International Airport (SFO)
1 McDonnell Road, San Francisco; tel: 650-821-8211; www.flysfo.com
SFO is the major international airport for northern California. From Europe, all the major airlines offer non-stop flights or connections via New York, Chicago, or Los Angeles. It also receives non-stop, or one-stop, flights from all the principal Pacific airports. For foreign travelers, many of the US airlines offer deals for visiting several American cities.

Despite being 13 miles away, downtown San Francisco is easy to get to. Taxis and shuttles line the inner circle of the transportation zones of the Arrivals/Baggage Claim Level, while BART (Bay Area Rapid Transit), located at the Departures/Ticketing Level at the International Terminal and accessible from the Domestic Terminal by the Airtrain, takes passengers to downtown San Francisco and across the bay to various cities, for minimal cost. SFO is blanketed by Wi-Fi and can be used for a fee.

Everyday, airplanes dump 90 million pounds of carbon-dioxide and other noxious greenhouse gasses into the atmosphere. To 'offset' this big carbon footprint, travelers can purchase carbon credits that, based on the distance traveled, invest money into renewable energy and energy efficiency programs. For more information visit www.sustainabletravelinternational.org, or www.climatecare.org/responsibletravel.

Oakland International Airport (OAK)
1 Airport Drive, Oakland; tel: 510-563-3300; www.flyoakland.com
The Oakland airport is located 4 miles south of the city's downtown, and is accessible by BART. A hub for low-cost carriers, OAK is a more economical alternative to the bigger and busier SFO.

San Jose International Airport (SJC)
1732 North 1st Street, San Jose; tel: 408-501-7600; www.sjc.org
The smallest of the three airports, Mineta San Jose International Airport is nearly 50 miles from downtown San Francisco.

BY TRAIN

Amtrak
Emeryville depot, 5885 Horton Street, Emeryville; information line: 800-USA-RAIL; www.amtrak.com; tel: 510-450-1087
While Amtrak, the cross-continental passenger rail line, does not connect directly to San Francisco, it has a free shuttle to deliver passengers to and from the depot in Emeryville, located in the East Bay. For longer trips, Amtrak can be frustrating as passenger trains share the rail lines with, and must defer to, the freight lines, causing significant delays. Nonetheless, it still remains a green alternative to air travel and some routes are quite picturesque.

BY BUS

Greyhound
San Francisco Transbay Terminal, 425 Mission Street; information line: 800-231-2222;

Left: San Francisco's most iconic mode of transportation.

For help navigating the entire Bay Area public transit system, including Muni buses and metro streetcars, and BART, call 511, or look online at **www.511.org**. 511 offers assistance with planning trips using public transportation, traffic and drive time information, tips for traveling with bikes, and links to various municipal transit agencies.

www.greyhound.com; tel: 495-1555; map p.135 D1
Downtown, just east of Market Street, the Transbay Terminal is a major hub for the transcontinental Greyhound bus service.

Green Tortoise
Hostel and headquarters, 494 Broadway; information line: 800-TORTOISE; www.greentortoise.com; tel: 956-7500; map p.135 C2
The Green Tortoise is a great alternative to Greyhound or even Amtrak. Each trip makes frequent stops at National Parks of other points of interest and their buses have communal areas that convert to reclined sleeping quarters at night. The San Francisco headquarters is also the site of the Green Tortoise hostel.

BY CAR
Despite congestion, hills, and the problem of what to do with your vehicle upon arriving, San Francisco is easy to reach by car. Interstates 101 and 80 pass through the city, while Interstates 5 and 99 are not too far away in the Central Valley. State Highway 1 runs along the coast of California and the western part of San Francisco.

Getting Around San Francisco

MUNI
Buses and Metro
Muni, the San Francisco Municipal Transit Agency, encompasses the city's diesel and electric buses, streetcars which run on lightrail lines underground through downtown, the historic F-line streetcars (comprising a collection of vintage trams from all over the world), and of course, the cable cars.

Purchasing a map is highly recommended and will make a stay in San Francisco infinitely simpler. They are $3 and available at the Muni kiosks at the Powell and Market and Powell and Beach Cable Car terminals, and in most stores where general maps are sold. They are also posted at many Muni metro and bus stops.

For all Muni metro and bus lines, adult fare is $1.50. Exact change is necessary, but transfer slips are given, allowing you to transfer twice to different Muni metro or bus lines within a 90-minute time frame. 1, 3, or 7-day visitor passports provide unlimited rides on Muni-operated transport, including the cable

Below: the sleek BART system in action.

cars. They are available at baggage claim at San Francisco International Airport, and on the mezzanine level of the Montgomery Muni metro station, as well as at the major cable car terminals, and the kiosk at Bay and Taylor streets. For route planning and general information, see www.sfmta.com.

Cable Cars

Cable Cars are also operated by Muni, but are the exception to most of the Muni rules. Fares can be purchased at the kiosk at each terminal, or when you board. Drivers do give exact change, but no transfers. They are also considerably more expensive at $5 per trip. Often crowded with tourists, they ride over San Francisco's famous hills.

Above: ferries from the Hyde Street Pier are a great way to see more of the Bay Area.

BART (BAY AREA RAPID TRANSIT)

www.bart.gov

Fast, quiet, and efficient, BART allows passengers to get around the Bay Area in comfort. All BART lines travel through San Francisco, extending to San Francisco International Airport, and under the bay to Oakland, Berkeley, and beyond.

Its stations provide maps that clearly explain routes and fares, and nearby ticketing machines allow passengers to purchase tickets. For buying a ticket without exact change, passengers may carry a balance on their ticket for future use, or utilize one of the change machines also located in the stations.

Four BART lines run through downtown and provide the quickest way to reach the Mission district, or Oakland and Berkeley.

> Taking a cable car ride is one of the classic San Francisco experiences. However, waits to board at the cable car turnaround at Fifth and Mission can be long. A better bet for speed and a seat may be to board the California line at Van Ness or the Ferry Building; the hills are steeper, so the views on this route of Nob Hill, Chinatown and the Financial District are extra-spectacular.

TAXIS

Taxis are a great, though expensive, way to get about when the majority of San Francisco's public transit shuts down, around 12.30am. They hover around popular tourist or nightlife spots, but in out-of-the-way locations it is advisable to call a radio-dispatched taxi.

Green Cab
Tel: 626-GREEN

Yellow Cab
Tel: 333-3333

DeSoto Cab Company
Tel: 970-1300

Luxor Cab Company
Tel: 828-4141

CYCLING

Around San Francisco, there are plenty of places to ride that are reasonably flat and far from exhaust fumes. Cycling through Golden Gate Park is a favorite, especially on Sundays, when many of the roads are automobile-free. Riding along the Golden Gate Promenade and crossing Golden Gate Bridge is a stunning ride, although difficult if the wind is up. In Sausalito, visitors can catch the ferry back to San Francisco. Bikes can be rented hourly or for the day, with rates varying by type of bike, but it is usually $20–60 per day, and $7–10 per hour.
SEE ALSO SPORT, P.116

Bay City Bike
2661 Taylor Street and 1325

Below: legs of steel are required for riding up the hills.

> The Muni Owl service replaces some lines between 1–5am. For more information, *see also Nightlife, p.95.*

Columbus Avenue; tel: 346-BIKE; www.baycitybike.com; daily from 8am; bus: 10, 30, 47; map p.138 C4 and map p.134 B4

Blazing Saddles
1095 Columbus Avenue, including a number of locations on Fisherman's Wharf; tel: 202-8888; www.blazingsaddles.com; daily from 8am; metro: F to Fisherman's Wharf; bus: 10, 19, 30; map p.134 B3

Golden Gate Bike and Skate
3038 Fulton Street; tel: 668-1117; Mon–Tue 10am–6pm, Fri 10am–6pm, Sat–Sun 10am–7pm; bus: 5, 21, 31, 33; map p.136 B3

WALKING

The best way to see San Francisco is by walking. Only 7 square miles, it is easy to cover great distances while seeing many different neighborhoods and glimpsing how residents live. Walking the hills provides spectacular views of the city and the rest of the Bay Area. Bring a map, comfortable shoes, and an extra layer of clothing in case the famous San Francisco fog rolls in. Always be alert while crossing intersections. Taxis can be particularly aggressive.

DRIVING

San Francisco is a difficult city to drive and park in, often taxing the most experienced local drivers. It is crisscrossed with one-way streets, and the fast paced driving culture can easily unnerve any visitor. If it is necessary to rent a car, all the major car rental companies have outlets at San Francisco International Airport and around the city.

Avis Rental Car
821 Howard Street; tel: 957-9998 or 800-822-3131; www.avis.com; map p.139 C4

Enterprise
350 Beach Street; tel: 474-9600 or 800-261-7331; www.enterprise.com; map p.134 B4

Hertz Rent A Car
433 Mason Street; tel: 771-2200 or 800-654-3131; www.hertz.com; map p.134 C1

Getting Around the Bay Area

FERRIES

Many locals use ferries to get to and from work, but for visitors, they provide a great scenic and environmental alternative to driving. Departing from Fisherman's Wharf or the Ferry Building, they travel to Angel Island, and throughout the North and East Bay areas. Tickets can be purchased at the ticket windows next to the ferry terminals.

Blue and Gold Fleet
Pier 39 Marine Terminal, The Embarcadero at Beach Street; tel: 705-8200; www.blueandgoldfleet.com; map p.134 C4

Golden Gate Ferry
Ferry Building, The Embarcadero at Market Street; tel: 455-2000; www.goldengateferry.org; map p.135 E2

CALTRAIN

Main San Francisco depot, 700 4th Street; information line: 800-660-4287; www.caltrain.org; map p.139 D3

Caltrain runs alongside Highway 101 to San Jose, with limited extensions all the way to Gilroy. It is largely a commuter train, but for visitors headed to the Peninsula or the South Bay, it is an enjoyable ride, complete with comfortable seating, an upper deck with tables, and a car to accommodate passengers with bikes. Caltrain's terminus is near the AT&T Ballpark and many San Francisco Muni bus and metro lines, helpful for geting passengers around the city. Every Caltrain stop has an electronic ticket machine at which passengers can purchase tickets.

INTERCITY BUSES

Neighboring transit systems also connect San Francisco with other Bay Area cities. These buses can be caught at various stops downtown, or at the Transby Terminal, located at 1st and Mission streets.

Golden Gate Transit
Information line: 455-2000; www.goldengate.org

Alameda Contra-Costa County Transit District
Information line: 510-891-4700; www.actransit.org

San Mateo County Transit District
Information line: 510-817-1717; www.samtrans.org

Below: Muni buses remain one of the most picturesque and efficient ways of getting around town.

Walks and Views

While strenuous, San Francisco is a pedestrian's paradise. Its many peaks offer sweeping vistas of the city, its parklands make walkers feel like hikers, and its condensed topography makes it easy to jump from one neighborhood to the next. There are hiking trails, strolls through residential areas, and even guided walking tours where knowledgeable locals offer insight into the depths of Chinatown, the highs of Haight-Ashbury, and the city's Victorian past. Below are a few suggestions to get the most out of your footwear, and a few places to find inspirational views without the perspiration.

Bird's Eye Views

Carnelian Room at the Bank of America Building
555 California Street, 52nd floor; tel: 433-7500; www.carnelianroom.com; daily 3–9.30pm; bus: 3, 4, 9X, 30, 45; cable car: California Street; map p.135 C2
For the price of a cocktail, albeit an expensive one, guests can get a bird's eye view of San Francisco from the top floor of its tallest building. The view lounge opens at 3pm, and dinner is available after 6pm.

Coit Tower
1 Telegraph Hill Boulevard; tel: 362-0808; daily 10am–5pm; entrance fee for the elevator; bus: 39; map p.135 C3
The crown of the landmark Coit Tower adds another 210ft to the 275ft Telegraph Hill, making it a pinnacle of the northern part of the city. Views extend all the way to the Golden Gate, North Bay, and Mount Diablo, and to the south, downtown and Mount Sutro.

Tower at M.H. de Young Memorial Museum
50 Hagiwara Tea Garden Drive; tel: 750-3600; www.deyoungmuseum.org; Tue–Thur 9.30am–5.15pm, Fri 9.30am–8.45pm, Sat–Sun 9.30am–5.15pm; entrance charge, under 13 free, 1st Tue of month free; metro: N to Irving Street and 9th Avenue; bus: 5, 21, 44; map p.136 B2
From the top of the de Young's twisting 144 ft copper tower, the amazing panorama of San Francisco's cityscape is a work of art. The 360 degrees of floor to ceiling windows reveal with postcard-like clarity the city's central highs and lows, its range of greenery and architectural styles, and the distant landmarks that make the skyline famous.
SEE ALSO MUSEUMS AND GALLERIES, P.83

Below: the striking tower at the de Young Museum offers spectacular views.

Into the Wild

While remaining a tight urban metropolis, San Francisco

Left: the Coit Tower and the tip of the Transamerica Pyramid stand out dramatically in North Beach's skyline.

Lover's Lane is the oldest foot trail in the Presidio. As early as 1776, soldiers began walking the 3-mile trail to Mission Dolores, the only other Spanish settlement on the San Francisco peninsula.

has managed to keep part of itself a little wild. Hiking boots can indeed be necessary within city limits, what with the bare hills in the south and the vast Presidio covering the north-west coast. Unusually for a metropolitan center, San Francisco offers the opportunity to get some mud on your feet while admiring its breathtaking skyline.

For all hikes, be sure to wear layers, including a windbreaker if available. Comfortable shoes with good, sturdy traction are a must. Throughout the various parks, paved trails frequently give way to rough terrain demanding attention and surefootedness.

San Francisco is known for its wildlife, including rare bird species. Coyotes have also been seen in Golden Gate Park and the Presidio. If one is sighted, give it enough space and do not try to approach it. They are not known to bother humans and will usually run away once spotted.

GOLDEN GATE PARK

Strawberry Hill

Start: Stow Lake Road; metro: N to Irving Street and 9th Avenue; bus: 5, 21, 33, 44; **map p.136 A2**

Crossing Stow Lake are two stone bridges off Stow Lake Drive, making it is easy to access this island peak. It is a leisurely walk on a network of unpaved paths to the top of Golden Gate Park's highest hill. The elegant Chinese pavilion and beautiful waterfall may provide easy distractions, as do the early morning congregation of waterfowl on the lake. The wooded summit of Strawberry Hill overlooks the Japanese Tea Gardens and Stow Lake, and on clear days, is blessed with views of the Golden Gate Bridge and Mount Diablo.

AROUND SAN FRANCISCO

Mt Davidson Park

Start: Dalewood Way and Myra Way; daily 6am–10pm; bus: 36

Covered in eucalyptus and anointed with a 103 ft cross commemorating the Armenian Genocide, Mt Davidson is San Francisco's highest peak. Fortunately, it is not necessary to climb its entire 927 ft to reach the top. From the park entrance, it is an easy, moderate walk to the summit, less than a half mile. The south-eastern side is bare and has commanding views of the Financial District, Hunter's Point, and San Bruno Mountain. The western side, thick in foliage, descends to the foggy Sunset District and the Pacific Ocean. The park's 40 acres are criss-crossed with walking trails.

Twin Peaks

Start: Twin Peaks Boulevard and Crestline Drive; bus: 37

The Crestline stop on the 37 bus brings passengers to the trailhead between the peaks.

Below: admiring the view of Ocean Beach.

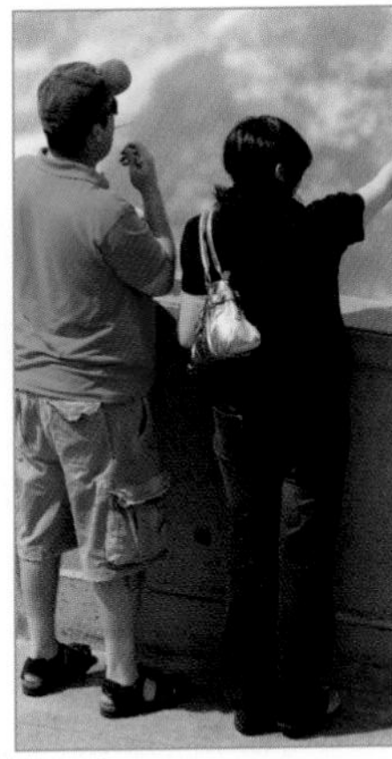

Above: the coast around San Francisco is an area of great natural beauty.

From here, hikers can walk the rocky ridgeline north or south, and summit each peak. Celebrated as the best panoramic view of the city, it is also home to redtail hawks, cottontail rabbits, and the endangered Mission Blue Butterfly. A guided map of the park can be downloaded from: www.parks.sfgov.org.

The Presidio: Ecology Trail-Lovers' Lane
Start: Presidio Boulevard Gate at Pacific Avenue; bus: 43, 3; map p.133 D1
End: Arguello Boulevard Gate; bus: 1, 4, 33; map p.132 C1
The Presidio's nearly 1,500 acres is as diverse at it gets in any urban park. With views of the Golden Gate Bridge and San Francisco Bay, and historic buildings, woods, grasslands, and coastal walks, complete with old gun batteries from the turn of the 20th century, it is easy to spend an entire day here. The 1.8 mile Ecology Trail-Lover's Lane is a good start, however.

From the Presidio Gate, head straight down Lovers' Lane, which runs parallel to Presidio Boulevard into the residential Tennessee Hollow. Continue on, crossing Liggett and MacArthur streets and eventually making a left on Presidio Boulevard. Make another left on Funston Avenue, and continue, passing Officers' Row. After crossing Moraga Avenue, the Ecology Trail begins.

On the trail, head straight up the hill, but keep right when it intersects with other unmarked trails. Here it begins to pass through groves of cypress trees and fields of native plants. To the left will be a large trail leading to Inspiration Point, a popular lookout. Going straight, the Ecology Trail will continue and terminate at the Arguello Boulevard Gate. For more details, and a map of the Presidio with its other hiking trails, visit www.bahiker.com/sfhikes/inspoint.html.

Land's End Trail
Start: Merrie Way and Point Lobos Avenue; bus: 38, 18
End: El Camino del Mar and 32nd Avenue; bus: 1, 18, 2
Many consider Land's End to be the wildest part of San Francisco. At the far end of the Merrie Way parking lot, the trail begins under a canopy of cypress trees and quickly rises high above the sharp cliffs plunging into the Pacific Ocean. Keep an eye out for the remnants of shipwrecks on the rocks below.

The trail is an easy 3½ mile round trip, with spectacular views of the Marin Headlands and the Golden Gate Bridge. It also passes the **Palace of the Legion of Honor** and ends in the fashionable Lincoln Heights neighborhood.
SEE ALSO MUSEUMS AND GALLERIES, P.83–5

Neighborhood Walks

MARINA DISTRICT–THE PRESIDIO

Golden Gate Promenade
Start: Aquatic Park at Van Ness Avenue and Beach Street; bus: 30, 47, 49; map p.134 A4
End: Fort Point; bus: 28; map p.132 A4
Beginning at the 1930s Aquatic Park, the Golden Gate Promenade follows the edge of the city to Fort Point, under the Golden Gate Bridge. Begin by heading west away from Fisherman's Wharf. Soon the wide cement walkway rises to the top of

When the city converted its many cemeteries into parks, workers were ordered to use the unclaimed headstones for the new trails and gutters. Out of respect for the dead, many decided to leave the pieces facing up, where they can still be seen today in Buena Vista Park.

A great resource for those interested in checking out San Francisco hikes is: www.bahikes.com

Fort Mason and offers views of the Marina District and the Golden Gate Bridge. Continue on the path down to Laguna Street, and stay to the right. Follow the sidewalk as the street turns and becomes Marina Boulevard. From here, it passes through the Marina Green, alongside the Saint Francis Yacht Club, and into the newly restored Crissy Field.

You can either stay to the left, or cut through the orderly row of cypress trees to the water. The nearby Crissy Field Center and Warming Hut Café, located at the end of the promenade, offer coffee and other delicious rewards. Early morning at the lagoon is a great time for bird watching.

RUSSIAN HILL

Hyde Street and Macondray Lane

Start: Lombard and Hyde streets; bus: 41, 45, 30; cable car: Hyde-Powell; map p.134 B3
End: Taylor and Union streets; bus: 41, 45, 30; cable car: Hyde-Powell; map p.134 B3

At the crest of the curviest street in the world, head south on Hyde Street. Across the street is George Sterling Park, which offers tennis and great views of the Golden Gate Bridge and Marina District. Continue down the leafy Hyde Street until Green Street. Turn left, which will be a bit of a climb, but lasts only one block. At Jones Street turn left again, and continue for half a block. On the right, the lush Macondray Lane, looks like a private walkway with an imposing 'Private Property' sign. Do not worry, it is there to discourage illegal parking.

Turn right down the pedestrian alleyway, and continue down the narrow path and rickety stairs to Taylor Street. Turn left and continue to Union Street. If wishing to go on to North Beach, head down the hill for two more blocks.

TELEGRAPH HILL

Filbert and Greenwich Steps

Start: Coit Tower; bus: 39; map p.135 C3
End: Sansome Street; bus: 10; map p.134 B3

Through gardens and quaint stairways, this steep descent down to the waterfront is one the most picturesque walks in the city. Both steps begin at the south-east corner of the Coit Tower lookout and parking lot. For the Filbert Steps, turn right down the paved path that runs next to and slightly below Telegraph Hill Boulevard. Where the road bends to the right at Filbert Street, a street in name only, turn left down the steps. Cross Montgomery Street, and descend the staircase on the other side. Beginning on either side of a row of parking spaces are the Filbert Steps. Continue down to Sansome Street at the bottom of the hill.

For the Greenwich Steps, descend the narrow brick steps beginning at the southeast corner of Coit Tower parking lot. It will end at the cul-de-sac at Montgomery Street. Take the lower road to the left-hand side. After about 200yds, there is a wide walkway angling down on the left. This will become the Greenwich Steps, which is largely a long cement walkway until it sharply descends to Sansome Street.

Below: (from top) ascending the Filbert steps; 'Victorians' in North Beach and the Haight.

Above: Mission Dolores Park is a great place to finish a walk.

HAIGHT ASHBURY–CASTRO DISTRICT
Buena Vista Park and Castro Street
Start: Haight Street and Central Avenue; bus: 6, 43, 66, 71; map p.137 D2
End: Castro and Market Streets; bus: 24, 33, 37; map p.137 E1
In addition to great city views and the lush beauty of Buena Vista Park, this walk also journeys past grand and beautifully restored Victorians, including the Spreckels Mansion, built in 1897. Beginning at the foot of Buena Vista Park, head up the steep sidewalk clinging to the edge of the park. This is Buena Vista Avenue West, which soon becomes Buena Vista Avenue East when it, and the park, turn sharply to the north-east.

At this point, a path into the park leads to a breathtaking view of downtown. Continue circling the park on Buena Vista Avenue East until Buena Vista Terrace. Turn right. At 14th Street turn left. Continue until Castro Street and turn right. Here Castro descends toward Market Street, where the rainbow-flagged neighborhood begins.

THE MISSION DISTRICT
Around Mission Dolores Park
Start: Market and Dolores streets; bus: 22, 37; metro: F, K, J, L, M, N, T to Church; map p.138 A2
End: Mission and 18th streets; bus: 22, 33, 49, 53; BART: to 16th Street; map p.138 B1
Beginning at the base of the California Volunteers' Monument and across from the US Mint, follow the wide palm tree-lined Dolores Street. At 16th Street, the historic **Mission Dolores** sits next to the ornate Basilica. Both are open for visitors; a small donation is requested. Continue on until 18th Street. Here Dolores Park begins, sloping up to the beautiful Liberty Heights district with spectacular views of the city. At 18th Street, turn right. After a block or so, the Mission begins in earnest. Continue until Mission Street, where stores, bars, cafés, and restaurants lure in any visitor.
SEE ALSO CHURCHES, P.45

THE WESTERN ADDITION
Lower Haight–Alamo Square
Start: Haight and Pierce streets; bus: 6, 7, 66, 71; map p.137 E2
End: Fulton and Divisadero streets; bus: 5, 16, 24; map p.137 E3
Surrounded by large 1920s era apartment buildings, sprawling Queen Anne's, ornate single home Victorians (notably the 'Painted Ladies' on the eastern side), and high enough to capture the splendor of City Hall, Alamo Square is the crown jewel of the Western Addition and Lower Haight districts. To get there, follow Pierce Street north, up the hill. It is a steep climb, but worth the exertion.

After crossing Fell and Oak streets, Pierce narrows, eventually colliding with Alamo Square. Cross Hayes Street and take the stone steps into the park, keeping to the left. Alamo Square is a favorite neighborhood spot where locals love to unleash their dogs. Take the cement path across the park, and at the corner of Fulton and Scott streets, turn left on Fulton Street, heading away from the dome of City Hall. On the corner of Divisadero and Fulton

Below: colorful murals adorn the Women's Building in the Mission; the Precita Eyes tour takes you all over the district.

Above: evening falls on Russian Hill.

streets sits Café Abir, a wonderful place to grab a relaxed cup of coffee or a beer.

Guided Walks

There are countless walking tours available throughout San Francisco, focusing on different cultural and historical aspects of the city. Most are about 2 hours with prices ranging from $15 to $30.

A free alternative is City Guides, sponsored by the San Francisco Public Library. It offers tours daily on a variety of subjects around the city. For details, visit www.sfcityguides.org.

Barbary Coast Trail
Tel: 454-2355; www.barbarycoasttrail.org
This self-guiding tour travels through San Francisco's bawdy past. Starting at the old Mint near Market and Mission streets, and lead by a series of bronze sidewalk markers, it tours North Beach, Chinatown, and Fisherman's Wharf. Additional books, maps, and audio tours are available.

FOOT! Tours
Tel: 793-5378; www.foottours.com
Laugh your way through San Francisco on the only walking tour lead by comedians. Offering a wide range of tours, the guides are not only funny but experts at San Francisco culture and history.

Precita Eyes Mural Arts
Tel: 285-2287; www.precitaeyes.org
Head to the Visitor Center and Art Store at 2981 24th Street for this distinctive and fascinating tour. Beginning in the lush Balmy Alley between 24th and 25th, the non-profit Precita Eyes Mural Arts tours the colorful and distinctive murals adorning the fences and building faces throughout the Mission. The guided walks, Saturdays and Sundays 11am and 1.30pm, explore the cultural, political, and artistic influences of the city's most accessible public art.

Wok Wiz Walking Tours
Tel: 650-355-9657; www.wokwiz.com
To get a taste of Chinatown, sign up for Shirley Fong-Torres' tour. While including the history and architecture of the area, Fong-Torres' focus is on food. Daily tours include an optional dim sum lunch, so come with an empty stomach.

Victorian Walking Tours
Tel: 252-9485; www.victorianwalk.com
Starting every day at Union Square at 11am, this 2½ hour tour travels Pacific Heights and other grandiose neighborhoods, and includes an inside tour of a Victorian house in the Queen Anne style.

Overgrown and lined in paths of uneven brick and stone, Macondray Lane inspires the romantic in everyone. Armistead Maupin used it as inspiration for his Barbary Lane in *Tales of the City*, a series of books chronicling life in San Francisco from the mid 1970's to the mid 1980's.

Atlas

The following streetplan of greater San Francisco makes it easy to find the attractions listed in our A–Z section. A selective index to streets and sights will help you find other locations throughout the city.

Map Legend

Freeway	Metro
Divided highway	Cable car
Main roads	Bus station
Minor roads	Ferry
Footpath	Tourist information
Railroad	Sight of interest
Pedestrian area	Temple
Notable building	Cathedral / church
Park	Mosque
Hotel	Synagogue
Urban area	Statue / monument
Non urban area	Post Office
Cemetery	Hospital
	Viewpoint

p132	p133	p134	p135
p136	p137	p138	p139

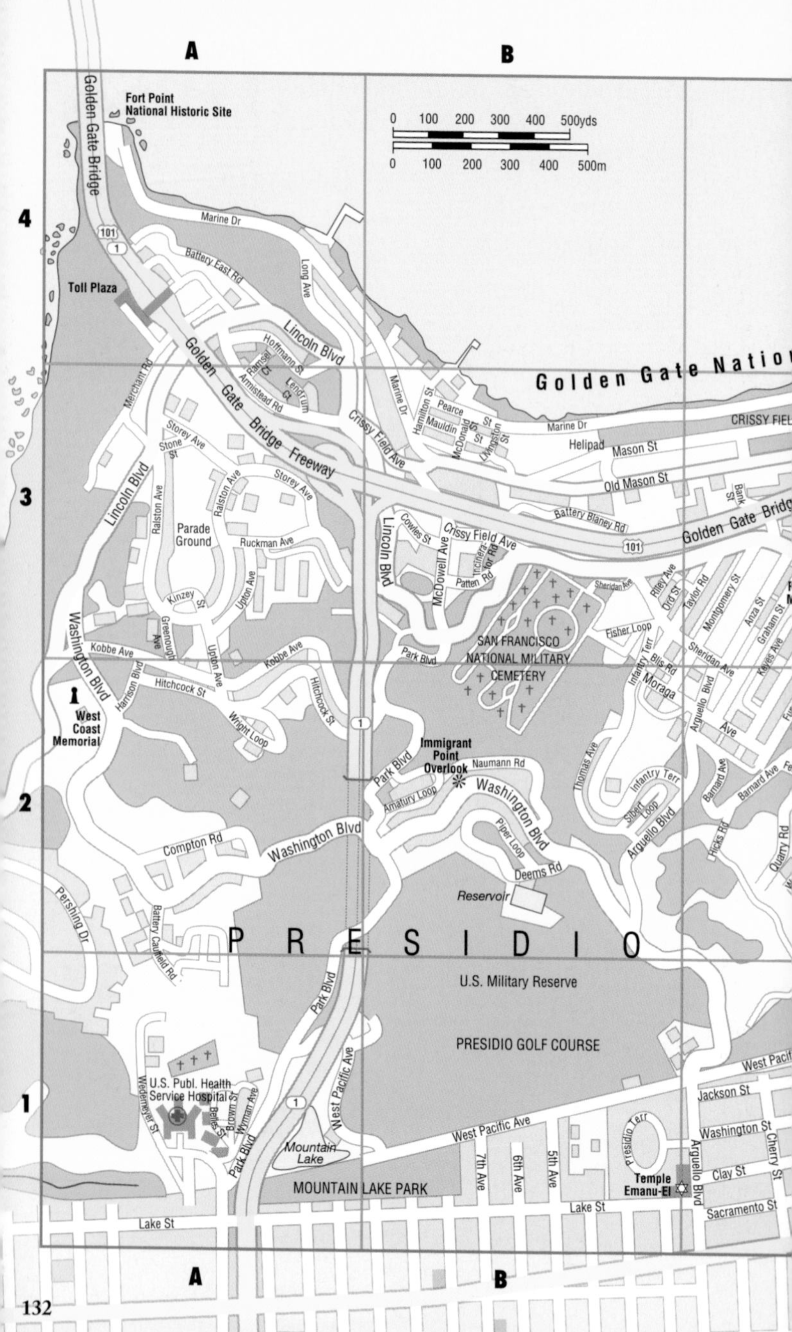
A
B
Fort Point
National Historic Site
Golden Gate Bridge
0 100 200 300 400 500yds
0 100 200 300 400 500m
4
Marine Dr
101
1
Battery East Rd
Long Ave
Toll Plaza
Lincoln Blvd
Hoffmann St
Ramsell Ct
Lendrum Ct
Armistead Rd
Golden Gate Bridge Freeway
Merchant Rd
Marine Dr
Crissy Field Ave
Hamilton St
Pearce St
Mauldin St
McDonald St
Livingston St
Golden Gate National
Marine Dr
CRISSY FIEL
Helipad
Mason St
Old Mason St
Bank St
Storey Ave
Stone St
Ralston Ave
Storey Ave
3
Lincoln Blvd
Ralston Ave
Parade Ground
Ruckman Ave
Lincoln Blvd
Cowles St
McDowell Ave
Crissy Field Ave
Incinerator Rd
Patten Rd
Battery Blaney Rd
101
Golden Gate Bridg
Kinzey St
Upton Ave
Greenough Ave
Washington Blvd
Kobbe Ave
Kobbe Ave
Upton Ave
Sheridan Ave
Riley Ave
Ord St
Taylor Rd
Montgomery St
Anza St
Graham St
Fisher Loop
SAN FRANCISCO NATIONAL MILITARY CEMETERY
Park Blvd
Infantry Terr
Blis Rd
Moraga
Sheridan Ave
Keyes Ave
Harrison Blvd
Hitchcock St
Hitchcock St
West Coast Memorial
Wright Loop
1
Arguello Blvd
Ave
Immigrant Point Overlook
Naumann Rd
Park Blvd
Amatury Loop
Washington Blvd
Thomas Ave
Infantry Terr
Sibert Loop
Barnard Ave
Barnard Ave
2
Washington Blvd
Compton Rd
Piper Loop
Arguello Blvd
Hicks Rd
Quarry Rd
Deems Rd
Pershing Dr
Reservoir
Battery Caulfield Rd
PRESIDIO
U.S. Military Reserve
Park Blvd
PRESIDIO GOLF COURSE
West Pacif
West Pacific Ave
Jackson St
1
U.S. Publ. Health Service Hospital
Wedemeyer St
Brown St
Wyman Ave
Belles St
1
West Pacific Ave
Presidio Terr
Washington St
Cherry St
Mountain Lake
Park Blvd
7th Ave
6th Ave
5th Ave
Clay St
Temple Emanu-El
Arguello Blvd
MOUNTAIN LAKE PARK
Lake St
Sacramento St
Lake St
A
B

D
E
p132
p133
p134
p135
p136
p137
p138
p139
4
3
2
1
Recreation Area
Marina Small Craft Harbor
East Harbor
Fort Mason Center
S.F. Craft & Folk Art Museum
Marina Green Dr
MARINA GREEN
Marina Blvd
Yacht Rd
West Harbor
Marine Dr
Jauss St
Marshall St
Allen St
Mason St
Doyle Drive
Exploratorium
Lagoon
Palace of Fine Arts
Jefferson St
Beach St
North Point St
Bay St
Francisco St
Chestnut St
Lombard St
Divisadero St
Scott St
Prado St
Avila St
Casa Way
Rico Way
Retiro Way
Cervantes Blvd
Mallorca
Pierce St
Capra Way
Alhambra St
Toledo Way
Fillmore St
Buchanan St
Laguna St
FUNSTON PLAYGROUND
MARINA
Magnolia St
Hotel Del Sol
Greenwich St
Moulton St
Steiner St
Webster St
Pixley
Filbert St
Vedanta Temple
Union St
Green St
Vallejo St
PACIFIC HEIGHTS
Convent of the Sacred Heart
Broadway
Pacific Ave
Bromley Pl
Jackson St
Webster St-Historic District
Washington St
ALTA PLAZA PARK
Clay St
Pacific Medical Center
FILLMORE
Sacramento St
Perine Pl
California St
Orben Pl
Pine St
Wilmot St
St Dominic's Catholic Church
Bush St
Gorgas Ave
Birmingham Rd
Thornburg Rd
Eddie Rd
Letterman Army Institute of Research
Kennedy Ave
Truby St
Letterman Digital Arts Center
Dewitt Rd
Letterman Dr
Presidio Blvd
Summer Ave
Lombard St
Sherman Rd
Simonds Loop
Ruger St
Shafter Rd
Morton St
Ligett Ave
Clark St
Sanches St
Sibley Rd
Richardson Ave
Lyon St
Baker St
Broderick St
COW HOLLOW PLGD
Normandie Terr
West Broadway
Raycliff Terr
Hotel Drisco
KAHN ROUND
PRESIDIO HEIGHTS
Presidio Ave
Walnut St
Laurel St
Locust St
PRESIDIO HEIGHTS PLGD
Laurel Inn
LAUREL HEIGHTS
101

A
B
Alcatraz
S.S. Jeremiah O'Brien
U.S.S. Pampanito
Municipal Pier
Hyde Street Pier
Historic Ships
Alma
Balclutha
Eureka
Eppleton Hall
C.A. Thayer
Pier 45
Pier 43
Pier 47
Fisherman's Wharf
Musée Méchanique
Fort Mason Center
S.F. Maritime National Historic Park
The Embarcadero
Jefferson St
Wharf Inn
Beach St
AQUATIC PARK
Argonaut
Anchorage
The Cannery
Mexican Museum
Museo Italo Americano
FORT MASON
Maritime Museum
VICTORIAN PARK
Ghirardelli Square
North Point St
Bay St
Tuscan Inn
African American Historical & Cultural Society
North Point Street
Columbus Ave
Vandewater St
Francisco St
Golden Gate National Recreation Area
RUSSIAN
Reservoir
HILL PARK
San Francisco Art Institute
Houston St
Water St
San Remo
Fielding St
Van Ness Ave
Octavia St
Gough St
Franklin St
Polk St
Larkin
Hyde St
Leavenworth St
Jones St
Taylor St
Mason St
Powell St
Stockton St
Chestnut St
North Beach Playground
Tuscany Alley
Powell-Hyde-Line
Powell-Mason-Line
RUSSIAN
HILL
NORTH BEACH
Lurmmont Terr
The Marina Inn
Lombard St
Grenard Terr
Michelangelo PLGD
Jansen St
Greenwich St
Filbert St
Harris Pl
Laguna St
Allen St
Havens St
Macondray Ln
Washington Square
Beach Blanket Babylon
Union St
Eastman St
Rockland St
Coolbrith Park
Octagon House
Holy Trinity Russian Orthodox Cathedral
Allyne Park
Green St
Bonita St
Vallejo St
White St
Waldo Alley
Glover St
Florence St
Fallon St
R. Levy Tunnel
Bernard St
Himmelman Pl
Salmon St
Broadway
Helen Wills PLGD
Morrell St
McCormick St
Lynch St
Wall Pl
Burgoyne St
John St
Auburn St
Pacific Ave
Cable Car Museum
Doric Alley
Whittier Mansion
Haas-Lilienthal House
Jackson St
Buchanan St
Sprecl Mansion
Washington St
Reed St
Priest St
Pleasant St
Sproule Ln
Miller Pl
Ewer Pl
Wetmore St
Codman Pl
Freeman Ct
NOB HILL
Lafayette Park
Clay St
Troy Alley
Kimball Pl
Acme Alley
Huntington Park
Grace Cathedral
Mark Hopkins
Huntington
Masonic Center
Pacific Medical Center
Sacramento St
California St
California Street-Line
Helen St
Petite Auberge
Golden Gate
Cartwright
Pine St
Austin St
St Francis Memorial Hospital
Joan Pl
Bush St
Fern St
York
Cosmo Pl
Andrews
Cable Car Theatre
Stage Door Theatre
Sutter St
Hemlock St
Daniel Burnham Ct
Hotel Majestic
Mea-cham Pl
Post St
Cedar St
Hotel Cosmo
Curran Theatre
Shannon St
Geary St
Geary Theater
The Serrano
Japan Center
1
2
3
4

D
E
p132
p133
p134
p135
p136
p137
p138
p139
0 100 200 300 400 500yds
0 100 200 300 400 500m
Pier 35
Pier 33
Pier 31
Pier 29
Pier 27
Pier 23
Foreign Trade Zone
Pier 19
Pier 17
Pier 15
Pier 9
Pier 7
Pier 3
Pier 1
Pier 2
Pier 24
Pier 26
Pier 28
Pier 30
Pier 32
4
3
2
1
Sausalito & Larkspur
Tiburon
Richmond & Vellejo
Harbour Bay Isle Ferry
Alameda & Oakland
Coit Tower
Levi's Plaza
N.E. Waterfront Hist. Dist.
The Embarcadero
SIDNEY WALTON PARK
Custom House
Golden Gateway Center
Ferry Building
Ferry Plaza East
Ferry Building Market
Justin Herman Plaza
Maritime Plaza
Transamerica Pyramid
Embarcadero Center
Hyatt Regency
Hotel Vitale
Federal Reserve Bank
Wells Fargo History Museum
Embarcadero
Rincon Center
Harbor Court
Folsom
Bay Bridge
Ricon Point
80
Mandarin Oriental
Bank of America
Pacific Stock Exchange
FINANCIAL DISTRICT
Transbay Terminal
Hallidie Bldg
Crocker Galleria
Montgomery St
Palace
Cartoon Art Museum
Museum of the African Diaspora
San Francisco Museum of Modern Art
The Four Seasons
Buddha's Universal Church
Chin. Culture Center
Portsmouth Square
CHINA-TOWN
St Mary's Church
Lombard St
Greenwich St
Filbert St
Union St
Green St
Vallejo St
Broadway
Pacific Ave
Jackson St
Washington St
Clay St
Sacramento St
California St
Pine St
Bush St
Sutter St
Post St
Geary St
Market St
Mission St
Howard St
Folsom St
Harrison St
Bryant St
Steuart St
Spear St
Main St
Beale St
Fremont St
1st St
2nd St
3rd St
New Montgomery St
Minna St
Natoma St
Tehama St
Kearny St
Montgomery St
Sansome St
Battery St
Front St
Davis St
Drumm St
Columbus Ave
Grant Ave
Stockton
Boheme
Pacific Inn
Lights kstore
en Hau emple
inatown Gateway
tel Triton
Jackson Square
Gold St
Merchant
Commercial St
Halleck St
Promenade

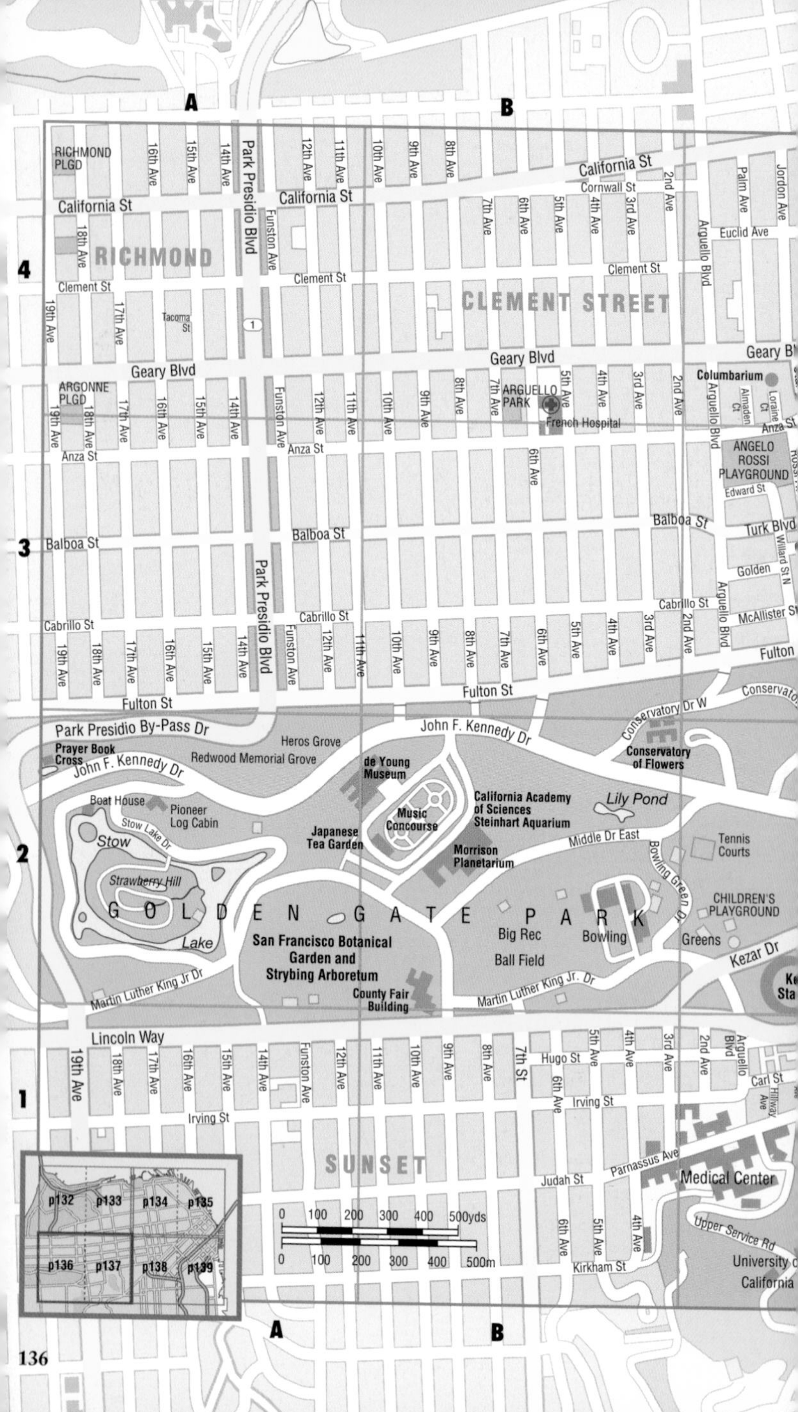
A
B
RICHMOND PLGD
California St
RICHMOND
Clement St
Geary Blvd
ARGONNE PLGD
Anza St
Balboa St
Cabrillo St
Fulton St
Park Presidio Blvd
Funston Ave
CLEMENT STREET
ARGUELLO PARK
French Hospital
Columbarium
ANGELO ROSSI PLAYGROUND
Turk Blvd
Golden
McAllister St
Park Presidio By-Pass Dr
John F. Kennedy Dr
Prayer Book Cross
Heros Grove
Redwood Memorial Grove
de Young Museum
Music Concourse
California Academy of Sciences Steinhart Aquarium
Conservatory of Flowers
Lily Pond
Boat House
Pioneer Log Cabin
Stow Lake
Strawberry Hill
Japanese Tea Garden
Morrison Planetarium
Middle Dr East
Tennis Courts
CHILDREN'S PLAYGROUND
GOLDEN GATE PARK
San Francisco Botanical Garden and Strybing Arboretum
County Fair Building
Big Rec Ball Field
Bowling Greens
Kezar Dr
Martin Luther King Jr Dr
Lincoln Way
Irving St
SUNSET
Judah St
Parnassus Ave
Medical Center
Upper Service Rd
University of California
Kirkham St
p132 p133 p134 p135
p136 p137 p138 p139
0 100 200 300 400 500yds
0 100 200 300 400 500m
4
3
2
1

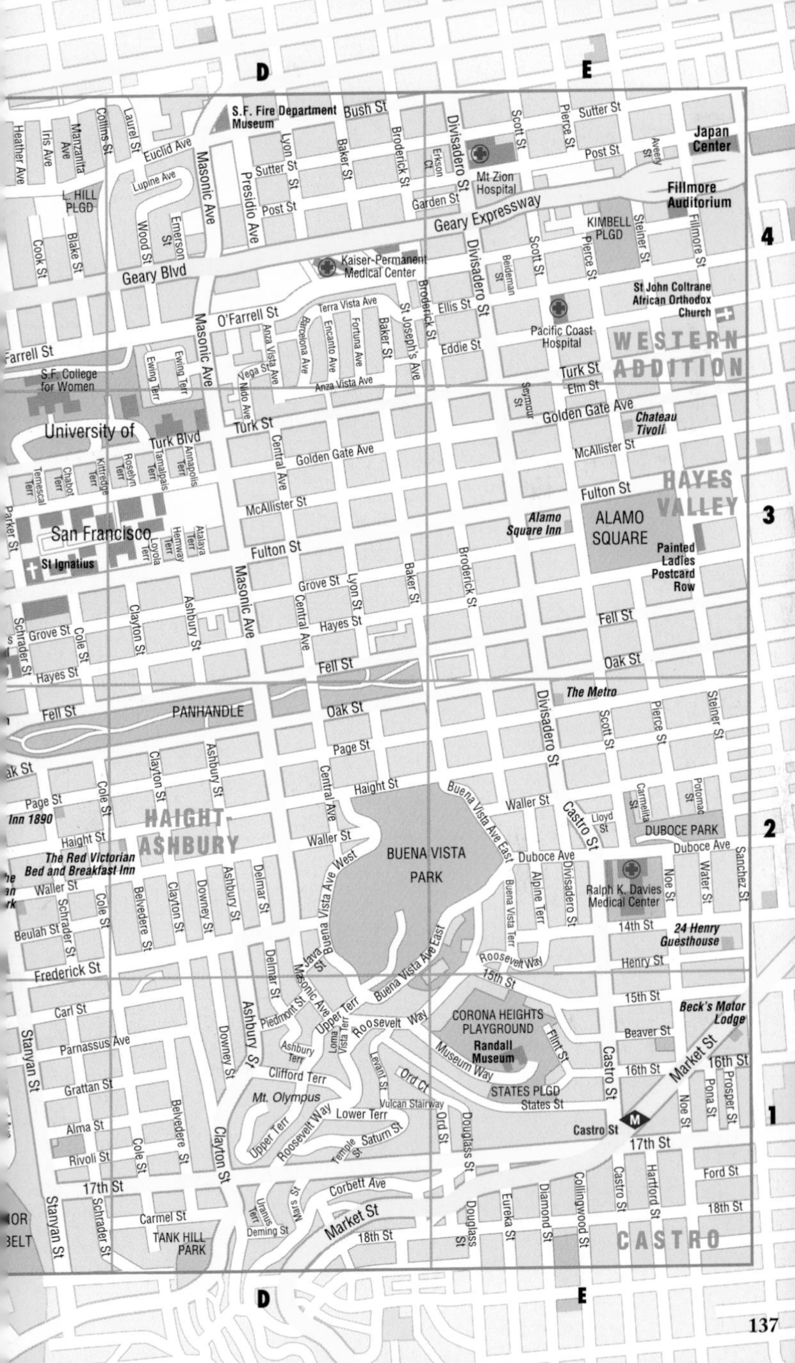
D
E
1
2
3
4
S.F. Fire Department Museum
Bush St
Sutter St
Post St
Geary Expressway
Geary Blvd
Japan Center
Fillmore Auditorium
Mt Zion Hospital
Kaiser-Permanent Medical Center
KIMBELL PLGD
St John Coltrane African Orthodox Church
Pacific Coast Hospital
WESTERN ADDITION
L. HILL PLGD
O'Farrell St
Ellis St
Eddie St
Turk St
Elm St
Golden Gate Ave
McAllister St
Fulton St
Grove St
Hayes St
Fell St
Oak St
Page St
Haight St
Waller St
Chateau Tivoli
HAYES VALLEY
Alamo Square Inn
ALAMO SQUARE
Painted Ladies Postcard Row
S.F. College for Women
University of San Francisco
St Ignatius
Turk Blvd
PANHANDLE
The Metro
HAIGHT-ASHBURY
Inn 1890
The Red Victorian Bed and Breakfast Inn
BUENA VISTA PARK
DUBOCE PARK
Duboce Ave
Ralph K. Davies Medical Center
24 Henry Guesthouse
Beck's Motor Lodge
CORONA HEIGHTS PLAYGROUND
Randall Museum
STATES PLGD
Mt. Olympus
Vulcan Stairway
Castro St
17th St
18th St
Market St
CASTRO
TANK HILL PARK
Frederick St
Carl St
Parnassus Ave
Grattan St
Alma St
Rivoli St
Carmel St
Stanyan St
Masonic Ave
Divisadero St
Broderick St
Baker St
Lyon St
Central Ave
Ashbury St
Clayton St
Cole St
Scott St
Pierce St
Steiner St
Fillmore St
Buena Vista Ave East
Buena Vista Ave West
Roosevelt Way
Museum Way
Clifford Terr
Corbett Ave
Douglass St
Diamond St
Eureka St
Collingwood St
Hartford St
Noe St
Sanchez St
Ford St
14th St
15th St
16th St
Henry St
Beaver St

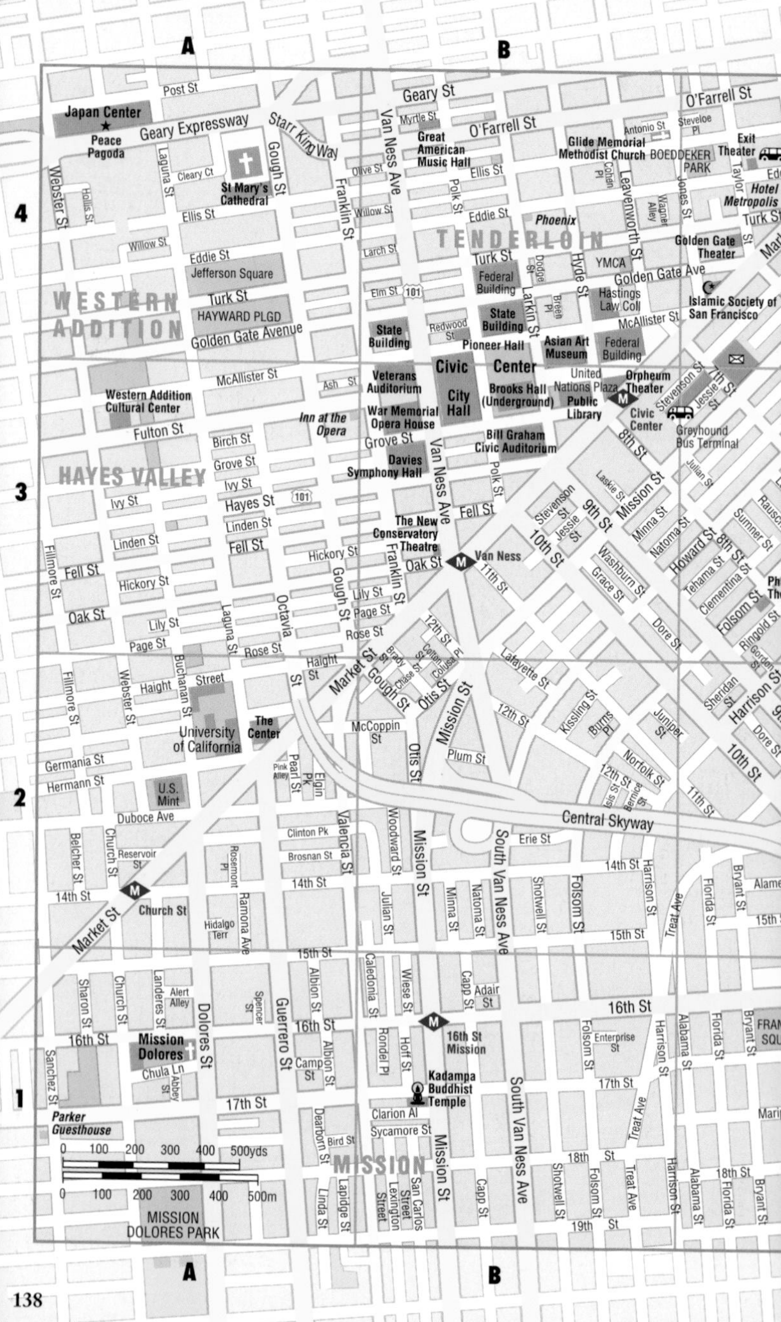

A
B
4
3
2
1
Japan Center
Peace Pagoda
Post St
Geary Expressway
Starr King Way
St Mary's Cathedral
Gough St
Van Ness Ave
Geary St
O'Farrell St
Great American Music Hall
Glide Memorial Methodist Church
BOEDDEKER PARK
Exit Theater
Hotel Metropolis
TENDERLOIN
Phoenix
YMCA
Golden Gate Theater
Islamic Society of San Francisco
WESTERN ADDITION
Jefferson Square
HAYWARD PLGD
Golden Gate Avenue
Federal Building
State Building
Hastings Law Coll
Pioneer Hall
Asian Art Museum
Civic Center
City Hall
Veterans Auditorium
Brooks Hall (Underground)
United Nations Plaza
Orpheum Theater
Public Library
Civic Center
Greyhound Bus Terminal
Western Addition Cultural Center
Inn at the Opera
War Memorial Opera House
Davies Symphony Hall
Bill Graham Civic Auditorium
HAYES VALLEY
The New Conservatory Theatre
Van Ness
University of California
The Center
U.S. Mint
Central Skyway
Church St
Market St
Mission Dolores
Parker Guesthouse
16th St Mission
Kadampa Buddhist Temple
MISSION
MISSION DOLORES PARK
0 100 200 300 400 500yds
0 100 200 300 400 500m
Mission St
South Van Ness Ave
Dolores St
Guerrero St
Valencia St

D
E
Mexican Museum
(Opens 2009)
Contemporary Jewish Museum
San Francisco Museum of Modern Art
San Francisco Museum of Craft & Folk Art
YERBA BUENA GARDENS
Center for the Arts
Metreon
Yerba Buena Square
Moscone Convention Center
Zeum
SOMA
InterContinental San Francisco
Bay Bridge Inn
Hall of Justice
SOUTH PARK
2nd & King
AT&T Park
McCovey Cove
SAN FRANCISCO PARK
San Francisco Caltrain Depot
4th & King
Brannen
Pier 32
Pier 34
Pier 36
Pier 38
Pier 40
South Beach Marina
Pier 48
Newsprint Terminal
Mission Rock Terminal
Pier 50
Boat Launch Ramp
Pier 52
Pier 54
Pier 64
CHINA BASIN
AGUA VISTA PARK
JACKSON PARK
POTRERO
The Embarcadero
James Lick Skyway
Southern Embarcadero Freeway
James Lick Freeway
Mission Creek Marina
Stevenson St
Mission St
Minna St
Howard St
Folsom St
Harrison St
Bryant St
Brannan St
Townsend St
King St
Berry St
Hawthorne St
2nd St
3rd St
4th St
5th St
6th St
7th St
8th St
Essex St
Rincon St
Bayside Village Pl
1st St
Federal St
De Boom St
Colin P Kelly Jr St
Stanford St
Clarence Pl
Ritch St
Zoe St
Welsh St
Freelon St
Clyde St
Lusk St
Bluxome St
Channel St
China Basin St
Mission Rock St
Illinois St
El Dorado St
Owens St
16th St
17th St
Mariposa St
18th St
19th St
Division St
Alameda St
15th St
Vermont St
Henry Adams St
Rhode Island St
De Haro St
Carolina St
Hooper St
Irwin St
Hubbell St
Daggett St
Wisconsin St
Arkansas St
Connecticut St
Missouri St
Texas St
Mississippi St
Pennsylvania Ave
Kansas St
San Bruno Ave
Indiana St
Minnesota St
Tehama St
Clementina St
Shipley St
Clara St
Langton St
Kate St
Decatur St
Gilbert St
Boardman Pl
Lucerne St
Butte Pl
Morris St
Grove St
Merlin St
Oak St
Welsh St
80
280
4
3
2
1
p132
p133
p134
p135
p136
p137
p138
p139

Selective Index for Street Atlas

PLACES OF INTEREST

PARKS

STREETS

Index

M

N

O

P

Insight Smart Guide: San Francisco
Compiled by: **Lisa Crovo Dion; Dan Dion; Elizabeth Linhart Money; Barbara Rockwell**
Proofread and indexed by: **Penny Phenix**
Edited by: **Sarah Sweeney**

Photography by: **APA/Abe Nowitz, Richard Nowitz, and Daniella Nowitz** except: **Alamy** 65tl; **Bancroft Library** 64tl, 64cl; **Corbis** 46b, 65bl, 66cr, 67tl, 67br, 78, 93; **APA/David Dunai** 127t; **Getty** 62t; **Rex** 80/81; **Eyevine** 94/95, 118/119; **Istockphoto** 64tr; **Lee Foster** 67bl; **Ronald Grant Archive** 80l; **Catherine Karnow** 119; **Terence Sweeney** 124b

Picture Manager: **Steven Lawrence**
Maps: **Tom Coulson (Encompass Graphics Ltd); James Macdonald; Neal Jordan-Caws**
Art Director: **Ian Spick**

Series Concept: **Maria Lord**
Series Editor: **Jason Mitchell**

First Edition 2008

Printed in Singapore by Insight Print Services (Pte) Ltd

Worldwide distribution enquiries:
Apa Publications GmbH & Co. Verlag KG (Singapore Branch) 38 Joo Koon Road, Singapore 628990; tel: (65) 6865 1600; fax: (65) 6861 6438
Distributed in the UK and Ireland by:
GeoCenter International Ltd
Meridian House, Churchill Way West, Basingstoke, Hampshire RG21 6YR; tel: (44 1256) 817 987; fax: (44 1256) 817 988
Distributed in the United States by:
Langenscheidt Publishers, Inc.
36–36 33rd Street 4th Floor, Long Island City, New York 11106; tel: (1 718) 784 0055; fax: (1 718) 784 0640l

Contacting the Editors
We would appreciate it if readers would alert us to errors or outdated information by writing to:
Apa Publications, PO Box 7910, London SE1 1WE, UK; fax: (44 20) 7403 0290; e-mail: insight@apaguide.co.uk

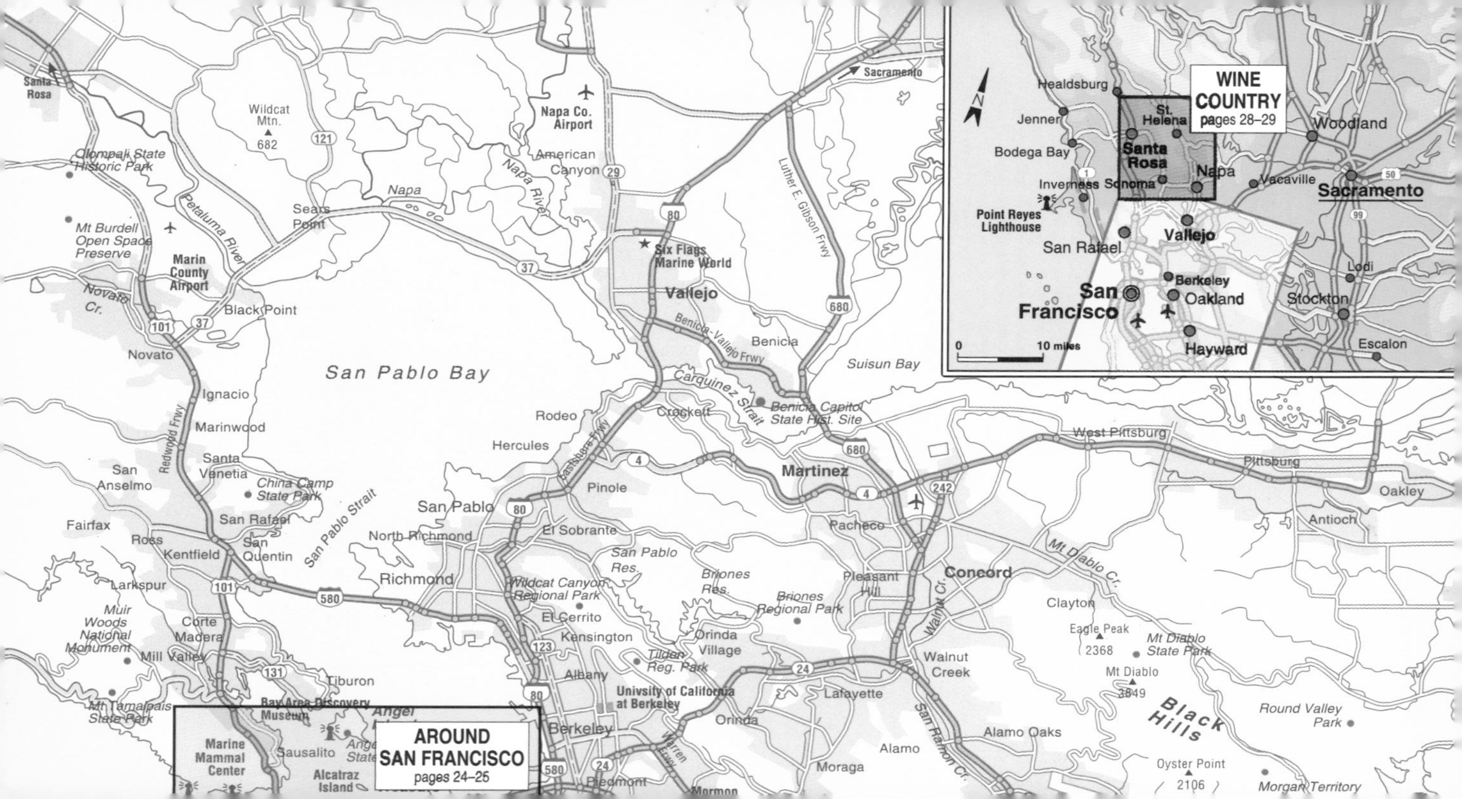

WINE COUNTRY
pages 28–29
Healdsburg
Jenner
Bodega Bay
St. Helena
Santa Rosa
Napa
Sonoma
Inverness
Point Reyes Lighthouse
Vacaville
Woodland
Sacramento
Vallejo
San Rafael
Berkeley
Oakland
San Francisco
Hayward
Lodi
Stockton
Escalon
0
10 miles
Santa Rosa
Wildcat Mtn.
682
Olompali State Historic Park
Mt Burdell Open Space Preserve
Marin County Airport
Petaluma River
Novato Cr.
Black Point
Novato
Sears Point
Napa
Napa River
Napa Co. Airport
American Canyon
Sacramento
Luther E. Gibson Frwy
Six Flags Marine World
Vallejo
Benicia-Vallejo Frwy
Benicia
Suisun Bay
San Pablo Bay
Carquinez Strait
Benicia Capitol State Hist. Site
Crockett
Rodeo
Hercules
Ignacio
Marinwood
Redwood Frwy
Santa Venetia
San Anselmo
China Camp State Park
San Pablo Strait
San Rafael
San Quentin
Fairfax
Ross
Kentfield
Larkspur
Muir Woods National Monument
Corte Madera
Mill Valley
Mt Tamalpais State Park
Tiburon
Bay Area Discovery Museum
Sausalito
Marine Mammal Center
Alcatraz Island
AROUND SAN FRANCISCO
pages 24–25
North Richmond
San Pablo
Richmond
Pinole
El Sobrante
San Pablo Res.
Wildcat Canyon Regional Park
El Cerrito
Kensington
Albany
Berkeley
Univsity of California at Berkeley
Tilden Reg. Park
Orinda Village
Orinda
Briones Res.
Briones Regional Park
Warren Frwy
Piedmont
Moraga
Lafayette
Martinez
Pacheco
Pleasant Hill
Concord
Walnut Cr.
Walnut Creek
Alamo
Alamo Oaks
San Ramon Cr.
West Pittsburg
Pittsburg
Oakley
Antioch
Mt Diablo Cr.
Clayton
Eagle Peak
2368
Mt Diablo State Park
Mt Diablo
3849
Black Hills
Round Valley Park
Oyster Point
2106
Morgan Territory